INSIDE THE
DEPARTMENT OF STATE

The Department of State Building, Washington (South Front)

Frontispiece.

INSIDE THE
DEPARTMENT OF STATE

By

BERTRAM D. HULEN

New York WHITTLESEY HOUSE *London*

McGRAW-HILL BOOK COMPANY, INC.

PUBLISHED BY WHITTLESEY HOUSE
A division of the McGraw-Hill Book Company, Inc.

Printed in the United States of America by the Maple Press Co., York, Pa.

PREFACE

DURING a conversation on various aspects of foreign policy, with a Secretary of State in his office in the Department of State building, the author asked what the Secretary thought of the Department and American diplomacy. His reply was one that many others who have occupied that high office could have made:

"I have found frank dealing," he said. "I used to think that diplomacy was mysterious, a combination of intrigues run by hard-boiled men who were not frank or honest with us; that they were sleuths on the trail finding out things on the other fellow. I have found nothing mysterious about it. It is complicated because it deals with so much."

What the Secretary of that time remarked—and he must remain anonymous because he was not speaking for personal attribution—epitomized the Department and its activities. There is nothing mysterious about its operations or the conduct of American diplomacy. There are victories and defeats, farseeing statesmanship and mistakes, but to anyone who looks behind the scenes there is nothing mystifying. It is complex, for foreign affairs are conducted in the United States from many fronts and are subject to democratic controls that on great issues are decisive.

The Department may be subordinated below its normal position, as when Woodrow Wilson assumed dominating personal direction of foreign affairs in the critical years

[vii]

before the United States entered the World War and during the Peace Conference. It may not be consulted, as when President Franklin D. Roosevelt on his own responsibility in 1937 advocated a quarantine of aggressor states. It may find itself on the side lines, as was the case during the great political battle over foreign policy when the Versailles Treaty was submitted to the Senate, and again during the controversy over policy implicit in granting facilities to France for the purchase of military airplanes in the United States in 1939.

These cases, however, constitute exceptions that do not prove the rule. Most Presidents prefer to rely on the Department of State and not get so far in front as to become a target, or to act so much alone as to invite serious consequences. In general the Department functions as it was intended to, as the active agent in the conduct of foreign affairs, the machine for carrying on relations with other governments. Through the Department and its Foreign Service, the government obtains information concerning conditions abroad and the actions and intentions of other governments, to aid in determining its own policies and actions. The Department is also the principal channel of the government for communicating with other governments. In addition, it renders a great variety of services for Americans abroad in respect to their travels, their business, and their protection when need arises.

Whatever the circumstances, the Department cannot be interpreted solely on the basis of problems of the moment, for it stands with a continuity of precedents and procedure and a permanent personnel as Presidents and Secretaries of State come and go. It is even surprisingly little affected by political changes from administration to administration. Its foundation remains the same as that laid down by the

first Congress, for although many statutes affecting it have been enacted since 1789, its primary functions have remained unaltered. Clear comprehension comes only from viewing it in its setting, not only in its relation to the rest of the government and the people, but also in the perspective of its growth and development through many vicissitudes in 150 years of uninterrupted existence. It is a living organism to which generations of men and women have devoted their lives. Year by year the Department accumulates experience in diplomatic and political relationships. Its functions consist of more than diplomatic procedure and consular practice. If this were all, technical experts could be placed in charge of the Department with a set of rules, and the President and the country could forget it.

A popular tradition of mystery attaches to its operations because diplomatic negotiations so often are conducted in confidence, but the facts either are made known as soon as arrangements have been advanced to a sufficiently definite point, or are revealed under the searching examination of Congress and the press. There is more truth than rhetoric in the assertion of Department officials "We have no secrets."

Since the World War, as much as at any time in its long history, the Department of State has been a center of interest because of the unsettled state of the world and the repercussions on the United States of the power politics and diplomacy of agitation of totalitarian states. A few decades ago these reactions might have been much less intense, but revolution in Europe and ferment in Asia have coincided with the assumption by the United States of a place as a world power—some maintain the most powerful of all nations. For the first time a great power has arisen outside Europe, causing a shifting of balance, with all that implies. The world consequences of that phenomenon

are yet to be measured by events; for the present it can only be said that the voice of the United States is powerful and carries far beyond the range of its direct national interests.

Because of these considerations the Department of State should be explained primarily in terms of the period since the World War, but it cannot be adequately understood without a glimpse behind the present era. It did not suddenly emerge full-grown. It has had a long history, as time is measured in the New World or in the life of governments, and a gradual, steady growth that merits consideration from the time of its origin. It could be dated even earlier than 1789, the year in which it was established, for it embraces the Diplomatic and Consular services that trace from the founding of the authority of the government in 1776.

The author, as a correspondent assigned to the Department of State, first for the Associated Press and since 1926 for the *New York Times*, has watched its wheels revolve under pressure of many circumstances and conditions, and the present volume is written in an effort to explain both what it is and how it operates. Although references are made by way of illustration to incidents and policies, no attempt has been made to write a history of American diplomacy or to describe the rules of diplomacy or to assess praise or blame. That is left to others, with the hope, however, that this book may place the reader in a better position to exercise his own judgment.

For that purpose it has seemed desirable to describe the place of the Department in the government, its growth and organization, and then to consider the position of the Secretary of State and his chief aides, as well as the operation of the chiefs of mission abroad and the Foreign Service.

PREFACE

A discussion of activities requires that attention be given to influences that beat upon the Department from the country and the outside world, as well as to the influences that the Department itself exerts in the opposite direction. In this, modern communication plays a vital part as it also does in the maintenance of contacts with foreign governments both through missions abroad and the foreign diplomatic corps in Washington. Finally, consideration must be given to the relations of the Department with the White House, with other departments and agencies of the government, and with Congress.

Naturally, the author has drawn upon his own observations. He has also had the generous assistance of officials both in and out of the Department. This has been necessary because of a dearth of literature on the subject. For that reason a bibliography would give a distorted impression of the sources. The basis in considerable part is original material. It seems best not to enumerate officials who have given their assistance and guidance but to express sincere appreciation to all of them through Michael J. McDermott, chief of the Division of Current Information in the Department of State.

It should be added that conversations are published with official permission.

BERTRAM D. HULEN.

WASHINGTON, D. C.,
June, 1939.

[xi]

CONTENTS

[xiii]

INSIDE THE
DEPARTMENT OF STATE

CHAPTER I

SOME GLIMPSES OF THE SETTING

ARCHITECTS shudder at the Department of State building.

A massive four-story structure, it fills the block west of the White House grounds, from which it is separated by narrow West Executive Avenue. Unlike the Treasury building flanking the Executive Mansion on the east, it is distinctive from all other government buildings in its ponderous French neoclassic style with porticos and mansards borrowed from Paris of the Second Empire. A great granite pile, it is expressive of the idea of grandeur of the 1870's.

For years it was admired. When General Grant returned from Europe he considered it more extraordinary than anything he had seen during his travels. John Hay when Secretary of State at the turn of the century considered it a masterpiece. Gradually views are changing, for it is completely out of harmony with the classic Greek or modern lines of other government buildings, and it has become a center of controversy at a time when the government is pressing a huge program that is transforming the national capital into a new and beautiful setting of public edifices and parks.

So far the Department of State building has defied all movements to modernize it. Yet before many years it may yield to the march of progress and appear in new face and form, to the bewilderment of the veterans who occupy its offices.

Regardless of its physical lines, within it lie the nerves of the nation's foreign policy, and its corridors and offices teem with activity, even though usually subdued. Ordinarily there is an unhurried atmosphere, an old-fashioned appearance which somehow escapes other departments of the government. Nevertheless, this impression is only on the surface, for grave events can quickly dispel the illusion.

A diplomatic crisis arises in consequence of a Japanese attack on Shanghai, where Americans are concentrated in the International Settlement, their lives endangered and their property threatened. Other powers are confronted with the same emergency. At once the machinery of the Department of State is thrown into action, sweeping in its operations from China to Geneva. Messages are despatched to Nanking and Tokyo, to London and Paris. Foreign ambassadors arrive and depart from repeated conferences with the Secretary of State until, with fact separated from rumor and all factors weighed carefully, the government's policy is determined. Garrisons in the International Settlement are reinforced, warnings are issued to Japan and China to exercise all precautions against endangering foreign lives and property, and treaty rights are reaffirmed. Once more a crisis has been met.

Europe totters on the brink of war over the status of Czechoslovakia, and the voice of the government is raised on broad humanitarian grounds for peace. Civil war breaks out in Spain and the Department is confronted with a major problem of evacuating Americans from an entire country. German troops march into the Rhineland and into Austria, and the issue is posed of what attitude shall be taken by this country. International exchange suffers a shock from a sensational political development, and the Department of State must participate in deliberations at the Treasury and the White House to decide how the United States shall meet the new situation. An American citizen is kidnaped by bandits

in Mexico. All possible measures must be taken to obtain his release and have the offenders punished.

History has been made behind the thick walls and dingy exterior of the building toward which the eyes of multitudes of Americans on so many occasions have been anxiously turned.

Quite appropriately, in view of the serious problems with which the Department deals, the building is placed nearer the Executive Offices of the White House than is any other division of the government. It is separated from Pennsylvania Avenue by a sunken garden where even large magnolia trees are dwarfed by the structure. Mounted on the broad flight of granite steps are ancient cannon which appear to belie the name "Department of Peace" by which the Department of State likes to be known. They are relics of the Revolution and other wars, captured in battle. They are there because the Secretary of War and the Chief of Staff and the Adjutant General of the Army long occupied a section of the building. Recently, however, these officials moved and left the building entirely to the Department of State, except for General John J. Pershing, General of the Armies, whose second-floor office overlooks the White House grounds.

Down Seventeenth Street, on the farther side from the White House, the length of the building stretches into distant perspective, broken slightly by the pairs of small columns which surmount the steps and support the portico roof. Around the next corner the setting changes abruptly from urban surroundings to a vista of parks. There is little activity here, though the outward appearance of the building is almost identical with the front.

On the West Executive Avenue side, next to the White House grounds, is the entrance customarily used by the Secretary of State and foreign diplomats who call on official

business, whether the negotiation of a treaty, the details of adjusting claims, or a conference on high diplomatic policy. Official automobiles with liveried chauffeurs are parked in front of the entrance. There every day ambassadors and ministers are seen alighting from sleek limousines with armorial insignia and low diplomatic license numbers, and entering the building for conferences with the Secretary of State. From the next entrance officials and messengers dodge traffic to cross the narrow avenue on errands to the Executive Offices of the White House.

The main entrance on Pennsylvania Avenue opens into a lobby, where guards in uniform are constantly on duty. Broad semicircular stairs with huge curved bronze balusters lead to the second floor, where the principal executive offices are located. Everything inside is in agreement with the massive proportions of the exterior. The floors are checkered in twelve-inch blocks of black and white marble, and the walls are tinted a light yellow, but the long corridors seem gloomy.

Lattice doors bar a glimpse into offices along the corridors, but principal interest centers in the group of offices in the south wing of this floor occupied by the Secretary of State and his immediate associates. On the right is a large reception room where Senators and Congressmen, delegations of civic organizations, and others await their appointments with the Secretary of State. The Secretary of State also holds his daily press conferences here. Leather chairs and sofas line the walls, and other chairs are placed around a long center table. A fireplace adds a touch of comfort, and portraits of former Secretaries of State look down from the walls.

The caller is escorted through an outer office occupied by the Secretary's administrative staff, thence through a small anteroom, and finally into the Secretary's own office directly above the south entrance to the building. This is the most

imposing and important of all the five hundred offices in the labyrinthian building. Slightly recessed from the corridor by a colonnade, it may also be entered directly from the corridor through a high mahogany door; but this entrance is reserved customarily for diplomats, who await their turn in a smaller reception room across the corridor.

Inevitably the office of the Secretary of State carries memories of the past that are unforgettably associated with it since the July day in 1875 when Hamilton Fish established himself there, with all the prestige of having recently brought about one of the greatest international arbitrations in the adjustment of the Alabama claims. The very atmosphere seems to recall the diplomacy of the Spanish-American War, the achievements of John Hay in his negotiation of the Hay-Pauncefote Treaty and his promulgation of the Open Door policy in China, the colorful career of William Jennings Bryan and the difficult days of the World War, and incidents connected with the Washington Naval Limitation Conference.

The office is large, with high ceilings and long windows through which the sun streams in both winter and summer. By turning his chair from his long, wide, flat-topped desk, the Secretary of State can look out upon the World War Monument to the First Division of the American Expeditionary Force in the park directly across the street and beyond to the Washington Monument. Chairs are here in ample numbers to accommodate the dozen or more officials who attend frequent conferences on foreign policy, and a few easy chairs for the more intimate conversations with foreign diplomats individually.

On one of the walls is suspended a plaque, a profile life-sized bust of James Madison in marble surrounded by a small gilt frame, the work of Giuseppe Ceracchi in 1792. Below it on standards are an American flag and the flag of

[7]

the Secretary of State with its blue rectangular field, a white disk in the center bearing the coat of arms of the United States, and a five-pointed white star at each corner. On other walls hang steel engravings of Washington, Madison, Andrew Jackson, Lincoln, and Grant, and at the far side of the room stands a huge grandfather's clock.

Here problems of state are discussed in private with chiefs of foreign diplomatic missions resident in Washington and at times with prime ministers and foreign ministers who come to take up pressing questions. At other times it is the scene of formal ceremonies, as when a treaty is signed after months of difficult negotiation or when distinguished foreigners who have come to Washington pay official calls of respect. A few years after the World War Georges Clemenceau and later David Lloyd George, on visits to this Country, were received here, after passing through lines of applauding officials and clerks in the corridor. Many long conversations were conducted in this same room by Prime Minister Ramsay Mac-Donald of Great Britain and Secretary of State Henry L. Stimson in their quest for a stabilized world order and peace.

The desk of the Secretary of State is littered with the papers of a hard-working official. Communications from subordinates, voluminous reports on special problems, and piles of cable messages from embassies, legations, and consulates in all parts of the world are here and are read closely by the Secretary, who must keep abreast of all that is going on, from the disappearance of an obscure American in a foreign port to a serious question of policy that has been raised by a foreign chancellery.

A telephone on the desk affords contact, not only with the White House, other departments, Congress, and the country at large, but with foreign capitals. Overseas conversations with American ambassadors, while not a daily occurrence,

have been held so often that they are regarded as routine. No longer is diplomacy the easygoing concern in point of time that it was in the days before the era of electrical communications.

Nevertheless the atmosphere is calm, in fact quieter than is usually found in the office of a busy business executive. The facilities are at hand for instant action, but diplomacy prefers an unhurried appearance. Strong words are sometimes spoken, yet always time is allowed for careful and thorough treatment. Good manners are part of the tradition of the Department. Its task is to create and preserve good will and confidence. The more disturbed or aroused a foreign diplomat or his government, the more consideration must be shown in the forms of diplomatic intercourse.

Consequently, when a diplomat calls on the Secretary of State there is ample time for conversation, no ringing of telephones, no rushing around of secretaries with papers and memorandums, from the moment the official caller arrives until he departs. There are times when the diplomat receives a strong message and departs knowing full well the disturbing implications of the communication, but the rule of courtesy is observed.

It is not unusual to see the door of the Secretary of State's office opened and an ambassador come out with a final bow and gracious words of farewell as he takes his leave of the Secretary, who has accompanied him to the door. A Negro messenger waits to escort the important visitor the few steps to the elevator, even as on his arrival the messenger had ushered him to the diplomatic reception room to await his appointment with the Secretary.

The messengers are humble but well-established functionaries who through long years of experience have themselves become schooled in the diplomatic tradition. Certainly there

was none more astute than Edward Augustine Savoy, the diminutive and, in the course of time, bent Negro who had the exceptional record of serving from 1869 until his retirement in 1933 as the messenger of twenty-one successive Secretaries of State, from Hamilton Fish to Cordell Hull. A diplomat in his own right through his long experience, he was suavity itself, in the early years of the World War before the United States entered the conflict, in seeing that ambassadors of enemy powers who entered the building at the same time did not meet. On sterner duty, it was he who in 1898 went to the Spanish Legation and handed the Minister, Luis Polo de Bernabé, his credentials on the eve of war. He performed the same service when Dr. Constantin Theodor Dumba, the Ambassador of Austria-Hungary, was dismissed from the country in 1915 for stirring up industrial strife in the United States.

Many of his associates at the offices of the Under Secretary of State and of assistant secretaries of state spent years in the White House before being transferred to the Department of State. They are always certain of a warm greeting from White House residents and Cabinet officers of former administrations calling at the Department. Their memories of previous administrations run far beyond those of the officials they serve.

Often the messenger is not the only one who meets the departing ambassador at the door of the Secretary of State. Frequently before the envoy can take the few steps to the elevator he is stopped by half a dozen men who have bobbed up in a miraculous way to ply him with questions. They are newspaper correspondents from the press room around the corner. If the matter under discussion is of a confidential nature, the ambassador amiably parries the questions and hurries back to his chancery to prepare a full report for

transmission in secret code by cable to his foreign office. Later, when the negotiation has proceeded to a definite point, an announcement of the terms is made by his foreign office and by the Secretary of State. At other times the subject of a conference is not of a nature to require secrecy and its purport is readily revealed to the correspondents.

Often calls of diplomats are merely for formal purposes. An ambassador comes to the Department and instead of requesting to see the Secretary of State goes to the office of the Under Secretary of State to whom he presents an official text of an important address on foreign affairs delivered the day before by his foreign minister to parliament. There is no new information conveyed, for the text of the address has appeared in the morning newspapers, but diplomatic procedure requires this courteous gesture.

Sometimes an ambassador appears regularly at the Department for weeks in conducting the negotiation of a treaty. If it is of a specially important and difficult character, he is assisted by a delegation of officials and experts from his home government. He acts under explicit instructions and keeps his foreign office fully informed by frequent cables of the progress of the discussions. Knotty points are debated, legal and technical divisions in the Department of State constantly advise the Secretary of State on the points at issue, every word is carefully scanned as the details are reduced to writing, and finally the long task is completed, the text is initialed, and a day is set for the ceremony of signing.

At the appointed time the ambassador, his assistants, and the chief diplomatic secretaries of his embassy appear. The Secretary of State is surrounded in his office by the Department officials who have assisted him in the negotiation. All are in formal dress. Functionaries of the Treaty Division of the Department who are familiar with the ceremonial routine

required are on hand with seals and wax, many-colored ribbons to be attached to the document, and pens carefully poised for the waiting hands of the Secretary of State and the ambassador who sign as the plenipotentiaries of their governments. News camera men are gathered at the end of the room to record the scene. In this setting the pact is duly signed. Then it is transmitted by the President to the Senate for approval by a two-thirds vote, and after this consent has been given ratifications of the treaty are exchanged and it comes into force.

All this activity takes place in a setting that recalls the past. In addition to the portraits in the Secretary's reception room, original likenesses of other Secretaries of State from the founding of the government look out from gold frames on the walls of the corridors. They include Thomas Jefferson in his fur collar, stern John Marshall, quizzical John Quincy Adams, leonine John C. Calhoun, the matter-of-fact William H. Seward, the bulldog-jawed Richard Olney, and the accomplished John Hay.

Ambassadors and ministers upon entering the diplomatic reception room find two significant reminders of traditional and basic American foreign policy. Bronze busts of Washington and Lafayette stand on marble pedestals, testifying to the historic friendship of France and the United States extending over a period of 160 years. Anglo-American friendship is reflected in contemporary portraits of Daniel Webster and Lord Ashburton that hang side by side in recognition of the importance of the Webster-Ashburton Treaty of 1842, which by settling the North American boundary removed a serious source of irritation in the relations of the two countries.

The most prized of all historic souvenirs is found in the small anteroom of the Secretary of State. It is a little Empire

flat-topped desk on which John Quincy Adams drafted the Monroe Doctrine. The desk has remained in the office of the Secretary of State ever since and is often used in the ceremony of signing treaties.

In these three reminders are to be discerned in broad outline basic American foreign policy: friendship with Great Britain, friendship with France, and America for the Americas.

The growth of the country and its Foreign Service is well illustrated in the history of the buildings that have housed the Department of State since the seat of government was established in Washington in 1800. When the government was formed in 1789, the founders anticipated growth and planned the national capital on generous lines, but they could not foresee the extraordinary expansion. They thought buildings of moderate size would be sufficient for the four original departments and planned for one at each corner of the White House grounds.

The Treasury was the first to be located, on the southeast, and the Department of State followed, after a few years in temporary quarters, on the northeast. Two buildings for the War and Navy Departments were placed on the site of the present Department of State building, west of the White House. Thus they stood until after the Civil War, except when gruff old Andrew Jackson decided that the Treasury should be enlarged and, walking out of the White House, pointed with his cane to the spot where the extension would be built.

With the surge of national development after the Civil War it was realized that much larger buildings were necessary. Accordingly, the structures which housed the State, War, and Navy Departments were razed, the north side of the Treasury was again extended by an addition to its present

proportions, and the Department of State building was erected to accommodate not only that Department but the War and Navy Departments. For many years it was known as the State, War, and Navy building.

During the World War, the Navy Department and much later the War Department moved to a temporary structure, leaving the Department of State building to that Department, which in the meantime had overflowed into neighboring office buildings.

The Department of State building required seventeen years to complete, from 1871 to 1888, but it was built a wing at a time, and Secretary of State Fish soon established his office in the south wing. From the Department one looks down on the White House grounds and upon the circular window of the Executive Offices behind which the President is seated at his desk. It is only a few steps from the one to the other, across West Executive Avenue and through a finished basement entrance of the Executive Offices. This path is frequently trod by the Secretary of State and the Under Secretary of State in the course of keeping the President constantly informed of all details of the government's foreign problems.

Tradition has it that the personnel of the Department of State and of the Foreign Service, which is its eyes and ears abroad, consists of dilettante sons of the wealthy who have entered a career of diplomacy for the social opportunities it affords. In the past this was much truer than at present, for with the expansion of American diplomacy since the World War encouraging the development of a large staff in the Department and in the foreign field, the Service has been placed on a merit basis. And it has been thoroughly reorganized to appeal to young men who do not have independent means with which to sustain their position.

When the Department of State was established under Thomas Jefferson, the first Secretary of State, its entire staff was comprised of five clerks, and the diplomatic corps of three ministers, while the consular corps had a personnel of sixteen. There were four foreign ministers-resident accredited to the United States government.

It was first known as the Department of Foreign Affairs, but its name was changed to the present one a few months later when Congress assigned to it a number of domestic functions, such as the safekeeping of Acts of Congress, records, and the Seal of the United States. From time to time more statutes were enacted giving it additional domestic duties. The country grew; responsibilities increased in the field of foreign affairs; and the Department gradually expanded, its most rapid growth resulting from the issues and aftermath of the World War.

Even a hundred years ago, however, the growth of the Department was noted with pride. Washington newspapers in 1838 took occasion to congratulate the country on this, boasting that, as compared with its small beginnings, the Department of State had fifty employes in Washington, nine ministers abroad, nine secretaries of legation, eleven chargés d'affaires, and six consuls at foreign posts.

The expansion continued steadily. The World War found an organization of several hundred officials and employes, but events demonstrated that staff inadequate. In consequence the Department of State now has an organization in Washington and abroad in the Foreign Service of seven hundred and thirty-nine Foreign Service officers and twenty-six hundred other officials, clerical workers, and other employes. Of the total, nine hundred are in the Department, the rest abroad. Diplomatic representation is maintained in sixty foreign countries and consular representatives at over

INSIDE THE DEPARTMENT OF STATE

three hundred posts abroad. In contrast with the small foreign diplomatic representation when Jefferson was Secretary of State there are at present fifty-four heads of foreign missions accredited to the United States government in Washington.

Yet the Department is the least expensive in Washington, where Congress is much more interested in farm relief than it is in the day-to-day operation of the Foreign Service. The annual appropriation for the Department of State is only $16,000,000, while consular, visa, and other fees that it collects and returns to the Treasury reduce the actual outlay to a net of $10,000,000 a year. Although this might be considered large, measured by the standards of a private business, it is modest enough for the greatest of all businesses, the government of the United States. In terms of factors with which the government deals, it is one-seventh the cost of a single battleship and a mere pittance of the amount carried in a farm relief bill.

It is this annual appropriation on which the Department operates a complicated mechanism. To carry out its duties it has evolved a structure of regional divisions, each dealing with a different part of the world; technical divisions for economic subjects and legal questions; and special divisions, such as one in charge of the negotiation of reciprocal trade agreements. Over all is superimposed a group of directing heads comprising three assistant secretaries of state, the Counselor, who is not to be confused with the Legal Adviser, and the Under Secretary, all immediately responsible to the Secretary of State. The higher officials are political appointees and so usually change with administrations. Because of their directing influence, the Department is very much a personal machine of the White House. Officers below the rank of assistant secretary, however, are governed by the merit system and the employes are under the civil service.

[16]

Possibly more continuity will some time be given to the Department to make it less subject to change at the top with administrations through the creation of the office of a Permanent Under Secretary of State. This has often been considered but never adopted, although other countries have found it highly useful.

The nearest approach to a Permanent Under Secretary was A. A. Adee, who served for nearly forty years as Second Assistant Secretary of State, a post he assumed in 1886 after several years of experience in the Department and abroad. On many occasions Adee served as Acting Secretary of State and once as Secretary of State *ad interim*, and he became a personage in the government. He was noted for his diplomatic skill, his literary talents, and his wit. Many times he performed services of the first importance for the United States. Since his death no one has risen to take his place.

Some of the older Washington newspapermen still recall with amusement an event which took place at the time the foreign legations were imprisoned in Peking in 1900 and official despatches were burning the cables. One evening Secretary of State John Hay had a long conference with Wu Ting Fang, the Chinese Minister, whose personality will long be remembered in Washington tradition. Secretary Hay left Washington at once on personal affairs, Minister Wu was unavailable, and when the inquiring press sought information, Adee was uncommunicative. He maintained that the conference was not important.

"But surely it must have been of some significance," the newspaper correspondents insisted.

"Oh, no," said Adee with a shrug. "The Minister talked and talked until the Secretary was Wu-zy; and then the Secretary talked and talked until the Minister was Hay-zy."

The present office of Under Secretary of State was established in 1919 and is usually held by an officer of long experi-

ence in the diplomatic service. He is selected by the President upon the advice of the Secretary of State, whose chief assistant he is. The circumstances of his appointment and service, however, are such as to make him a personal appointee of each administration. All questions reaching the Department come to his attention and he, more than the Secretary of State, keeps in constant, personal touch with the foreign diplomatic corps. It is he, more often than the Secretary of State, whom the diplomats see when they call at the Department to exchange information. On outstanding issues, the diplomats confer with the Secretary of State.

These informative discussions help the Department to keep informed of events and developing policy abroad. American diplomats in foreign capitals have access in the same way to the foreign offices for equally informative discussions, and report promptly to Washington.

Ceaselessly there pour into the Department, through its telegraph room, despatches in secret code from United States diplomatic and consular representatives in all parts of the world. These are promptly decoded and copies sent to all officials in any way concerned with the subject matter. The outside world also has its views and interests reflected through the daily newspapers, and through information and questions brought by newspaper correspondents, who maintain a constant vigil from offices provided for them a few doors from that of the Secretary of State.

The Department has even become so modern as to have a news ticker installed, conveying press despatches from the rest of Washington and from the entire world for instant transmission to officials and experts. Frequently these become the basis of inquiries abroad without the delay of awaiting an official report.

Certainly the Department has no humdrum existence and presents no picture of dry-as-dust routine.

CHAPTER II

ADEE AND EXPANSION

THE history of the Department of State is written almost as much in colorful personalities as in the documents stored in its archives, and far more vividly. Through the years these men have stamped their individualities on the organization and the traditions of a Department which, as time is measured in this country, is beginning to assume an aspect of respectable antiquity. They have been sufficient in themselves to relieve the atmosphere of any touch of the monotonous. Some are numbered among the great figures in American history; others, known only to the Washington of their time and the narrow ranks of professional diplomacy, have made invaluable contributions to the growth and development of the Department.

Under the guidance of directing officials who served from administration to administration the Department has expanded steadily with the increasing power and responsibilities of the country until today it is a structure that would astonish the founding fathers. For a long time life in the Department was marked by periods of comparative quiet, but it has been years since a Secretary of State has had the time that was available to Daniel Webster, one of the most distinguished occupants of the office, to compose a long letter for President Fillmore to the Sultan of Muscat insisting in colorful phrases on fair treatment for Americans in Zanzibar.

Gold had recently been discovered in California and Webster was impressed, so one can understand his boasting, for

its effect on the Sultan, of California "where the quartz
rocks of the mountains are filled with gold, and the rivers
flow over golden beds, and the sands of the ocean Shore
Sparkle with the richest ore." One still seems to hear his
sonorous voice describing the continental sweep of the United
States—"from whose eastern shores, which receive the first
beams of the rising sun, to those on the West, where rest his
Setting rays is one hundred and fifty days journey." Even
Webster could not conceive of the airplane.

Those days departed long ago. They were followed by an
era spanning the Civil and World Wars in which the personal
element was dominant in the administration of the Department. Yet the chief actors in the period of personal administration laid foundations on which the present impersonal and
highly integrated organization is based. No one played a
greater part in preparing the way for expansion than the
aforementioned A. A. Adee. More than anyone else he
personified the period when gradual transition took place
from the small beginnings of the Department to the present.
For nearly forty years he kept a skillful hand on the mechanism of foreign affairs. It was often remarked in the Washington of his time that he was the Department of State.

Adee and his colleagues planted roots that have sprouted
into offices and bureaus; assistants they trained now hold
key positions. The Department of this generation stands on
their shoulders. No sharp line of demarcation can be drawn
between the old and the new. Adee spanned them in his long
life. If any point could be assigned for the change, it would
be the World War. With the Department, as with so much
else in human activity, it is a case of "before the War" and
"after the War." It was not as disruptive a force as the
Army experienced in the Spanish-American War, when a
departmental chief ruefully exclaimed that he had had his

office functioning perfectly only to have the War shatter it; but increased burdens caused a change from the old order.

The transition was not accomplished overnight. A full ten years was necessary after the first impact of the World War before the new order was firmly implanted. There was no revolution. There was instead a carefully developed program of enlargement and of scientific organization. Successive administrations made contributions, testing and revising in the light of experience as they went along. There was a good foundation on which to build, for in the years prior to the War capable officials had been at the controlling positions, sensitive to their responsibilities and comprehending the national interest, and they had built well. Theirs was a compact though relatively small organization, and, even though department personnel was subject to the spoils system, they had made a beginning toward a career diplomatic service. Many of them left enviable records in the diplomatic history of their times and stamped their personalities on the Department.

There was John Bassett Moore, who was in and out of the Department several times as Assistant Secretary of State, as secretary and counsel to the American Commissioners who negotiated the Treaty of Peace with Spain in Paris in 1898, and early in the Wilson administration as Counselor, the title by which the present office of Under Secretary of State was then known. His monumental "Digest of International Law" is still the Bible of the Department, the final authority on questions that arise concerning the law of nations.

Several other assistant secretaries of state contributed valuable services in the same period. There were William F. Wharton, David Jayne Hill, and Francis B. Loomis. There was also W. W. Rockhill, whose sagacious counsel, although he had retired in 1897 as an assistant secretary, was a

powerful influence in Far Eastern diplomacy at the turn of the century. A little later, in the period of "dollar diplomacy," Huntington Wilson as the right hand of Secretary Philander C. Knox was a decisive force in the Department.

There were others less known to the public but equally effective in their special fields. Some are still in the service. There was Wilbur J. Carr, who rounded out his career at a focal point in European politics as Minister to Czecho-slovakia, a post where he was subjected to the greatest strain and performed ably when war seemed a matter of hours. Yet he is principally known as "the father of the Foreign Service" because he organized and supervised the modern consular service. As administrative officer of the Department in the years he was an assistant secretary of state, his control of the budget amounted almost to a rite. Secluded in his office, with secretaries moving silently and mysteriously about, he pruned figures conscientiously down to the last cent.

There was Charles Lee Cooke, in active harness until his death in 1937, who was the outstanding authority on social and ceremonial usage and diplomatic procedure. He was constantly consulted by Cabinet officers and other high ranking officials of the government and by the members of the foreign diplomatic corps, who placed great dependence upon his judgment and guidance. If they wanted to be sure about seating arrangements at an official dinner, or the order of precedence at a public ceremonial, they knew to whom to turn.

Entering the Department in 1901, Cooke became a specialist on ceremonial and protocol, but he was so busy he never had time to place his knowledge on record. Fortunately, a few years before his death the Department painstakingly obtained the information from him and used it as

the basis of rules and regulations in this field of its activities. However, something is missing, for there is lacking the personal authority with which Cooke imbued his pronouncements. He was a mild, friendly man whose grasp of his subject inspired unquestioned reliance in his judgments. Rules and regulations have their place, but they do not replace him.

Cooke abhorred vacations and could be found at his desk day in and day out twelve months in the year. For many years he arranged the seating for official White House dinners, first acting as behind-the-scenes adviser when arrangements were supposed to be made by officials of the Executive Mansion and then more openly (although his modesty kept him from the spotlight) when this function was formally transferred to the Department of State. Weeks in advance he would work out the details on table charts, carefully using red and blue pencils to distinguish between the gentlemen and ladies. Difficulties inevitably were encountered, but he was equal to every situation and never made a mistake.

His problems were trying, especially when the straight table ordinarily used for official dinners in the State dining room of the White House was replaced by a much larger horseshoe table to seat the ninety or a hundred guests at the annual diplomatic dinner given for the chiefs of foreign missions resident in Washington. Diplomats, jealous of their prerogatives, often have been observed quietly counting to ascertain whether any of their colleagues of lesser rank were seated more favorably in the numerical order following the line of their precedence in the diplomatic list of the Department of State. Cooke never misfired, although his skill was sorely taxed.

Once the American-born wife of the ambassador of one of the smaller Allied powers soon after the World War objected

to being escorted to her place at the diplomatic dinner by the German Ambassador. War hatreds were still strong and it was a coincidence in the order of seniority that her escort happened to be the ambassador of the former enemy country. An embarrassing incident was averted because she discovered the arrangement a few hours in advance and declared positively that she would plead illness in order not to attend, if the seating were not changed.

Cooke was called upon and managed to adjust matters satisfactorily; and his ingenuity forestalled other difficulties on that ticklish occasion. That experience was enough for the White House. It was early in the Coolidge administration, and the President promptly issued an order officially and formally transferring White House protocol to the Department of State. It had always been exercised there in fact, but Coolidge did not want any public misunderstanding on that score.

Cooke and Carr were of a type that has not entirely disappeared from the Department, for there is Sidney Y. Smith, still in service as an assistant in the Treaty Division at the age of eighty-one. He entered the Department in 1881, and from 1897 until its abandonment in 1918 was chief of the Diplomatic Bureau, where he had charge of diplomatic correspondence with foreign states. This work has since been absorbed by other divisions. A skillful expert in the drafting of treaties and conventions with an encyclopedic mind for precedents, he now attends to details of these special diplomatic instruments and the technical requirements in the ceremony of signing treaties. He sees that the plenipotentiaries affix their signatures properly, that wax, seals, and ribbons are attached, that everything proceeds according to protocol. Word that a treaty is to be signed during the day often spreads through the Department for the first time when

Smith is observed in the corridors attired in the frock coat he always wears at the ceremonies, and accompanied by his inevitable pipe.

Yet the dean of all this group was Adee. He was born in Astoria, New York, on November 7, 1842, and because of deafness resulting from illness in childhood was privately educated. He never married. He gave his undivided attention to official duties, except for annual summer bicycle trips through Europe, when he freshened his viewpoint through personal contact with lands to which he gave official attention the rest of the year. Entering the service in 1870 as secretary of legation in Madrid, he quickly won attention by discovering the presence in Vigo of Boss Tweed and being instrumental in his capture and return to New York.

Eight years later he returned to Washington as chief of the Diplomatic Bureau. He became Third Assistant Secretary of State in 1882, and four years later, in 1886, was promoted to Second Assistant Secretary of State upon the death of William Hunter, the only one who had previously held the office. For a brief time in 1898 he was Secretary of State *ad interim*, and at other times he was Acting Secretary of State during the absences of the Secretary from the Capital. He continued in the rank of Second Assistant Secretary of State until the office was abolished and all assistant secretaries of state were placed on the same level with the reorganization of July 1, 1924, under the Rogers Act. He was appointed an assistant secretary of state, but three days later he died.

This is the brief record by which he preferred to be remembered, for he was without vanity and desired no personal credit. It was for this reason he had all his personal papers burned upon his death. His acts were carefully inscribed in the official records, but his personal association with them, down to the penciled notations he liked to make from

[25]

"Alice in Wonderland," his favorite book, were carefully destroyed.

A wise adviser on policy, he knew the roots which nourish peoples and governments, and so largely determine their foreign policies. A master of the diplomatic phrase, with an extraordinary talent for drafting official communications, he was also a reservoir of diplomatic history and precedents, with an astonishing memory. The esteem in which he was held was gladly conceded by his official superiors.

Secretary Hay referred to him as "*semper paratus* Adee; an invaluable man." On the fiftieth anniversary of his government service, Secretary of State Bainbridge Colby spoke of its significance to the Department "which at so many points bears the impress of your learning and remarkable abilities." Secretary Hughes described him as "the constant and most trusted adviser of Secretaries of State." He was the only man who could write a despatch that President Cleveland would sign without altering. President Wilson in refusing his resignation said that was also the wish of the entire Cabinet.

On one occasion not so many years ago an indignant Secretary of State was bent upon giving a prominent foreign ambassador papers of dismissal because of an official affront, real or fancied. He refused to listen to calming counsels until Adee recommended that no action be taken. The Secretary immediately adopted the advice. It averted an international sensation over a question the details of which have never been revealed. Possibly the Secretary of State of that day may some time disclose them, if he ever writes his memoirs.

One after another, Presidents relied upon Adee's counsel. President McKinley valued it especially. On the eve of the War with Spain, the President was informed only a few minutes in advance that the ambassadors of six European powers were coming to the White House to make an official appeal for peace on behalf of their governments. McKinley,

who kept a firm grasp on foreign affairs, knew what his answer would be. He considered the situation "intolerable." At least it was out of control of diplomacy. The question was how to inform the ambassadors of his refusal. They represented an impressive group of nations—Germany, Austria-Hungary, France, Great Britain, Italy, and Russia. They were coming to the White House under instructions of their governments and had their appeal framed in a formal communication couched in careful diplomatic phraseology.

McKinley hastily asked Adee how he should tell the envoys of his refusal. In the few minutes available Adee scratched a statement on the back of an envelope and McKinley made it as his own to the ambassadors. It meant "No." It consisted of two paragraphs. The first thanked the envoys for their good will. The second, of a single sentence, said, "The Government of the United States appreciates the humanitarian and disinterested character of the communication now made on behalf of the powers named, and for its part is confident that equal appreciation will be shown for its own earnest and unselfish endeavors to fulfill a duty to humanity by ending a situation the indefinite prolongation of which has become insufferable."

It was a fine example of Adee's art. It also met completely McKinley's requirement, so often expressed in the form of a question to Adee and others, "It sounds pretty. Will it wash?"

After making the statement President McKinley crumpled the envelope and threw it into a wastebasket, from which it was recovered and copied in the official records. Adee preserved the envelope until his death, when it was burned with his other papers.

As time passed an expanding organization took over functions he had long exercised, but he retained this facility in diplomatic expression until the end. Shortly before his death

he was called upon by Secretary Hughes to draft a note to Great Britain on a commercial subject. It required delicacy in phrasing but unmistakable point and insistence. Others had attempted it unsuccessfully. Seated at his desk in a corner of the small office he occupied, Adee promptly completed the task and an assistant took the note to Secretary Hughes. He read it, paused, and, as he turned to it again with an appreciative gesture, said, "I shall now give myself the pleasure of a second reading."

The old system passed. It had gradually been changing in Adee's time, and even before. As early as 1833 the Department had been reorganized from its very small beginnings through the establishment of seven bureaus. In 1853 the office of an assistant secretary of state was created, a second assistant secretary of state was provided in 1866, and eight years later, in 1874, the office of third assistant secretary of state was added.

In the meantime, Secretary Hamilton Fish had carried out, in 1870, a reorganization through the establishment of diplomatic and consular bureaus. The next important reorganization was conducted in 1908 by Secretary of State Elihu Root, who set up the first of the regional divisions having jurisdiction in departmental affairs over geographic areas. This operated so successfully that it was followed by others in the course of the next fourteen years. Through these divisions the work of the Department was carried on with countries by areas, for western and eastern Europe, the Near and Far Easts, and Latin America. As an administrative device it worked well.

Then the World War and the Peace Conference produced their shocks and lessons. Gradually divisions were reorganized, better technical services were provided through selection of expert personnel in greater numbers, and new

offices and bureaus were provided as circumstances justified. Each succeeding Secretary of State after the World War made improvements, while Secretary Hughes made an outstanding contribution by placing the Foreign Service on a merit basis in a sweeping reorganization.

Still the duties of the Department continued to grow. Finally, Secretary Hull carried out a broad reorganization in the light of new requirements and of the more than fifteen years' experience since the War. The office of Under Secretary of State was retained, along with assistant secretaries of state, but the geographic divisions were rearranged and consolidated.

As at present constituted there are four geographic divisions: Europe, the Near East, the Far East, and the American Republics. They are directed by career diplomats, but only one of the four chiefs is still classified as a Foreign Service officer. The others are rated as permanent departmental officials. Now that the Foreign Service is on a sound basis, this represents an evolution that is taking place toward the establishment of a permanent home service in the Department where chiefs and assistant chiefs of divisions may serve without the interruption of periodic tours of duty abroad.

Between the division chiefs and the assistant secretaries of state stand two political advisers to the Secretary of State. They are diplomats of long experience who inform him of political aspects of relations abroad, one for Europe and the other for the Far East. Undoubtedly a third will be provided for Latin America. Around the geographic divisions stretch other bureaus, offices, and divisions dealing with technical questions. There are legal and economic divisions, passport and visa offices. There is also an historical and research section in charge of the Department's library founded by Thomas Jefferson and now containing two hundred thousand

volumes. And of course there are many others for carrying on the far-flung duties of the Department.

Some would astonish Adee and his coterie. There is, for example, a Division of Controls which issues licenses for the export of munitions, sees that arms embargoes are not violated, and registers domestic arms manufacturers. It represents a far cry from a period only a score of years distant when gun running to Mexico and Central America was one of the most irritating problems confronting officials. One division alone represents an enormous increase in the business of the Department in recent years. It is the Trade Agreements Division, which conducts the details of negotiating tariff treaties. This also is a far cry from the days when the tariff was a local issue and subject to logrolling in Congress. An indication of the volume of work the modern method of scientific tariff making entails may be gathered from the fact that in the Department of State and other agencies of the government are fifty subcommittees engaged in this activity. All head up into the Trade Agreements Division of the Department.

There is one office very recently established that represents the ultramodern in American diplomacy. It is a Division of Cultural Relations and is designed to spread good feeling and understanding among the nations to the South, and, incidentally, meet propaganda drives of Germany, Italy, Great Britain, and other European countries in South America where markets are eagerly sought, as well as to combat the ideologies of totalitarian states. The radio, unknown to Adee in its modern development, is one of the principal instruments for carrying on these activities.

While there are many permanent department officials on the staffs of the geographic and other divisions, Foreign Service officers continually flow in and out of them from the

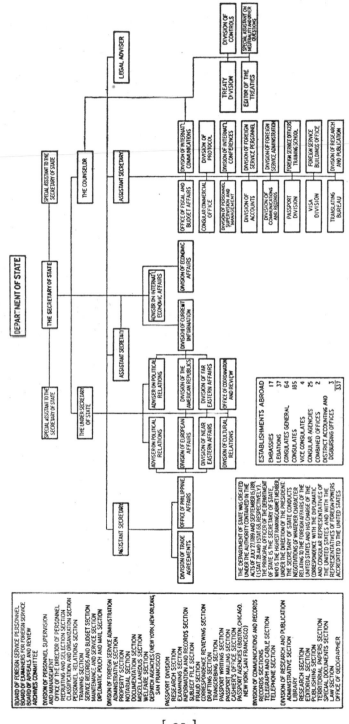

DEPARTMENT OF STATE

THE SECRETARY OF STATE

SPECIAL ASSISTANT TO THE SECRETARY OF STATE

THE COUNSELOR

LEGAL ADVISER

SPECIAL ASSISTANT ON NEUTRALITY AND OTHER QUESTIONS

TREATY DIVISION

EDITOR OF THE TREATIES

DIVISION OF CONTROLS

SPECIAL ASSISTANT TO THE SECRETARY OF STATE

THE UNDER SECRETARY OF STATE

ASSISTANT SECRETARY

OFFICE OF FISCAL AND BUDGET AFFAIRS

CONSULAR COMMERCIAL OFFICE

DIVISION OF PERSONNEL SUPERVISION AND MANAGEMENT

DIVISION OF ACCOUNTS

DIVISION OF COMMUNICATIONS AND RECORDS

PASSPORT DIVISION

VISA DIVISION

TRANSLATING BUREAU

DIVISION OF INTERNAT'L COMMUNICATIONS

DIVISION OF PROTOCOL

DIVISION OF INTERNAT'L CONFERENCES

DIVISION OF FOREIGN SERVICE PERSONNEL

DIVISION OF FOREIGN SERVICE ADMINISTRATION

FOREIGN SERVICE OFFICERS' TRAINING SCHOOL

FOREIGN SERVICE BUILDINGS OFFICE

DIVISION OF RESEARCH AND PUBLICATION

ASSISTANT SECRETARY

ADVISER ON POLITICAL RELATIONS

ADVISER ON INTERNAT'L ECONOMIC AFFAIRS

DIVISION OF ECONOMIC AFFAIRS

ADVISER ON POLITICAL RELATIONS

DIVISION OF EUROPEAN AFFAIRS

DIVISION OF NEAR EASTERN AFFAIRS

DIVISION OF CULTURAL RELATIONS

DIVISION OF CURRENT INFORMATION

DIVISION OF THE AMERICAN REPUBLICS

DIVISION OF FAR EASTERN AFFAIRS

OFFICE OF COORDINATION AND REVIEW

ASSISTANT SECRETARY

OFFICE OF PHILIPPINE AFFAIRS

DIVISION OF TRADE AGREEMENTS

ESTABLISHMENTS ABROAD

EMBASSIES	17
LEGATIONS	37
CONSULATES GENERAL	64
CONSULATES	185
VICE CONSULATES	4
CONSULAR AGENCIES	25
COMBINED OFFICES	2
DISTRICT ACCOUNTING AND DISBURSING OFFICES	3
	337

THE DEPARTMENT OF STATE WAS CREATED UNDER THE AUTHORITY CONTAINED IN THE ACTS OF JULY 27, 1789 AND SEPTEMBER 15, 1789, (1 STAT 28 AND 1 STAT 68, RESPECTIVELY). THE PRINCIPAL OFFICER OF THE DEPARTMENT OF STATE IS THE SECRETARY OF STATE, WHO IS THE HIGHEST RANKING CABINET MEMBER. UNDER THE DIRECTION OF THE PRESIDENT, THE SECRETARY OF STATE CONDUCTS NEGOTIATIONS OF WHATEVER CHARACTER RELATING TO THE FOREIGN AFFAIRS OF THE UNITED STATES, AND HAS CHARGE OF THE CORRESPONDENCE WITH THE DIPLOMATIC AND CONSULAR REPRESENTATIVES OF THE UNITED STATES AND WITH THE REPRESENTATIVES OF FOREIGN POWERS ACCREDITED TO THE UNITED STATES

BOARD OF FOREIGN SERVICE PERSONNEL
BOARD OF EXAMINERS FOR FOREIGN SERVICE
BOARD OF APPEALS AND REVIEW
ARCHIVES COMMITTEE

DIVISION OF PERSONNEL SUPERVISION AND MANAGEMENT
OFFICE OF THE DIRECTOR OF PERSONNEL
RECRUITING AND SELECTION SECTION
CLASSIFICATION AND ORGANIZATION SECTION
PERSONNEL RELATIONS SECTION
TRAINING SECTION
SERVICE RECORDS AND BUDGET SECTION
MAINTENANCE AND SERVICE SECTION
DIPLOMATIC POUCH AND MAIL SECTION

DIVISION OF FOREIGN SERVICE ADMINISTRATION
ADMINISTRATIVE SECTION
PROPERTY SECTION
NOTARIAL SECTION
DOCUMENTATION SECTION
MISCELLANEOUS SECTION
WELFARE SECTION
DESPATCH AGENCIES (NEW YORK, NEW ORLEANS, SAN FRANCISCO)

PASSPORT DIVISION
RESEARCH SECTION
EXAMINING SECTION
INFORMATION AND RECORDS SECTION
SUBJECT FILE SECTION
FRAUD SECTION
CORRESPONDENCE REVIEWING SECTION
DRAFTING SECTION
TRANSCRIBING SECTION
PASSPORT WRITING SECTION
PASSPORT MAILING SECTION
CASHIER'S OFFICE SECTION
PASSPORT AGENCIES (BOSTON, CHICAGO, NEW YORK, SAN FRANCISCO)

DIVISION OF COMMUNICATIONS AND RECORDS
RECORDS SECTION
TELEGRAPH AND CABLE SECTION
TELEPHONE SECTION

DIVISION OF RESEARCH AND PUBLICATION
ADMINISTRATIVE SECTION
LIBRARY
RESEARCH SECTION
EDITORIAL SECTION
PUBLISHING SECTION
TERRITORIAL PAPERS SECTION
SPECIAL DOCUMENTS SECTION
LAW SECTION
OFFICE OF GEOGRAPHER

field. They supervise the work concerning different countries in which they are specialists. There are experts on Spain, China, Japan, Cuba, Mexico, and all other countries. All together the arrangement provides an organization of non-partisan experts who read, evaluate, and assemble all the information bearing upon matters calling for decisions.

The expert personnel is a combination of men acquainted with the records of the Department and the precedents of the past, and men from the Foreign Service with the specially valuable background which experience in the foreign field has given them. Some return quietly to the Department and take over routine desks with laurels and practical rewards won in tight and dangerous places.

One whose distinguished service was equalled by his modest demeanor when he returned from the Spanish Civil War was Eric C. Wendelin. He had been in the service only five years and was serving as third secretary in the Embassy in Madrid, where he was the only officer on duty when the Spanish revolution suddenly broke out in the summer of 1936. The Ambassador and the rest of the staff were cut off without warning at the summer capital on the seashore and were unable to return to Madrid. Wendelin found himself in charge and in a grave emergency with American lives and interests at stake.

He was thirty-one years old. He was in the third Foreign Service grade from the bottom, rating the modest salary of $3,000 a year when this responsibility so unexpectedly devolved upon him. The situation would have given the gravest concern to an older and more experienced official. It caused the most serious apprehensions in the Department of State and the White House. Wendelin, however, was undismayed and rose to the emergency. A chance which occasionally comes to a Foreign Service officer was before him and he seized it.

He remained in Madrid under heavy bombardments and the stress of war service at the front, worked all hours, gathered Americans into the Embassy building, where he organized them into work squads to care for the building and the routine of daily life and even saw that there were amusements for dull hours by organizing bridge parties and nursery entertainment for the children. At the same time he made vigorous representations at the Foreign Office in behalf of Americans as circumstances required, and kept in touch with consular officers at posts of danger throughout Spain. When the capital moved, he moved with it.

His performance was so brilliant the Department refused to supersede him with a higher ranking officer. The Ambassador was stationed on the French frontier to watch developments from that quarter. In the meantime Americans were evacuated from Spain in the largest operation of that character that had been carried out since the outbreak of the World War found Americans in the summer of 1914 at danger points throughout Europe. Finally, after the crisis for Americans was over, Wendelin, being due for a tour of home duty, was recalled to the Department. He was officially commended and promoted one grade. His new rank carries a salary of $3,900.

As the official in charge of the Spanish desk in the Department he is directly available to the Secretary of State for consultation when important questions of policy arise. However, the system does not operate so simply. The advice of a young official is not the only guidance. As a junior official he sits at the foot of the table when staff conferences on his special subject are held in the office of the Secretary of State. There are present older and more experienced heads, the Under Secretary of State, two or more assistant secretaries of state, the political adviser on European affairs, the chief of the European division, and the legal and economic advisers

to the Secretary of State. There all angles of the situation are canvassed and decisions reached, subject to the approval of the President.

The same method is applied for all other areas of the world under the present organization of the Department, which is designed to withstand strain and not be thrown out of gear by an emergency. It represents a degree of refinement that was unknown when Adee was at the summit of his powers. Then there were three assistant secretaries of state, but no Under Secretary of State, as the chief guides for the Secretary. There were a number of bureaus but no such elaborate network of divisions and offices staffed by a multitude of experts and operating in close coordination with each other. Now there is a degree of specialization that suggests the right-eye doctor and the left-eye doctor. Nevertheless, a return to the old order would manifestly be impossible. Without doubt it would not be desired by officials of a quarter of a century ago, if they should miraculously reappear at their former posts.

The extent to which the system is utilized naturally depends upon the temperament of the Secretary of State. It runs automatically up to a point, but whether or not it performs beyond that point depends upon the demands made of it. The machinery is completely under the control of the Secretary and it is for him to decide how he will employ it. Here the personal equation enters. Secretary Hull has used the coordinated method to the utmost. Another Secretary of State might turn the machinery over very largely to his immediate subordinates, if he had a one-track mind and was concentrating on a single great problem.

There have been Secretaries with one-track minds and others of a different type. Secretary Hughes, for example, had an extraordinary capacity for turning swiftly from

[34]

problem to problem, yet such was his intellectual energy that, looking back on the four years he directed the Department, officials remark that "he did it all himself." The work he accomplished was prodigious. Mail that is now distributed among several chief officials he signed in huge volume daily. And he knew what he signed. While he relied upon subordinates, he knew for himself every angle of every situation and made incisive decisions. He labored long hours at the Department during the day and at home far into the night.

He permitted no time to be wasted. If a caller wished to see him, that was made known through a brief written memorandum which he would sweep with one glance, rather than lose time in unnecessary conversation with his secretary. Yet he knew how to relax and, when he wished, could spend time in pleasant conversation. The newspaper correspondents who met him daily in press conferences discovered that he had a fine sense of humor.

His power of concentration, of turning from one subject to another with extraordinary speed, and of getting at the facts himself, however, was a distinguishing trait. He demonstrated it repeatedly. Many instances could be given, but perhaps one will suffice. Just before he assumed office, on March 5, 1921, the day after the inauguration of President Harding, Panama and Costa Rica had become involved in a tense dispute over a boundary question which had been submitted years before to the arbitration of Chief Justice Edward D. White of the United States. His award had not been accepted by both governments, although the parties were pledged in advance to abide by it. Fortunately, when administrations change in Washington there is close cooperation between the outgoing and incoming Secretaries of State and their chief assistants, even though they may be of

opposite political parties. Possibly Panama and Costa Rica had counted on a period of indecision in the Department of State during the change of administrations. At any rate, Secretary Hughes had not had time to acquaint himself with the details of the Central American controversy.

It was in these circumstances that a newspaper correspondent, having received a report telling of actual hostilities, sought him in his hotel rooms one night at 10:00 P.M. He found the Secretary alone, seated in a chair in the center of a dozen chairs that were covered with official reports and latest despatches to the Department of State.

Secretary Hughes by his cordial manner at once dispelled his reputation as a "human icicle." He removed papers from one of the chairs to make a place for his caller and waved toward the others as he explained that the boundary dispute was the matter occupying him. Using a favorite expression, he said he was attempting to separate the wheat from the chaff in order to determine the facts. As soon as he had completed his study he would be prepared to act.

The United States was interested in the preservation of peace on this continent. It also did not want war to break out close to the Panama Canal. Moreover, there was the issue of governments observing their plighted word if a sound basis of good relations was to be maintained. Secretary Hughes did act. Having marshaled and analyzed the facts, he promptly sent a note demanding a cessation of fighting. He then opened the way for Panama and Costa Rica to adjust their dispute through mediation of the United States.

He had an adequately large department for disposing of that question, but he made use of its services in his own way. Other Secretaries of State might have used the conference method, and probably have arrived at the same result.

Secretary Hughes did not disdain the Department. On the contrary, he used it to the utmost. Before he left office he demonstrated conclusively that he appreciated its importance by making the great contribution to its operation of a scientifically reorganized Foreign Service. That achievement still stands. The Service has been improved since in the light of experience but fundamentally the present organization of the Foreign Service is what Secretary Hughes, in collaboration with Representative John Jacob Rogers of Massachusetts, bequeathed to the Department.

Other Secretaries of State when they succeeded to the office made important contributions to the organization, and future ones will make changes to meet new conditions as the Department continues to grow with the country. It operated at first on a small scale, surged forward after the Civil War, when the personal factor dominated in administration—but not in policy, for that rested as always in international law, the precedents, the national interest, and the controlling force of political opinion; and emerged during the aftermath of the World War as a full-grown organization, highly specialized and expertly staffed.

Originally it was a one-cylinder machine. Today it is a sixteen-cylinder car, geared to high speed but not free of engine trouble.

CHAPTER III

THE DIRECTING FORCE

WHETHER the Department of State operates effi- ciently or loosely, vigorously or mildly, wisely or shortsightedly, depends primarily upon the Secretary of State. Lesser officials have their place in administering its affairs, contributing expert knowledge and judgment as well as diplomatic technique, and providing continuity from administration to administration, but it is the Secretary of State who gives direction and vitality to foreign policy. He is completely in control, subject to limitations of law, his own force of character and abilities, and the will of the White House.

It was with this in mind that President Coolidge was wont to say, "Bear in mind that the Secretary of State IS the Department of State." Yet Coolidge did not intend the definition as a comprehensive description of the office. If he had, it would have been more illuminating for him to say that the Secretary of State is the Federal chancellor, keeper of the great seal, and foreign minister.

His duties as foreign minister are almost always the most important. As custodian of the Seal of the United States they are perfunctory, for he merely affixes the seal to presidential proclamations and other legal documents—an act usually performed for him by the Chief Clerk of the Department. Important as is his role of foreign minister, it has at times been overshadowed by his place as Federal chancellor, or

premier of the Cabinet, a circumstance that has been the only inducement for some men to accept the office. It is recognized at every Cabinet meeting where the Secretary of State sits at the right hand of the President, and in the presidential succession ordained by Congress under which he would be the first to succeed to the Presidency in event of the permanent incapacity or death of both the President and Vice President.

This has never occurred in the history of the country, but frequently the Secretary of State finds himself the senior official in the executive branch of the government in Washington because of absence of the President. Notwithstanding the fact that the President, wherever he is, may now keep in direct contact with the seat of government, the Secretary of State follows the custom of horse-and-buggy days and invariably remains in the capital during absences of the Chief Executive prepared to act in an emergency.

The political character of the office is often lost sight of in the country; it is never forgotten in the government. It attaches in some degree to all Cabinet posts. In fact, there have been many times when Presidents have considered the political side of greater importance than the administrative in certain of their Cabinet officers. The selections frequently are dictated by political considerations in the first place.

This was very frankly conceded on one occasion by President Theodore Roosevelt when he was bluntly asked what use his Secretary of the Navy was. He had five in seven and a half years. Roosevelt liked impertinent questions—if they were not asked too often—and so he paused a moment to enjoy this one before replying. Then flashing his famous white teeth, he said, "You should remember that a Cabinet officer has two functions, one to administer his department and the other to serve as a political adviser to the President;

and, *politically*, the Secretary of the Navy is of *some* use to me."

This may not have been very complimentary to his Secretary of the Navy of the moment, but it stated a truth—one that cannot be overlooked in considering the office of Secretary of State.

On the other hand, even though the office is dominant in the Cabinet and in the Department of State, the Secretary of State does not serve long. He is not appointed for a fixed term but serves at the pleasure of the White House. He usually but not necessarily goes out of office with the President who has appointed him, and he always tenders his resignation when the administration changes. In a number of cases the Secretary of State has continued into the succeeding administration, remaining at the head of the Department for a short time until his successor has assumed the duties of the office.

Not one, any more than a President, has served more than eight years, and even this is not a long period in terms of foreign policy or the continuing life of the Department. Secretaries come, exercise their influence, make their contributions to diplomatic history, and go. The Department continues, with the records they have made inscribed in its traditions, and its life history more fully rounded because of their influence. Policy has been more sharply marked, and precedents have been established that will shape future action as new issues arise in a world that is never static.

Few Secretaries of State have served as many as eight years; in fact it is more than sixty years since the last one served that long. Of the forty-five Secretaries, from Thomas Jefferson to Cordell Hull, only four occupied the office for eight years, or within a few months of that span. They were James Madison and John Quincy Adams in the early

history of the country, and William H. Seward and Hamilton Fish in the Lincoln, Johnson, and Grant administrations. Another four held the office for approximately six years, James Monroe and John Forsyth in the early period, John Hay, and now Cordell Hull, who may well carry on to join the select company that has eight years to its credit. Sixteen served four years, and the others for lesser periods. The average throughout the entire history of the government is three and a quarter years, and it is an average quite closely maintained both before and since the Civil War.

This relatively low average is in general due to normal political or natural causes, for most of those who have held the office have acquitted themselves creditably and to the satisfaction of the White House. After all, in the past 100 years only four Presidents were in office eight consecutive years. Many Secretaries of State passed out of office when their administrations came to a close; others retired voluntarily in order to recoup their private fortunes after years in public office, or for other personal reasons. Four died in office, Abel P. Upshur, who was killed in the explosion of a naval gun on the Potomac River in the Tyler administration, Daniel Webster, Walter Q. Gresham in the second Cleveland administration, and John Hay.

James G. Blaine retired when political differences arose between him and President Benjamin Harrison. Fortunately for the country, never since has there been as sharp political rivalry between a President and his Secretary of State. A few have been dismissed in the course of the long history of the Department. In fact, it was an early experience, for Timothy Pickering, who entered the office under President Washington, was ousted by President John Adams because of his attitude during years of strained relations with revolutionary France. In recent history Robert Lansing was

forced to resign and William Jennings Bryan voluntarily resigned because of differences with President Wilson. Many have continued in public office after leaving the Department of State, several having enriched the Senate with their experience and abilities. A few have gone higher, for six became President and two Chief Justice of the United States. The last to become President was James Buchanan. In the early years of the Republic the office of Secretary of State was a direct steppingstone to the Presidency, but it is no longer. Jefferson became President; so did Madison, Monroe, John Quincy Adams, and Martin Van Buren, while several, including Henry Clay, Lewis Cass, and Blaine, were unsuccessful candidates for the Presidency. It is interesting to note that not one Secretary of State has become President since before the Civil War.

John Marshall, who was Secretary of State less than a year under John Adams, became the great Chief Justice, an office not held again by a former Secretary of State until Charles Evans Hughes was appointed to that high post. Both served as Chief Justice during critical periods in the history of the Supreme Court.

This record is sufficiently extensive to point to the political character of the office. It is true that as a rule men of exceptional qualifications have been selected to preside over the Department of State. The greatest care is exercised by the President in making the appointment, because the Secretary of State is the chief of his Cabinet as well as his chief adviser in the conduct of that most delicate subject, foreign affairs.

Yet it is a curious fact that of the entire list of forty-five, only two have come from west of the Mississippi River: William Jennings Bryan and Frank B. Kellogg; and the appointment of Bryan was dictated by political necessity without regard to foreign affairs, while Kellogg was born in

New York State, even though he lived in the West as an adult. The most acceptable explanation is that with the growth of the country proceeding from East to West, the regions first settled and so more firmly established have developed more interest in foreign problems than sections where questions associated with pioneering have held first place. If so, it can be expected that in the future more Secretaries of State will be found coming from the West.

It also is an interesting circumstance that few Secretaries of State have been international lawyers by profession. That is only one of many reasons why a solid and efficient Department of State is essential. Several Secretaries have had wide diplomatic experience, especially in the earlier years of the government, a few have been men of literary attainments, many have been outstanding corporation lawyers, and others have been great political leaders. Nearly all have had political experience.

On a number of occasions the President has selected for the office the leading figure, next to him, in his political party. Thus it was that Blaine was selected; that Wilson appointed Bryan, whose qualifications for directing foreign policy were widely open to question; and that, among other reasons, President Harding appointed as his Secretary of State Charles Evans Hughes, who had been the unsuccessful candidate of the Republican party for the Presidency four years before.

A political selection of the chief of the Cabinet obviously makes for unity and cooperation in the party. It bears immediate fruit, as when Bryan performed yeoman service in assisting President Wilson to have Congress adopt his legislative program the first two years he was in the White House. Occasionally it has only multiplied troubles because of overweening political ambition of the Secretary of State.

Nearly all who have held the office have had prior political experience, and two-thirds of them in the national arena. The record is a long one, but a few illustrations will give point to the observation. Henry Clay, for example, during a lengthy public career was thrice Speaker of the House of Representatives, Senator, and Whig candidate for President; Daniel Webster was the political leader of New England; Buchanan was for years an influential leader of Northern Democrats in the Senate at a time when Southern Democrats were in the White House; John C. Calhoun was a great Southern leader in the Senate and had also served as Vice President; William H. Seward all but won the Republican nomination for President in 1860 and had been for years a political leader in New York and in the Senate. Elihu Root in the course of a long public career was a directing force in a long series of Republican national conventions. Cordell Hull, in addition to service in both branches of Congress, was for several years chairman of the Democratic national committee. More than a score served in the Senate or House of Representatives, or both. Many were governors of their states.

Still other considerations have entered into the selections. John Hay, to be sure, had long been a spokesman for the Republican party, but he had also had valuable diplomatic experience and at the time of his appointment as Secretary of State was Ambassador in London. More than a quarter of a century later history was repeated when President Coolidge turned to the London Embassy and summoned the Ambassador, Frank B. Kellogg, to take charge of the Department of State.

While Kellogg had had a long public career, including a term of six years in the Senate, what counted even more in his favor was that as ambassador he had come to know the

leading statesmen of Europe, was thoroughly acquainted with the problems of European diplomacy, and no other man who was politically suitable and available could match these qualifications. As the writer learned in the White House at the time, Kellogg's selection was due to his practical equipment for the office.

Several Secretaries of State held other Cabinet portfolios before being transferred to the Department of State. This fact recalls an observation made by President Wilson to Franklin D. Roosevelt when he was Assistant Secretary of the Navy and often repeated by Roosevelt to official associates after he himself became President. It probably reflected an attitude of the academic mind. In any event, a good argument can be made for its soundness.

"A man who has had important experience and learned to discharge his duties with satisfaction," Wilson said, "finds that he has no difficulty in quickly learning and discharging the duties of another position to which he has been transferred. It is largely a matter of experience."

Many Secretaries of State have justified this observation.

Yet the office is more than administrative. The position of the Secretary of State in the Cabinet as a member of the President's official family and closest body of advisers is often as important as his departmental position. He is not expected to confine his observations in Cabinet meetings to foreign affairs. His advice on a wide variety of political problems is invited.

Sometimes this influence is of a peculiarly personal character, if he enjoys the close confidence of the President. Many have had this confidence, and perhaps none more than Elihu Root. Between Root, with his legal brain, and Theodore Roosevelt, the impulsive President, was a firm bond of sympathy and understanding, so strong that, had it been

politically possible, Roosevelt would have preferred to have Root succeed him in the White House.

It is still recalled in the Executive Offices of the White House how the two would be heard in eager discussion at the President's desk, their voices growing louder as the argument proceeded and finally, above the vigorous voice of the President, Root would say firmly, "Now, Theodore—" and prevail upon him with his moderating counsel.

The political service performed by Bryan for President Wilson is remembered by veteran members of Congress who were in the House of Representatives and Senate a quarter of a century ago. There have been innumerable other instances when the Secretary of State has appeared in a political role behind the scenes or on the stump in open and active support of the administration. His political talent, however, may be overdeveloped for the successful conduct of the duties of foreign minister.

James G. Blaine was a Secretary of State who through long years of controversy on the political stump and in the legislative forum was unsuited for the more delicate tasks of diplomatic negotiation. Yet his political talents were put to great public service when he initiated the movement for Pan-Americanism in the Western Hemisphere and by his vigorous championship of the cause from the public platform won for it a popular support without which diplomatic efforts in this field might have failed for many years.

Obviously, within proper limits political experience and skill is an essential part of the equipment of the successful Secretary of State. The great problems which come before him in the Department of State are in their essence political and call for shrewd and farsighted wisdom. Moreover, the Secretary of State has his own personal political problem of keeping in step with the President, and also of winning the

support of the Chief Executive and often of Congress to his own views.

The fact remains, however, that the great Secretaries of State stand out in history by virtue of the records they made in conducting foreign affairs. Their political side has been important at the moment but has not given them enduring reputations, save as they may have moved higher, into the Presidency. Moreover, their administrations of the Department of State usually stand out for some single achievement. This is true even of several of the lesser figures who have occupied the office. Irrespective of what they have accomplished in many directions, some single event in their administration of the Department captures the public imagination or so overshadows all else that forever they are stamped with its distinguishing mark.

There are many examples. In the early history of the country the part John Quincy Adams played in drafting the Monroe Doctrine will always be associated with his name. A few years later Webster's negotiation of the boundary treaty with Lord Ashburton of Great Britain stands out as a landmark in his two periods of service as Secretary of State. Seward is remembered not only for his Civil War diplomacy but even more for his purchase of Alaska.

Coming to a later period, at the turn of the century, John Hay, who will always rank high among Secretaries of State, even though Theodore Roosevelt did not consider him of great stature, is known for his application of the Open Door policy in China. Elihu Root was a leader in the movement for legal determination of international controversies and negotiated many arbitration treaties, a work which Secretary Kellogg later pressed vigorously until he had even more to his credit than Root. The name of Philander C. Knox is associated with the phrase "dollar diplomacy"

because of his policies in Manchuria and South America. Bryan's reputation in the office, scant as it is as a foreign minister, is based on his passion for peace and his negotiation of a wide-flung series of conciliation treaties.

Charles Evans Hughes is remembered for many activities but chiefly for his leadership in the limitation of navies by international agreement; Secretary Kellogg for his negotiation of the treaty outlawing war as an instrument of national policy, a contribution to international diplomacy for which he was awarded the Nobel peace prize; and Secretary Stimson for his implementation of that pact, in the course of his endeavors to mobilize world public opinion for peace in Manchuria, by refusing to recognize gains won contrary to the terms of the peace treaty. Secretary Hull, while pressing persistently a sane peace program, is known principally for his reciprocal trade agreements program.

The question may well be asked, who was the greatest Secretary of State? Obviously, there are so many phases of their careers to take into consideration that a categorical answer would produce only disagreement. Surprising as it may seem, in efforts to assess the qualities of Secretaries of State since the Civil War the palm is often given to Richard Olney who served for only two years, at the end of the second Cleveland administration. Interestingly enough, it is a view that finds considerable acceptance in the Department of State.

At least Olney made a deep impression on Washington because of his courage. It is sometimes contended that when through his vigorous note to Lord Salisbury he forced arbitration of the Venezuelan controversy with Great Britain he practiced shirt-sleeve diplomacy. This strong-arm technique is occasionally necessary to produce results. Some of his predecessors had done the same thing, as when Seward

terminated the Maximilian venture in Mexico, first by adroit and then by forceful diplomacy culminating in the ordering of an army to the border. Probably Olney knew exactly what he was doing. He had previously served as Attorney General and was an accomplished lawyer. And in the arbitration, Venezuela, while losing on several points, won on the principal issue, namely, control of the mouth of the Orinoco River; and Great Britain explicitly recognized the Monroe Doctrine.

The records have been made by men who were of different types; they were confronted in their times by widely varying foreign and domestic conditions. To review only partially the list of Secretaries of State since the Civil War, there was Seward, a tower of political strength in two administrations and a skillful negotiator who could be cool in times of stress. Hamilton Fish was a source of strength to the Grant administration and an efficient administrator of his department. Although William M. Evarts was considered a profound student of international law, he was confronted by no tests that would produce large achievement.

Hay was one whose success in the field of diplomacy was sometimes offset by his inability to cooperate with the Senate. The fault, however, was not entirely on his side. Knox was lazily indifferent to secondary matters but could act with promptness and decision on large questions. He admitted to his friends that in accepting the office he was moved by the desire to be premier; and he dominated the Cabinet of the Taft administration.

Secretary Hughes did not dominate the Harding Cabinet, but he directed the diplomacy of that short administration with a strong hand. For his own peace of mind he was fortunate in having in Harding a President who was content to let him direct foreign policy; and he found in Coolidge

a basis of complete confidence and mutual understanding. These two Presidents gave his abilities full and free scope for pursuing his task of regularizing relations with Europe after the chaos of the World War and dispelling the political clouds over the Pacific through the Washington Conference on Armament Limitation and Pacific Questions.

Of the incidents remembered vividly in the Department of State, probably more are associated with Secretary Hughes than with any other Cabinet officer in the memory of officials. As we have already seen, he was possessed of an incisive brain which enabled him to turn rapidly from subject to subject. His photographic memory was astonishing. At a glance he could take in the printed page and retain it. Many instances could be recalled but none more striking than when an official handed him a typewritten three-page memorandum for public announcement as he was leaving his desk to hold his daily press conference. Secretary Hughes took the memorandum, walked slowly to the reception room where the correspondents were awaiting him, and as he walked read the three pages, then folded and thrust them into an inside pocket.

Entering the reception room, he greeted the correspondents and made the announcement from memory. Later when the stenographic report of the conference was compared with the memorandum it was found that he had made one error, on a single, unimportant word.

Not all Secretaries of State had the same experience with Presidents as Secretary Hughes. McKinley retained close control of foreign affairs, yet Hay had more latitude under him than under Theodore Roosevelt. Woodrow Wilson was of a temperament that inevitably would have made him his own Secretary of State, even had the Great War not compelled that course. Harding, as has been pointed out, was a

far different type of executive, a fact that accounts for the persistence of a favorite story still told in Washington.

A Senator was asked by Harding how he intended to vote on a treaty pending in the Senate, it is related, and admitted after some equivocation that he had not read it. To which Harding made the frank reply, "You haven't got anything on me; I haven't read it either."

It should be said in justice to Harding, however, that from the first he was determined to let his Secretary of State direct foreign policy. He made this known when he presented newspapermen of his party at St. Augustine, Florida, to Charles Evans Hughes in February, 1921, a short time before inauguration, and announced the selection. He then told the correspondents that from that moment they should look exclusively to Mr. Hughes for information on foreign affairs.

Nevertheless, it would be an unusual President who would refrain from assuming close supervision of foreign affairs in a grave emergency. McKinley so acted when war loomed with Spain. Wilson, of course, had a continuous record of personal direction of foreign policy. At other times conditions have produced the reverse of this situation. Abraham Lincoln was forced by the great emergency of civil war to leave much of the direction of foreign policy to Seward, although there were times when he restrained his Secretary of State from taking too brusque action. President Hoover had an able and forceful Secretary of State in Henry L. Stimson, who kept him constantly informed of developing foreign policy. But President Hoover, although he gave his approval to foreign policy in its various stages, did not have the time for the subject that he would have had, if he had not been confronted with urgent domestic problems incident to a great depression.

As a general rule the President, if he will, can use his Secretary of State as a shield by permitting him to make announcements of policy and keeping silent himself. Not that this is a counsel of cowardice, but Presidents are open to attack on many fronts and it is unnecessary for them to rush into the open and court direct attacks when the Secretary of State might just as well bear the brunt of criticism. His line of vulnerability is much shorter than that of the President.

Secretary Hughes had this in mind when he advised President Coolidge late in 1923 on the reply that should be made to the appeal of Georgii V. Tchitcherin, Peoples Commissar for Foreign Affairs, for recognition of the Soviet government by the United States. Notwithstanding the absence of diplomatic relations, Commissar Tchitcherin addressed a telegram to President Coolidge on December 16th suggesting negotiations looking to recognition. The telegram was referred to Secretary Hughes, who two days later had a reply drafted and took it to the White House. It was a rejection of the appeal.

"If the Soviet authorities," it said, "are ready to restore the confiscated property of American citizens or to make effective compensation, they can do so. If the Soviet authorities are ready to repeal their decree repudiating Russia's obligations to this country and appropriately recognize them, they can do so. . . . Most serious is the continued propaganda to overthrow the institutions of this country. This government can enter into no negotiations until these efforts directed from Moscow are abandoned."

Coolidge approved the reply and it was decided to instruct the American consul in Riga to deliver it to the Soviet representative there for transmission to Tchitcherin. It was also decided to make it public immediately in the form of a

statement, and it was then that Secretary Hughes was asked by Coolidge why the President rather than the Secretary of State should not issue it. The President could, Secretary Hughes replied, but he should reflect on the fact that the administration would be attacked by elements at home for rejecting the Russian overture and that the Secretary of State could take that burden from the President's shoulders. Secretary Hughes was promptly told by the President to issue the statement. He made it public through the Division of Current Information in the Department of State and when four hours later President Coolidge was asked for comment and elaboration at a White House press conference he refused and referred the inquirers to the Department of State.

Thus Coolidge was more cautious than Woodrow Wilson who did not hesitate to go in person to the Versailles Peace Conference. This is considered by many the cardinal political mistake of his career, for he was held responsible for the failure of the Conference. Had someone else headed the delegation and the President remained at home, direct responsibility would have fallen elsewhere. But that was not Wilson's way.

There have been many times also when Presidents have deliberately acted independently of their Secretaries of State and made pronouncements of foreign policy which came as a surprise to the head of the Department of State. In such circumstances that official could only subscribe to the program, maintain silence, or resign. Such a situation arose when President Franklin D. Roosevelt in a speech on foreign policy in Chicago on October 5, 1937, suggested the quarantining of aggressor nations. A draft of the speech had been prepared after consultation with ranking officials in the Department of State who were familiar with its contents, and it did not then contain the dynamic phrase that aroused

so much comment. When, having re-dressed the draft to his own satisfaction, the President uttered the suggestion it caught Secretary Hull as much by surprise as anyone else.

On a more historic occasion, President Roosevelt took over direct supervision of foreign policy when he considered what measures the United States should take to encourage a peaceful adjustment of the Central European controversy in the fall of 1938 over Germany's demands on Czechoslovakia. In that case there was complete teamwork between him and his Secretary of State, with the President making the decisions and embodying them in direct appeals for peace to the heads of the governments involved. Likewise he directed the enunciation of the position of the United States toward the occupation of Czechoslovakia in March and of Albania in April, 1939, and later appealed to Chancellor Hitler for non-aggression pledges against thirty-one countries.

Not infrequently the President also makes decisions affecting the Department of State when other agencies of the government are more immediately concerned. This is true of naval limitation and international financial matters which affect the Navy or Treasury Departments directly and the Department of State only through their reactions on foreign policy. It has been especially so in regard to war debts owed by Europe to the United States, a subject in which Congress is also a directly interested party.

It was in such a situation that President Coolidge once acted promptly when he was spending a few days at his family homestead in Plymouth, Vermont, during the summer of 1926. It was a Sunday evening and the President was reading in the room where he had so dramatically taken the oath of office in the light of an oil lamp. Word was unexpectedly received that Georges Clemenceau, the wartime Premier of France although no longer in an official capacity,

had given out in Paris an open letter to the President urging sharp reduction or, preferably, cancellation of war debts. Only a short time before, the debts had been scaled down in refunding operations that had produced formal agreements supposed to stand inviolable until the obligations had been gradually paid off over a period of more than sixty years.

The word did not come officially; it never did. But it was apparent that a movement backed by powerful support was under way to upset the agreements and that prompt action was necessary to block it. In fact, a few years later they were upset under the impulse of forces which focused in the great depression.

The writer, having received a summary of the Clemenceau letter by telegraph, wrote a memorandum giving its terms and sent it by a Secret Service agent into the temporary White House with a suggestion that the President might care to comment. He did. Through the open window he could be seen studying the memorandum and occasionally walking around the room with the paper in his hand. In adjoining houses his friends and neighbors, many of them relatives who bore marked resemblances in features to the President, were occupied, not with problems of state, but with the humbler cares of farm life and thoughts of the week's work ahead.

In a few minutes the Secret Service agent returned with a penciled note from the President. With Coolidge brevity, it consisted of two sentences. It read, "This Government will conduct its relations with the French people through their duly constituted diplomatic authorities. The negotiations relative to the French debt are closed."

It was the only reply ever made to the Clemenceau letter, and was in due time copied into the official records of the Department of State. It was sufficient for the purpose,

effectively stopping the movement, a circumstance which the President realized the next morning and which his smiling face attested.

Long afterward, Secretary Kellogg in discussing the incident with the writer remarked that the doctrine enunciated concerning diplomatic intercourse was regarded as basic in the Department of State, that foreign negotiations will be conducted through official representatives and not through private individuals. It was a reaffirmation of a purpose long written into the laws of the United States, through the Logan Act passed in consequence of irregular diplomatic practices during the troubled era of the French revolution. The Act prohibits private American citizens from conducting diplomatic negotiations abroad.

The Secretary of State may be of large or mediocre calibre, but at least it is written in the laws that he as head of the Department of State is to conduct the diplomatic correspondence of the government, and that he is the right hand of the President in directing foreign affairs.

CHAPTER IV

THE GENERAL STAFF

AN engagingly frank Attorney General of the United States once confessed to the writer that when he assumed office and took over the direction of the legal arm of the government he was "scared to death." He was new to official life in Washington, but in a few weeks his trepidation was only an amusing memory. He had become adjusted to his surroundings, had tested the machine, and realized that he had as supporting aides a staff of competent lawyers and administrators, many of whom had had long experience in the Department.

Other Cabinet officers without previous experience in high office probably would admit the same feeling of uncertainty as they entered upon their duties. Secretaries of State are no exception, and many of them must in their private thoughts regard the years before them in the Department of State with emotion tinged with uncertainty. After all, nothing is more sobering than grave official responsibility. But, like the Attorney General in the Department of Justice, they know they have in the Department of State an organization that has been developed and tested through the years. Nevertheless, at the outset of an administration safeguards are erected against inexperience through the careful selection of the immediate official family of advisers of the Secretary of State.

Like the Secretary of War, with his trained circle of professional army officers headed by the Chief of Staff of the

Army and concentrated in a General Staff, the Secretary of State has at his right hand a body of professional advisers who may well be termed a general staff. They are to be found in the Under Secretary of State, who is virtually the chief of staff of the Department of State, the Counselor and the assistant secretaries of state. Not all of them but nevertheless a sufficient number are selected with an eye to professional experience in order to provide the Secretary of State with seasoned guidance, and also to assure continuity in basic foreign policy.

There is no more superficial assumption than that basic foreign policy changes from administration to administration. Temper and tone change, emphasis is often shifted here and there, but in its fundamental character American foreign policy changes surprisingly little. There are important differences in administrations as they conduct foreign affairs, but on close examination they usually will be found to concern principally details. After all, American diplomacy is imbedded in national history, has long been tested, and is little affected by partisan politics. Foreign affairs are not confined to the narrow channels of party programs.

In fact, one of the first discoveries a Secretary of State makes is that every question of any magnitude before the Department of State has both a *tale* and a *tail*. Before him stretch long histories of foreign policy carefully built up by preceding administrations in every important area of the world. He finds that the attitude of the government has been developed toward the economic, financial, and political problems of Europe step by step over the years. If a new administration would forget some aspects of the government's relations in the past with Latin America, nothing is more certain than that it will learn it cannot disregard the record. And in the Far East the pages of diplomacy are filled

with complications of the past forty years and a chain of
events extending back a century and a half.

The task of catching up with the record occupies the new
Secretary of State for weeks; and the study is never completed, for it is a continuing story. Although there is close
cooperation between an outgoing and an incoming Secretary
of State, and assistant secretaries of state sometimes remain
in the Department for weeks to aid their successors during
the period of transition, this would be insufficient except for
the guidance available from experienced and trained personnel which does not change with administrations every four
or eight years.

Even this would be inadequate, if ways had not been found
to offset the disadvantages of political appointments of the
chief advisers to the Secretary of State as represented in the
Under Secretary and assistant secretaries of state. True,
they must be of the same political party or politically in
sympathy with the White House; and it is equally proper
that the Secretary of State should have the opportunity to
select his own official family. Yet this would not assure continuity and experience in the conduct of foreign affairs if
every administration did not appoint a number of veteran
diplomats to the key positions.

Otherwise there would be serious objection to the custom
of an incoming President appointing a new Under Secretary
of State and several assistant secretaries of state as the
official family and immediate group of administrative assistants and consultants of the Secretary of State. From time to
time the suggestion has been advanced that there should be a
permanent Under Secretary who would remain in office
regardless of changes in administrations. Sometimes an alter-
native proposal has been offered calling for a permanent group
of elder statesmen sitting as an advisory council to give

continuity to policy. Neither has been adopted and for well-defined reasons. In the first place, the present system works very well, while there has been no convincing reply to the simple statement that the functions of an advisory council can be performed satisfactorily by the Committee on Foreign Relations of the Senate if it is kept promptly and adequately informed concerning policy by the Department of State.

Inasmuch as the Department derives benefit from new ideas contributed by officials with fresh viewpoints, it is probable that suggestions for a change in the system will not prevail as long as administrations in selecting the higher officials guard against a break with the past. In no other department of the government is so great care exercised to assure continuity through the selection of ranking officials. A career diplomatic service, the beginnings of which were laid nearly forty years ago, has made it possible.

Comparison is often made with the British Foreign Office where there is a Permanent Under Secretary of State, but under the practice that has grown up with respect to the Department of State there are more points of similarity than of difference between the two. This is the opinion of officials in the Department and also of foreign diplomats of long experience in Washington. In discussing the question with the writer, a British diplomat who himself had been Permanent Under Secretary in London remarked that "the two systems work out quite similarly."

His observation may be better understood through an explanation of the office of Under Secretary of State. He is the chief of staff and main reliance of the Secretary of State. They occupy adjoining offices that are connected by a door continually used as they constantly confer. Often, as the Under Secretary is at his desk engrossed in a study of documents, reports, and cable despatches, he is interrupted by

the Secretary of State who has walked in unannounced to discuss a knotty problem. At other times the Secretary summons the Under Secretary to his own office by the convenience of a buzzer. Physically their offices are separate. Actually they are very much one and the same.

The Under Secretary becomes Acting Secretary of State in the absence from the Capital of the Secretary, and he takes practically exclusive jurisdiction of important questions assigned him by the Secretary when he is required to concentrate on other matters. In addition, the Under Secretary relieves the Secretary of a large part of a duty that in the aggregate consumes an immense amount of time, by receiving many of the diplomatic callers from foreign embassies and legations who come to the Department with their problems.

In the ordinary routine of the day and in the consideration of major issues, he is the chief adviser of the Secretary of State. In the course of keeping the President informed of developing policy he is almost as frequent a caller at the White House as the Secretary himself. While his duties are sufficiently important in themselves, the position of the Under Secretary is doubly vital because so many Secretaries of State come to their high office without previous training in diplomacy or international law. Seldom has their experience given them the technical equipment for conducting foreign affairs alone.

Naturally, the selection of the Under Secretary is approached with unusual care. It is important enough when an incoming administration is of the same political party as its predecessor; it is of even greater importance when the incoming administration is of the opposite political party. The solution has been found by appointing one who is steeped in the traditions of American diplomacy. Since the office was created, the practice usually has been to select a

[61]

career diplomat or an official of long experience and training in the home service of the Department of State.

Since the office of Under Secretary was established in 1919 there have been two outstanding instances of this careful procedure to assure continuity in the direction of foreign policy at the top. When in 1921 President Harding, a Republican, succeeded Woodrow Wilson, a Democrat, the appointment of Under Secretary of State was given to Henry P. Fletcher, who had been a member of the diplomatic service since 1902, first as secretary at legations and embassies, and then as Ambassador to Chile and to Mexico. After serving as Under Secretary of State he was appointed Ambassador to Belgium and then to Italy.

When in 1933 Franklin D. Roosevelt, a Democrat, succeeded Herbert Hoover, a Republican, President Roosevelt, for the express purpose of maintaining continuity in the conduct of foreign affairs, selected William Phillips as Under Secretary, a post he had filled before for two years under Charles Evans Hughes in a Republican administration. Phillips entered the diplomatic service in 1903, served as secretary at foreign posts, as chief of the Division of Far Eastern Affairs in the Department, as Third Assistant Secretary of State, and as Minister to The Netherlands, Ambassador to Belgium, and Minister to Canada before becoming Under Secretary the second time. He left that office after three years to become Ambassador to Italy.

Even before the office of Under Secretary was created the same practice had been followed. For all practical purposes many of the functions, and particularly those dealing with continuing policy and precedents, were performed by A. A. Adee from the time of his appointment as Second Assistant Secretary of State in 1886 until 1909 when the office of Counselor of the Department of State was established.

Adee then carried on in his office of an assistant secretary of state as the great authority on precedents and as a valued consultant on policy until his death in 1924.

The office of Counselor was superseded by that of Under Secretary, but the change was more one of title than duties. The importance attached to it by President Wilson was indicated when he succeeded President Taft, a Republican, and appointed as Counselor, John Bassett Moore. Aside from his professional life in the private practice of law, Moore had previously served as a law clerk in the Department of State, as an assistant secretary of state, as secretary and special counsel to the American Peace Commissioners in Paris in 1898, and as a delegate to international conferences. In no one were the traditions of American diplomacy more completely instilled or the authority of international law more completely personified. His appointment as Counselor took on added significance because he served under William Jennings Bryan, who had had no training for the specialized duties of the office of Secretary of State. When Moore resigned after a year, he was succeeded as Counselor by another international lawyer, Robert Lansing, who later was promoted to the office of Secretary of State when Bryan resigned.

There have been few exceptions to the practice of obtaining the services of experienced diplomats as Under Secretary. President Hoover soon after entering the White House appointed Joseph P. Cotton, a distinguished New York lawyer. The appointment was made largely at the instance of Secretary Stimson, who held Cotton in personal and professional esteem. However, since the Hoover administration represented no change in the political party control of the government and most of the other ranking officials of the Department of State carried on, there was no break with the past.

In one other instance there was a personal appointment, when Secretary Kellogg summoned his former law partner, Robert E. Olds, who served as Under Secretary of State for one year, from July 1, 1927, to June 30, 1928. But that was in the middle of an administration which adhered closely to traditions and policies of the past.

The term of the Under Secretary is for no set period, but in most cases has been from one to three years. The longest period served was by Frank L. Polk of New York, who was in office continuously for five years, first as Counselor and then as Under Secretary when the title of the office was changed. The record compares fairly well with that of the Permanent Under Secretaries of the British Foreign Office. Several of their terms have been of two and three years, although one served for five years, and the first to hold the office retained it for fifteen years. This record, however, falls far short of the long service of Adee, who performed so many of the functions of an Under Secretary of State.

In some respects the two offices are different. The American Under Secretary of State is a political appointee, while the Permanent Under Secretary in London is a civil servant protected by civil service laws. He is also buttressed by a more highly developed and organized permanent Foreign Office staff, which exercises a deep influence because of its character, long tradition, and personnel selected by very strict competitive examination for an administrative career. There is encouragement in the fact that since the American career service was placed on a scientific basis in 1924 it has been improving to the point that it may in a few years begin to rival its counterpart in Great Britain.

Apart from the continuity the Under Secretaries assure and their technical competence as professional diplomats, the type selected has been successful in personal contacts

with foreign envoys. Like seeks like, and persons of the same type speak the same language. In no profession is an atmosphere of mutual understanding more essential for successful relations than in diplomacy. Moreover, professional diplomats speak a language all their own. They understand the shades of meaning in well-turned phrases that are the accoutrement of the diplomat. In none of his duties does the Under Secretary of State make a greater contribution to the conduct of foreign affairs than in these contacts.

There are several who because of their varied training and experience have been outstanding. The present (1939) Under Secretary of State is Sumner Welles. A native of New York City and forty-six years old, he is a graduate of Groton and Harvard, and entered the diplomatic service in 1915. The leading authority in the Department of State on Latin-American affairs, he specialized in that field through service in South America and as chief of the Division of Latin American Affairs in the Department. Relatively early in his career he spent three years in the Dominican Republic with the rank of Minister, assisting in straightening out tangled affairs. He later performed a similar service in Honduras but subsequently resigned, although in 1929 he was a member of the Dawes Financial Mission to the Dominican Republic.

With the administration of Franklin D. Roosevelt, Welles returned to diplomacy as an assistant secretary of state but almost immediately was sent to Cuba as Ambassador, where he went through the turmoil incident to the overthrow of the regime of President Machado. He then resumed his former post in the Department of State as assistant secretary with supervision of Latin-American affairs, a duty he continues in his present office. After attending the Inter-American Peace Conference in Buenos Aires in 1936 he was made Under Secretary of State.

[65]

A man of icy exterior to those unacquainted with him, he is the typical career diplomat. Correct and formal, faultlessly groomed, ambitious, he possesses a mind as keen as a razor blade and is an indefatigable worker. He drives himself even harder than he does his subordinates, and is close in the confidence of the President and the Secretary of State.

William R. Castle, Jr., who served as Under Secretary from 1931 to 1933, was equally close to President Hoover. Of a prominent Honolulu family and a Harvard graduate in 1900, he entered the Department at the time of the World War, became chief of the Division of Western European Affairs, then an assistant secretary of state, and Ambassador to Japan during the London Naval Conference of 1930, when he performed important services in facilitating naval understanding. Soon after his return to this country he was appointed Under Secretary and frequently served as Acting Secretary of State, notably during the negotiations for the moratorium on war debts. No one possessed more urbanity, or a greater facility and ease in diplomatic negotiation and in daily informal conversations with ambassadors and ministers.

Phillips and Fletcher are much of the same school; they entered the diplomatic service at approximately the same time and rose together as the first of the present-day type of career diplomat. Both were close to Theodore Roosevelt. Fletcher served under him as a Rough Rider in Cuba in 1898, and both were frequent visitors at the White House during his administration. Fletcher is a Pennsylvanian, Phillips a Bostonian and Harvard graduate. While Phillips continues in the service, Fletcher resigned a few years ago.

Bracketed with them is Joseph C. Grew, a Bostonian, and a Groton and Harvard graduate. He also is one with associations that trace back to Theodore Roosevelt, whose admira-

tion he won for prowess as a tiger hunter. He entered the diplomatic service in 1904, and was Under Secretary from 1924 to 1927. He left that office to become Ambassador to Turkey and then Ambassador to Japan in the present difficult period.

Of a somewhat different type is J. Reuben Clark, Jr., who was Legal Adviser, or Solicitor as the office was then known, of the Department of State from 1910 to 1913, and who was Under Secretary from 1928 to 1929. An able international lawyer, he was chief assistant to Dwight W. Morrow when Morrow was Ambassador to Mexico, and succeeded Morrow as Ambassador there.

Nor should reference be omitted to Norman H. Davis, banker and international negotiator, who was Under Secretary of State from 1920 to 1921, after having served as an assistant secretary of the Treasury, and before that as a member of the Armistice Commission, the Supreme Economic Council, and financial committees in Paris at the close of the World War and during the establishment of peace. A specialist on international conferences, Davis was called upon for services of this character by Republican as well as Democratic administrations after he had left the Department of State. During the administration of Franklin D. Roosevelt he has had the unofficial rank of Ambassador-at-large because of his frequent trips to Europe to conduct diplomatic conversations with leading statesmen and to attend international conferences as chief of American delegations.

The effort so deliberately made to achieve continuity in practice does not stop with the methods used in selecting Under Secretaries. The process carries farther down through the assistant secretaries of state who stand as a bulwark for the Secretary of State and the Under Secretary of State.

While assistant secretaries usually change with administrations and are political appointees, and while some are selected without reference to any previous diplomatic experience, there are usually at least two who are reared in the diplomatic tradition and have had years of service in the Department and in the foreign field. This is an important consideration, because they are policy officials, specializing in subjects that are assigned them either permanently or as needs arise. They bring to the immediate command of the Secretary of State a rich equipment of experience and knowledge.

Ordinarily there are four assistant secretaries of state, one of whom is in charge of the Consular Service and is, in addition, the budget and administrative officer of the Department. The others are policy officials. At present there is a slight variation in the organization; there are three assistant secretaries and a Counselor, who, while having the title formerly given to the chief aide of the Secretary of State and enjoying equal rank with the Under Secretary, actually carries out duties that would be assigned to an assistant secretary.

One of the assistant secretaries directs policy affecting the negotiation of reciprocal trade agreements. This office is held by Francis B. Sayre, son-in-law of President Wilson and formerly professor in the Harvard Law School. He supervises all questions of a broad character entering into the consideration of trade agreements, a subject that has greatly increased the work of the Department under the liberal economic program of Secretary Hull. The details of negotiations are attended to by the Trade Agreements Division.

Another assistant secretary of state supervises policy on special questions that are assigned him from time to time as they arise, such as negotiations with Canada for a deeper St. Lawrence waterway. The administrative assistant secre-

tary is George S. Messersmith, a career diplomat who was formerly Minister to Austria, and a specialist on central European affairs. The office of Counselor is filled by R. Walton Moore, lawyer and former member of the House of Representatives from Virginia, and close friend of Secretary Hull, who induced him to enter the Department in 1933. Moore, vigorous and alert at the age of eighty is concerned with policy on legal questions and legislative matters, such as the neutrality statutes.

There have been purely political appointees with no special training in diplomacy serving as assistant secretaries of state, but it can scarcely be overemphasized that there have always been one and usually two who are grounded in the traditions and precedents, and who as specialists in foreign affairs can advise the Secretary of State directly on problems calling for their particular knowledge. Invariably they attend staff conferences with the Secretary of State when serious problems of policy are to be decided, and contribute valuable information, understanding, and judgment to the discussions. After they have served for a few years as assistant secretaries they return to the foreign field as ministers or ambassadors.

Hugh R. Wilson, Ambassador to Germany, served as an assistant secretary of state after ten years as Minister to Switzerland. There are others now serving as ambassadors who have been assistant secretaries of state in the course of diplomatic careers that began years before. Among them are Nelson T. Johnson, Ambassador to China; J. Butler Wright, Ambassador to Cuba; and Jefferson Caffery, Ambassador to Brazil.

Standing in almost a special class is Wilbur J. Carr, recently Minister to Czechoslovakia, who entered the Department of State in 1892, organized and then directed the

Consular Service for so many years that he is known as "the father of the Foreign Service," and who was the administrative assistant secretary of state from 1924 to 1937. After long years in the Department and when approaching the age of seventy, he found himself subjected to the exacting duties of a Minister in the focal point of the great central European crisis of the fall of 1938; and, be it added, met the test with credit to himself and his government. With the partition of Czechoslovakia the following spring, he retired.

Obviously, the method followed in selecting the Under Secretary and assistant secretaries of state means that as questions arise they are considered from the background of American diplomatic tradition. It is a system which has operated to lessen prospects of any abrupt break with the past and wild departures in the present. It represents a desire of successive administrations to ascertain what has been done by their predecessors in reference to similar problems. New policies, it is true, are charted; sometimes an administration turns away from old channels. But there is much to support the assertion that as a general rule basic policy is followed from administration to administration.

Perhaps a clearer picture may be obtained by comparing the American with the British system, by holding one against the other so that the outline may be seen in sharper detail. It is doubtful, for example, that a new President and Secretary of State make greater changes in foreign programs than occur when a British government falls. The Disraeli and Gladstone ministries viewed foreign questions from different angles; when the Labor government succeeded the Conservative government in Great Britain in the 1920's there were shifts in Egyptian and other policies; and it is difficult to conceive of a sharper and more abrupt shift in policy in this country than was reflected in the resignation

of Anthony Eden as Foreign Secretary when he finally disagreed over methods with Prime Minister Neville Chamberlain.

Nevertheless, there was no change at any of these times in Great Britain's basic foreign policy of predominant sea power. Under the Labor government there was a change in balance of power politics on the continent, a policy as old as sea power and inextricably woven into it but nonetheless subsidiary. Also, the strength of the Navy temporarily declined but only in proportion to others.

While the United States has shifted position on naval power, like Great Britain, it, too, has a basic foreign policy, one that has persisted from the time of President Washington and that is summed up in the phrase, "no entangling alliances," and, intertwined as a subsidiary, "no interference abroad." Some define it as isolation; others deny this description. In any event, it continues to stand. The Monroe Doctrine is an implementation of it, as well as a measure of defense. It is what Secretaries of State mean when they refer to "our traditional policies."

After all, the basic foreign policies of most countries tend to be permanent because they reflect inevitably the inherent natures of the people; but the basic policies of Great Britain and of the United States are singularly simple, and for an identical reason, if the opinion of experienced diplomats is to be accepted. Their simple character has been made possible because of the geographical positions of the two countries, bounded by the seas—Great Britain in an insular position, and the United States with the Atlantic and Pacific on either side. The insulation of the seas has kept a host of complications at a distance. Whether this insulation has broken down with the development of aviation is still for the future to answer definitely.

[71]

However, there is an important difference between the two countries, for the United States is a self-contained continental entity, while the British Empire is a great sea power encircling the globe, with far-flung territories, and, therefore, is a much more artificial structure. Manifestly, the character and application of policies by each of them must differ widely. Obviously, in the circumstances it would be impossible for them to give practical application to an all-embracing agreement to take parallel action in every situation. Some parallel action is possible, and is resorted to in special areas, like the Pacific Ocean or the Far East, where there is frequently an approximation of identity of interests but for them to attempt parallel action at all times would be impossible.

At the same time, it would be a mistake to assume that fundamental policies have always been followed rigidly. There have been temporary swings which can be likened to the forming of side eddies in a stream. Yet eddies disappear and the stream resumes its normal flow. The United States had an enormous eddy when she intervened in the World War. Great Britain has had many, as when she departed after the World War from balance of power politics on the continent for collective security.

There have been many eddies also in the American policy of noninterference. Diplomats picture this policy in three compartments; one for Europe, where there is a tradition of noninterference that was broken in the Great War; another for Latin America, where administrations have intervened only to have a successor withdraw; and a third for the Far East, where there has long been a measure of American interference but where withdrawal from the Philippines may mark the disappearance of an eddy into the main stream.

Yet, simple as basic policies are, and indoctrinated as directing officials are with traditions, difficulties arise in

applying fundamentals in special cases. No one denies, for instance, that economically the United States is far from isolated. Moreover, the American people desire peace and are glad to have their government cooperate abroad for peace, within proper limits. The practical question, accordingly, constantly arises of where to draw the line, of how far to proceed in a program of helpfulness abroad, or in registering disapproval of the acts of another government which do not directly affront the United States. The Department of State has all these problems to consider. Furthermore, it is not a free agent, for it is under the direct orders of the White House, has to consider the attitude of Congress, and when important issues arise must give heed to public opinion. The resultant of many forces determines policy. And it is here that any close parallel between the American and British systems definitely breaks down.

A British Foreign Secretary must defend his recommendations before the Cabinet and carry a majority with him. It is not enough to convince the Prime Minister alone, who, to be sure, usually has several ministerial votes in his pocket. The Secretary of State of the United States is under no such compulsion. He must convince the President, who will discuss the question with his Cabinet or not as he sees fit. The Cabinet is not drawn from Congress as the British Cabinet is from Parliament, and has no power of veto. If it takes a vote, it has no binding force. The President in submitting the question at a Cabinet meeting does so as an act of courtesy and information. He also may wish to obtain the benefit of its judgment and gain an insight into what the state of public opinion may be in the regions from which the Cabinet officers come, for being politicians they keep informed of their home viewpoints.

The President makes the final decision himself, but in so doing his thoughts are more often on the Committee on

Foreign Relations of the Senate, which at this juncture is more in the position of the British Cabinet than is the President's own Cabinet. This is invariably the case if the negotiation of a treaty is at issue; it is generally true because of the influence of the Committee on Foreign Relations.

This has never been more vividly illustrated than when Woodrow Wilson, one of the most unyielding of Presidents, on his first return from the Paris Peace Conference at the end of the World War chose to land in Boston. Europe thought he represented the last word but, while confident, he was under no illusions. New York or Washington would have been more convenient, but he chose Boston because Henry Cabot Lodge of Massachusetts, foe of the President, was chairman of the Committee on Foreign Relations. Anticipating opposition from Lodge, Wilson desired to impress him with the reception he would receive in the Senator's own state. It was the familiar device of seeking to build a backfire against an elected official in his own district.

Wilson was given a most flattering reception. The writer rode a few feet behind him as he motored to his hotel, and watched as he stood in his automobile, cloaked in a fur coat and doffing his silk hat in acknowledgment of a continuous ovation of applause and cheers. That afternoon the President presented his case calmly and confidently for the League of Nations and the Peace Treaty in a persuasive speech before leaving by special train for Washington. It was the beginning of one of the great battles over foreign policy in American history, one that led to an historic struggle in the Senate, a great national referendum in the presidential election of 1920, and a decisive verdict.

Wilson's reception in Boston could not have been more enthusiastic or flattering, and must have encouraged him to press the fight, but Lodge was not to be deterred, and in due

course the Senate demonstrated, as it often has, that its influence in the conduct of foreign affairs is almost always conservative.

In the last analysis, it is public opinion which prevails, and it often speaks through the Senate. With all the mechanism and all the precedents, in the end public opinion is the determining force. Sometimes, as in occasional periods of intense excitement or when, as in the 1890's and early 1900's there was a surge of sentiment for expansion, public opinion as expressed by the Senate is violent, but ordinarily it is a steadying and even restraining influence on the operations of the Department of State.

CHAPTER V

THE EYES AND EARS ABROAD

SURPRISING as it may appear at first, there is much more to the Department of State than is housed in the huge building flanking the White House on the west, with its elaborate organization of officials, experts, and civil service employes grouped in divisions, bureaus, and offices and supervised by the Secretary of State and his general staff of immediate assistants. The larger part of the Department is not to be found in the building at all. It is stationed in embassies, legations, and consulates in every foreign land. There are many more officials and employes abroad than in Washington.

Necessarily a far-flung organization is required to furnish the Department information for conducting foreign relations. It is this function which is performed by the Foreign Service. It provides eyes and ears abroad. More than that, its officers are representatives of the government in foreign lands. When in Washington on periodic tours of home duty they can find inconspicuous niches along with hundreds of other government officials in the numerous departments and agencies, but when abroad they lose their neutral tint. They stand out with distinctive color and glamor as the representatives of their government in a very personal sense, and must conduct themselves accordingly. They are not submerged in a mass of officialdom.

Some are located in peaceful surroundings, others on turbulent frontiers, but wherever they are they stand for the United States. Their judgment in tight situations can smooth

or mar the official relations of their government, for in emergencies Foreign Service officers at distant posts, while furnished with general instructions, have to be entrusted with a considerable amount of discretionary authority. And more often than the Department of State would have preferred, the country has been reminded in the troubled years since the World War that life in the Foreign Service has its grim as well as its pleasant side. Wars in China, Ethiopia, and Spain have found diplomatic and consular officers at the danger points. When the threat of war hung menacingly over central Europe in 1938, the newspapers published many accounts of embassies and legations and consulates hurriedly building bombproof shelters in anticipation of sudden attack or a long siege, while facing with a grin the arduous task of protecting American lives and property. Yet memories are short, and the impression has never been permanently erased that the life is more distinguished for its social activities.

This causes pain in the Department of State, but it was a diplomat who, inadvertently, gave the type so widely pictured its neatest characterization. The occasion has become historic to professional diplomats. It happened when one of their veteran and ranking members, Hugh S. Gibson, then Ambassador to Belgium, was testifying before a Congressional committee. In attempting to refute suggestions of Representatives who were not at all diplomatically minded that career diplomats were rich, good-for-nothing, idle playboys, he indignantly exclaimed that they were not "cookie pushers." The phrase stuck.

Gibson was not speaking in defense of himself. Everyone knew that he was of another class, dependent upon his salary for livelihood and hard working, but the phrase was pounced upon gleefully. It will be remembered as long as there is career diplomacy. Quite apart from its fairness as a charac-

terization, the Department of State, if not the country, knows that men spend their lives in the Foreign Service, just as they do in the Army and Navy. And just as in the military services, the officers rise by promotion on merit. The Foreign Service is now fully as well established as a career as the profession of arms.

The "cookie pushers" incident attracted attention only because of a popular conception that the Foreign Service is composed of bespatted young men whose chief ambition is to gossip at luncheons, quarrel over social precedence, and give only incidental attention to their duties. Anyone, however, who assumes that the life is an uninterrupted idyll of social engagements, luxury, and ease should pause on entering the main lobby of the Department of State building to read the inscription on a bronze plaque set in the wall facing the door and framed by American flags.

The plaque lists the names of sixty-six Foreign Service officers who have died heroically or tragically in active duty. It is a reminder that the men who constitute the eyes and ears of the Department abroad do not always live comfortably in the world's great capitals. Many are on the frontiers of civilization where wars and upheavals are epidemic; some have been overwhelmed at their posts by great natural catastrophes.

The first to die was William Palfrey, who was lost at sea in 1780 when on his way to France to serve as consul. The last name on the plaque is that of J. Theodore Marriner, consul general in Beirut, who was assassinated in 1937 as he was about to enter his office. Three others were murdered; several were lost at sea or drowned in attempting to save life. Many died of yellow fever, cholera, and other diseases; several died of exposure or exhaustion; and five gave up their lives in volcanic eruptions, earthquakes, and hurricanes.

Marriner died at a time when he was preparing to engage in larger duties with promise of a brilliant career. He was on the threshhold of appointment as minister after completing a period of duty as consul general. Previously he had been Counselor of Embassy and Chargé d'Affaires in Paris, diplomatic secretary at various European posts, and a division chief in the Department. His death was all the more tragic because it was due to a mistake. An applicant for a passport visa had been granted one but had neglected to give his correct post office address, and the document never reached him. Assuming his application had been rejected, he nursed a fancied grudge and shot down Marriner, who personally had had nothing to do with the case. It had been handled by one of his assistants. His death was a price the Service is sometimes called upon to pay.

The life is not always one of ease, of attending official receptions and conducting diplomatic affairs in the quiet of embassy rooms and foreign offices. London and Paris may capture the imagination of the socially ambitious, but there are Foreign Service officers also in unhealthful tropical seaports, and in fever-ridden posts in Africa and Asia, where the personnel is more familiar with difficult and hazardous living conditions than with cocktail parties. As Secretary Hull once said, "They have more experience of malaria than of spats."

Even in Europe times of crises produce long hours of intensive work for consular and diplomatic staffs. When revolutions or other wars break out, Foreign Service officers have to take their chances with the rest, for their mission is to protect insofar as possible American lives and property. The siege of the legations in Peking in 1900 when the fate of the foreign diplomats was unknown for weeks and their plight caused the gravest apprehensions throughout the

civilized world is still a vivid recollection. Probably it will never be repeated, but danger arises in other forms with all too great frequency. The experience of Wendelin and his diplomatic and consular associates during the Spanish Civil War is only one of many that have called for stern work.

Shortly before, in 1935, the Service had to bear the brunt of a similar situation when the Italian forces invaded Ethiopia. The American Legation in Addis Ababa then had its experience with the realities of life on the fringes of civilization. Panic ensued when the natives precipitately began their flight from the capital before the approach of the conquering forces, and the Legation found itself under fire. The staff had to resort to arms and stand off the mob. For a time the issue looked dubious. American interests in Ethiopia were in the charge of Cornelius Van H. Engert, a veteran career diplomat, who, because of his training and experience, had stepped spectacularly from a routine post in the Legation at Cairo to the zone of conflict. His conduct met all expectations and he was rewarded with two promotions within the space of a few weeks carrying him to the highest classification in the Foreign Service.

Had Europe in 1938 or the crises of the spring of 1939 toppled into the abyss of a general war, unquestionably there would have been many grim experiences in the Service. Bombings would not have contributed to the pleasures of life.

China has been an almost constant field of danger during the years of revolution and of warfare with Japan. Foreign Service officers along with others have run the risks of bombardment and street fighting. Some were on the United States gunboat *Panay* when she was bombed from the air on the Yangtze river. Others stuck to the Legation in Nanking during the fighting and disorders as the Japanese approached

and occupied the city. Bombproof shelters in the Legation compound only partly lessened the danger.

Because of a conflict of orders from Washington, Nelson T. Johnson, the Ambassador, and some of his staff at Nanking went to a gunboat at the dock for a few hours. But they did this reluctantly and only after the Ambassador in a public statement declared his regret at having to leave his official post for the first time in thirty years of service. The orders were due to a misunderstanding, and he promptly returned the few hundred yards to his official residence. He left it then only when the Chinese capital was moved, in order to proceed with the government and maintain official contact. That was in accordance with the tradition in which he was reared.

All is in the day's work, for, while Foreign Service officers are supposed to use discretion and run no unnecessary risks in order to avoid diplomatic complications insofar as is practicable, actually risks are unavoidable. These risks are not reserved alone for the officers and men of the military services. Moreover, discretion means nothing when dangers arise that cannot be foreseen. Two Foreign Service officers died in the eruption of Mt. Pelée on the Island of Martinique in 1902, several went through the horrors of the Japanese earthquake of 1923, and, for variety, some have had to beat off bandits in North Manchuria and other far places.

The dangers are faced as incidents in the main task of carrying on the business of the government in foreign lands and of listening to the diversified sounds of the world's activities. The demands are as various as the multiplicity of human interests can make them. Many are routine; some are filled with excitements; all are recorded as the Department of State daily receives a flow of reports from eight hundred career officers at more than three hundred posts abroad. The

record ranges from major problems of policy to misfortunes of individuals. These are incidents and details as the Service conducts its basic mission of creating good will and common understanding with foreign governments, promoting and protecting the interests of the United States and its citizens, and reporting on political and economic trends abroad.

Time was when the diplomatic branch negotiated treaties and conventions, while the consular staffs devoted their energies to technical questions of trade, shipping, and immigration. Consuls still issue visas, perform passport services for Americans abroad, and conduct other miscellaneous duties, but in the broader aspects the distinction which long existed between the two branches of the Service has broken down. Changing world conditions have forced a consolidation of functions. Economic, financial, and political questions have become so interwoven that they cannot be separated, and this trend has been accentuated by the centralization of functions in totalitarian states. Small wonder that the old division between political-diplomatic and consular-commercial activities is out of date. Keeping step with the march of progress, the two branches of the Service are now very largely consolidated. In many foreign capitals they are housed under the same roof.

One of the oldest agencies of the government, nevertheless, the Foreign Service reached its present estate only after a long struggle from a modest start. It antedates the Republic, for it was born during the Revolution. Long the prey of politics, it is now on a nonpartisan, scientific basis, undisturbed by storms that blow from administration to administration. A definite start toward the present order was made a little more than thirty years ago. The present organization, however, was not achieved until 1924 in consequence of the

long struggle for civil service reform, the growth of American trade abroad, and lessons of the World War and the Peace Conference at Versailles. It was at last realized that the older system was inadequate.

Until comparatively recently the Diplomatic and Consular Services operated as two separate organizations with personnel that did not transfer from one to the other. There was no appointment by examination. Political or personal influence was the dominant factor. This was especially so with regard to consuls, who notwithstanding the appearance in their ranks occasionally of men like Nathaniel Hawthorne as consul at Liverpool, Bret Harte as consul at Geneva, and John Howard Payne as consul at Tunis, were far too generally of a class that warranted the caricature painted by O. Henry based upon his Latin-American experiences. Content in their positions, they were secure as long as their political party remained in power or they retained an influential friend in Washington.

There were exceptions, however, and they stand out like beacons in American diplomatic history. One of the most conspicuous examples of merit and ability was furnished by Townsend Harris, who went to Shimoda as consul general in 1858 after Japan had been reopened to Western influence by the American Navy. One of the first achievements of his historic and fruitful mission was the negotiation of a Treaty of Commerce and Good Will. He continued as Minister Resident to contribute vitally to friendly relations that have ever since rested on his initial service.

Forty years later, and much nearer home, Fitzhugh Lee, a former Confederate general of the famous Virginia family, gave exceptional service as consul general in Havana during the insurrection that preceded intervention of the United

[83]

States. He performed his duties so successfully through a combination of tact and firmness that his return to Washington in 1898 took on the character of a triumph.

Still later, at the time of the Russo-Japanese War and the establishment of Japanese control in Korea and South Manchuria, a young consular officer, Willard D. Straight, attracted national attention by the ability with which he carried out his duties, first in Seoul, and immediately after the war as consul general in Mukden. He won the approval of Theodore Roosevelt in the White House and soon was summoned to Washington where be became acting chief of the Division of Far Eastern Affairs in the Department of State. He resigned in a few years to enter finance. When barely more than thirty years old be became a member of the firm of J. P. Morgan and Company.

There was another man, of more recent times, who bridged the old and the new, and, because of his knowledge of the region and his influence with all classes and nationalities was dubbed by Will Rogers "the Emperor of North Manchuria." He was George C. Hanson, who entered the consular service in 1909 and from 1921 to 1934 was consul general in Harbin.

He was one of a long line of American consular and diplomatic officers who have specialized on the Far East, acquired the languages, and known the region as well as the natives. Edwin S. Cunningham was another. He entered the Service in 1898 and only recently retired after many years as consul general in Shanghai. They belong to a breed who care only for the Far East. Apparently once the breath of the Orient enters the nostrils it never leaves. Such men have never had their heads turned over their shoulders looking toward London, Paris, or other European capitals and the day when they may be stationed there.

Specialists with a great tradition behind them, they have been unusually influential in the shaping of Far Eastern policy in the Department of State. Their *esprit de corps* is reflected in the efficiency with which the Division of Far Eastern Affairs has operated.

The same tendency has been noted with reference to the Near East, where experts live with problems little understood by most Americans but deeply involved in the politics of Europe. It is now being observed with regard to Latin America, where more and more in recent years diplomatic officers and consuls have been expressing a preference for service.

The trend is encouraging enough in itself. But, coincident with this geographic consciousness, another development is manifesting itself in a movement to have officers specialize in subjects for which they show a natural bent so that they may be assigned abroad on that basis without regard to geographical considerations. It represents a phase in an expansion of the Service that is constantly proceeding. One who demonstrates aptitude in economics, for example, is now encouraged to specialize in that subject so that he may be assigned anywhere in the world as a technical expert. He might be sent to Buenos Aires one year, and to Shanghai the next. In order to facilitate this, the Department has obtained appropriations from Congress with which to send a number of career diplomats each year to American universities for graduate study in special subjects in order that they may become more proficient experts.

For nearly fifteen years there has been little or no distinction between consular and diplomatic officers. Previously the distinction was not only deeply marked in law and administration but also in the type of official personnel.

[85]

In those earlier years circumstances produced on the whole a higher class of diplomatic officials than consuls.

There was no competitive examination, but the pay was low and the social obligations many. Therefore men of independent means usually sought the diplomatic offices. Some were idealists and sincerely desirous of performing public service. Others were eager for social position, bringing down the scorn of the man in the street who sneered at their airs and graces and aping of English and French manners. Nevertheless, the opportunities for appointment being relatively few, there was keen competition, and the result was a higher type of official in the Diplomatic Service than in the Consular Service.

Long before permanent reform was seriously attempted there were signs of a change, of a gradual improvement that might be made in time. It developed out of the personal interest of abler members of the diplomatic corps in encouraging through gradual evolution the growth of a class of career diplomats. They kept a watchful eye on the most promising of younger men and gave their assistance toward inducing them to remain in the Service and facilitating their promotion at a time when advancement was imperfectly grounded in merit. No one took a more active part in these efforts than Henry White, who is often referred to as the first career diplomat. He devoted his life to diplomacy and many times undertook delicate tasks for Presidents and Secretaries of State in administration after administration. For many years in the late nineteenth and early twentieth centuries he was stationed in the Embassy in London as first secretary, but he made frequent trips home, exercised an influencing hand in the Department, and was in close contact through personal correspondence with Presidents and Secretaries of State. At every opportunity he gave encouragement

to younger men, like Henry P. Fletcher and William Phillips, who showed signs of promise and with whom there appeared definitely for the first time signs of a really developing career diplomacy, and Hugh S. Gibson, who retired in 1938 after thirty years of service.

It was Gibson whose lot it was to gain national and international attention during the World War, when as a young diplomatic secretary in Belgium he led in the effort to save Edith Cavel, the British nurse, from a German firing squad. He was Ambassador to Belgium when he retired.

White left London to become Ambassador to Italy in 1905 and to France in 1907, and closed his official career as a member of the United States delegation to the Paris Peace Conference at the end of the World War. In all those years he exercised a most helpful influence toward the achievement of a permanent Diplomatic Service based on merit. He lived to see it established by law.

There was another man who had a determining influence in the gradual evolution that was taking place, one whose hand was exerted more directly on the Consular Service but whose efforts extended also into the diplomatic establishment. He was Wilbur J. Carr, who in 1902, ten years after entering the Department of State as a clerk, became chief of the Consular Bureau. There he devoted his attention to problems of personnel and administration, and concentrated on an effort to place it on a systematic basis in which merit would count, rather than political favoritism. He could not have succeeded except for the support of his superiors, but this was given and in 1906, with the help and approval of President Theodore Roosevelt and Secretary of State Root, a law was passed providing for appointments to the Consular Service by competitive examination. That marked the definite turn away from the old order to the present. The

reform was begun under Root; it was brought to fruition eighteen years later under Secretary Hughes.

The next year, in 1907, Carr became Chief Clerk of the Department but in 1909 he was appointed Director of the new Consular Service, and for nearly thirty years he directed its activities with a jealous eye. His discipline over personnel was exacting and there were grumblings of bureaucracy but also admissions of efficiency and singleness of purpose. He kept his hand on the Service as time went on and as he assumed additional duties. He was appointed budget officer of the Department in 1921 when the budget system was adopted throughout the government, and with the reorganization of 1924 he was made an assistant secretary of state to supervise the administration of the Department, direct the budget, and oversee consular activities. He remained in that office until he was appointed Minister to Prague in 1937.

There his service culminated during the tragic months that witnessed the disappearance of the Czechoslovak state.

The system of appointing consular officers by merit after competitive examination worked so well that almost immediately selection of diplomatic officers below the grades of ambassador and minister was made subject to examination. This method, however, was not applied strictly. Much more of the older order remained than in the case of consuls, although by 1917 political favoritism had largely disappeared in appointments. This situation continued through the World War when definite action was found to be necessary.

The war had projected the United States into a position of much greater world responsibility, but at the same time a supply of good personnel for new appointments had been restricted, for many young men who ordinarily would have turned to a career of diplomacy had entered the Army. It was a problem to which Secretary Hughes gave thoughtful

attention. Action could not be taken immediately, for thorough study was required, so for a few years there was a period of flux during which conditions did not improve.

Finally, in 1924, Secretary Hughes was prepared to act, and he moved in collaboration with Representative John Jacob Rogers of Massachusetts, who was the ranking Republican member of the Committee on Foreign Affairs of the House of Representatives next to Representative Stephen G. Porter of Pennsylvania, chairman of the committee. Congress was ready to help and the result was the Rogers Act, which stands as the great basic charter of the modern diplomatic service.

That Act marks the emergence of the Foreign Service from a political organization into a career service below the grade of minister. It does not touch ministers and ambassadors, but otherwise its scope is all embracing, even to the offices of assistant secretary of state, which it placed on a flat basis without numerical designation. It has prepared the way for the development of diplomats to the point that they will be trained and equipped to assume the duties of minister and ambassador.

Not only did the legislation consolidate the diplomatic and consular branches, but it was followed in 1939 by blanketing into the Foreign Service by Executive Order the foreign attachés of the Departments of Commerce and Agriculture. This represents an enormous gain from the standpoint of administrative convenience. The Rogers Act requires appointments to the Foreign Service on the basis of competitive written and oral examinations, with merit alone defined as the guide for selections. Promotion is also by merit.

Both men and women are eligible for the Service and many women have taken the examinations for admission. Several

have been admitted in consequence but few remain long with the Service. Often marriage accounts for their resignations. At present there are two in the foreign field, one as second secretary of embassy at Brussels, and the other as a consul. A third, Miss Margaret M. Hanna, for years was chief of the Office of Coordination and Review in the Department of State, then was transferred at her own request to Geneva as consul, and at the end of the year 1938 retired for age. She is associated in the departmental mind with Mrs. Bertha M. Shipley, chief of the Passport Division and the only woman chief of division now in the Department, for both were assistants for several years to A. A. Adee.

The Rogers Act envisages the advancement of the ablest officers to the higher positions through a system of classifications. Its administration has been attended by improvements in organization and the weeding out of less competent officials, so that in the past ten years the Department and the Foreign Service have been placed on a higher plane. A few years after enactment of the legislation a Congressional investigation led, not to adverse criticism, but to amendments to improve the operation of the Service. There is still room for standards to be raised, and complaints are sometimes heard that the system of promotion is marked by favoritism in the consideration of records of officers. At least no better arrangement has been devised and it is fairly comparable to the systems employed for promotions in the Army and Navy.

One of the most conspicuous benefits of the Rogers Act is found in increased salaries. No longer is it necessary for one to have independent means to be a member of the Foreign Service. Under the old arrangements salaries ranged from $2,500 to $4,000 a year, an inadequate scale in view of living costs and social obligations.

The result was that the Diplomatic Service was recruited very largely from a restricted class of the specially privileged. Periodically there arose cries of caste, of a Harvard or some other clique dominating the Service and the Department. The fault was in the system.

Now there are three unclassified and, above them, eight classified grades in the Foreign Service with salaries running from $2,500 to $10,000 a year. In addition, allowances are granted for costs of rent, lights, and other incidentals, including equalizations because of differences in exchange when officers are in the field. As a result the Service today presents a cross section of graduates of colleges and universities from all sections of the country. Some are wealthy, but the majority have to live on their salaries. A democratizing process has been accomplished in a very few years. As evidence of the representative character of the Service, every state is represented. New York, as might be expected, stands first in the number of officers. It is surprising, however, that one of the most distant states—California—ranks second.

The lure of the Foreign Service as a career always attracts many more applicants for the examinations than there are vacancies, but this is offset to a great extent by the fact that invariably there are many failures to pass. The examinations are long, severe, and require training beyond that covered in the requirements for the bachelor's degree in the average college. Many candidates spend months preparing for them at foreign service schools. They must be American citizens between the ages of twenty-one and thirty-five, but no political affiliations are considered.

No regular time is set for the examinations, but as a rule they are held once or twice a year in Washington, New York, Chicago, and other cities. They are conducted under the

[91]

supervision of the Civil Service Commission. There are four general examinations to test the applicants' knowledge of history, government, geography, art, literature, and similar subjects, and to reveal their all-round education and intelligence. In addition there are four special examinations: on modern languages; international, commercial, and maritime law; international relations; and economics. The two types of written examinations are conducted in four consecutive days with morning and afternoon sessions of from one and a half to three hours each.

But this is not all. Approximately three months after candidates have passed the written examinations they are summoned for oral examinations before the Board of Examiners for the Foreign Service in the Department of State, composed of veteran officials. These examinations are designed to ascertain their physical, mental, and temperamental qualifications, their character, ability, address, judgment, and contemporary information, as well as their experience and business ability. The test is grueling as question after question, carefully framed to reveal their fitness, is asked. The candidates are nervous as they stand before the critical eyes of the Board, forgetful of the fact that some of these same officials were in their places years before.

If a candidate averages 80 percent on the written and oral examinations, he is placed on the eligible list, where he is available for appointment to the Foreign Service as openings occur. These usually are made fairly promptly, but if he has not been appointed within two years, he loses his eligible rating and to regain it must pass the examinations again. When appointed to the Foreign Service he is placed at the foot of the ladder and paid a salary of $2,500 a year. As the years pass and he wins promotion, he passes through classi-

fications that gradually increase his salary until a maximum of $10,000 a year is reached.

When the candidate is summoned from the eligible list he is appointed a vice consul and sent into the field for a trial period of one year.

He is then recalled to the Department for a few months of intensive instruction in the Foreign Service School. Upon completing that instruction he is assigned to another post in the field and enters definitely upon his professional work and is rewarded by promotions and salary increases as his services justify. Junior officers are shifted to different stations fairly frequently in order to give them varied experience, but senior officers are transferred less often and for more specific reasons. Their transfers are based more on their equipment and capacity for meeting special situations as they arise in various parts of the world. Periodically they are assigned to duty in divisions of the Department of State in order that the Department may obtain at first hand the benefit of their fresher and closer viewpoints on foreign problems, and also to enable them to refresh their own national viewpoints by residence in the United States. In addition, every ambassador in foreign capitals is buttressed by seasoned counselors and secretaries from the career service. It would be a stupid ambassador who would blunder in these circumstances. In the absence from his post of the ambassador or minister, it is the professional staff which carries on the duties. Many of the ablest career diplomats eventually are appointed ministers and ambassadors.

There is an injustice in the system, however, for when a career diplomat accepts appointment as minister he must resign from the Foreign Service in which he has spent so many years, and he does not regain his standing as a Foreign

Service officer after his term as minister has lapsed. Congress is now considering proposals to preserve the career status of these officials by creating the rank of "ministers of career," so that they may still be members of the Foreign Service available for further diplomatic duties.

The question has not yet been solved, but it is easier of solution than what to do with our former Presidents.

CHAPTER VI

THE CHIEFS OF MISSION ABROAD

ONE evening shortly after the World War an official
dinner was being given in London. Members of the
Cabinet, diplomats of the Empire, admirals and generals, and
foreign envoys were present. Quite naturally the conversation
around the great table was in harmony with the thoughts of a
group that moved in the world of high politics and diplomacy.
The occasion was formal, but as the dinner went forward the
conversation relaxed. It was in this atmosphere that a lady
seated next to Arthur J. Balfour was prompted to ask a
question that had long intrigued her. She now had the opportunity to ask it of one who from long experience in public
life was qualified to give an authoritative answer.

"Who do you think is the best speaker in England?"
she inquired.

Balfour, who had demonstrated forensic ability himself
in the House of Commons and on the public platform, replied
unhesitatingly. Nodding toward one seated at the table a
short distance away, he said, "There he is." His glance was
directed toward John W. Davis, Ambassador of the United
States. It was a generous tribute, not only to the talents
Davis possessed as a speaker but also to the prestige he
enjoyed during his official residence in London and which
was reflected on his government and country.

The incident is one that might have occurred years earlier
in the case of Joseph H. Choate and other Ambassadors

to the Court of St. James. This tribute to Davis is remembered gratefully in the Department of State as an example of an ambassador whose position was unassailable. After all, while the Foreign Service provides the professional staffs of embassies and legations, it is through the ambassadors and ministers that the Department acts directly. They are the heads of the embassies and legations, and all communications are addressed to them. If they are equal to their responsibilities, chief reliance is placed upon them; if incompetent, there is no choice except to depend upon the subordinate staff.

At smaller posts where no great issues arise, the competence of the chief of mission is relatively unimportant, but in the great capitals the capacity of the ambassador can mean the difference between a smooth or a difficult handling of complicated problems. Even though he does not actually impair relations, he may throw the machinery out of gear. If he is a political appointee of indifferent capacity, the embassy proceeds under a discouraging handicap; if he is a vivid personality, he instills a force and vigor into the embassy and into the relations between his own government and the one to which he is accredited.

This has always been true. It is more than ever true now that modern communications have replaced the older classical diplomacy with a diplomacy of dynamics. Not that old forms and methods are not still used, but when the occasional great emergency arises, when the issue of war or peace hangs in the balance, speed becomes the order of the day. Suggestions are sent, appeals made with the aid of the overseas telephone, and decisions reached in a space of time that was undreamed of a few years ago. The formal note then merely confirms as an accomplished fact what has already been decided.

President Franklin D. Roosevelt had this in mind when, in discussing the Munich Accord after the breath-taking crisis of late September, 1938, he remarked that the radio and the airplane had expedited the meeting of the situation. A crisis now comes to a head more quickly, he explained, and with the facilities now at command, can be tided over, if that is at all possible. Not only can the theater of a crisis be reached, but the whole world in converging forces for a settlement.

Fortunately, the able ambassador at the major posts is the rule rather than the exception. Occasionally one of mediocre talent creeps in. Then the Department of State prayerfully hopes for his early disappearance from the scene, and when he resigns forgets him. His name is remembered only in the official records. The incident concerning John W. Davis, however, emphasizes the fact, readily conceded in the Department of State, that years of training in career diplomacy are not an indispensable requirement of an ambassador. Nevertheless, some solid qualifications are essential. To be successful he must have political sense. He also should be close to the President in the White House, enjoy his political as well as personal friendship and confidence, and know in advance what are to be the administration's foreign and domestic policies.

Davis had many attributes which qualified him for the London post, and among them political training and experience. He had been a member of Congress and had served brilliantly as Solicitor General of the United States. A few years after resigning as ambassador he became the candidate of his party for President. His defeat in the election of 1924 meant no loss of esteem in his own country, while in England his standing had long been secure. Because of it he had been able to perform valuable services as a diplomat for his government.

His two years in London showed how an ambassador may improve international relations. That is an ambassador's one opportunity, for, paradoxical as it may seem, he seldom can impair relations. If he is objectionable to the government to which he is accredited, he is either ignored and diplomatic relations are conducted through the embassy of that government in Washington, or, if his attitude is offensive, the fact becomes apparent to his own government and ways are found to encourage his resignation under circumstances that are outwardly placid. It is difficult to recall an occasion when it has been necessary to recall an ambassador or minister directly and so provoke a diplomatic incident. In any event, if he is objectionable the foreign government usually does not regard him as representative of the Department of State or the White House.

Not all ambassadors and ministers are selected from private life. Many are appointed from the higher brackets of the Foreign Service, and often these career men are to be preferred over the civilian diplomat when relations with other countries are of an especially delicate character requiring the exercise of judgments that are the product of long years of careful, technical training. Certainly Presidents for a number of years have demonstrated that under the conditions existing in the Far East the desirable type of Ambassador to both Japan and China is the man equipped through long experience in the field and in the Department of State. In those countries the problems are such that a careful hand and skillful diplomatic technique are essential.

On the other hand, in a country where business problems are to the fore the business type of diplomat, taken from successful private life, will usually produce better immediate results than the more narrowly trained professional diplomat. The choice of an ambassador allows for no general precepts

but only a rule of thumb method may be followed. And in the Department of State there is no list of sheep and goats.

At present (1939), approximately half the ambassadors and ministers have been selected from the career service. There are twenty-five from the professional ranks and twenty-six from private life. In accepting the appointments, career diplomats must resign from the Foreign Service because they then enter the official family of the President, just as the Secretary of State and other Cabinet officers are of his official family.

They serve during the pleasure of the President and at the end of his administration automatically tender their resignations, in order that the new President, whether he is entering upon a second term or is coming for the first time to the White House and beginning his first administration, may be free to start with a clean slate, unembarrassed by any question of getting rid of an undesirable or unwelcome member of his inner circle. If the President is continuing in office for another four years, he usually requests them to remain at their posts. However, if the President is just entering the White House, he probably will accept the resignations, even though his predecessor has been of the same political party, because he prefers to select his own official family.

Although much of this represents the processes of democratic government translated into diplomacy, the appointment of ambassadors in the principal capitals is anything but democratic. Due to a combination of circumstances, this small group is the last stronghold of exclusiveness in the government. It is a caste of wealth. Democracy has penetrated the Foreign Service, and has reached the more modest posts occupied by ambassadors and ministers, but the prize plums are left for multimillionaires.

Even the United States Senate has lost its traditional character of a rich man's club, but one need only call the roll of ambassadors to London, Paris, and Rome during the past quarter of a century to reveal the gulf that separates them from Americans with moderate incomes. A few representative names will suffice. In London, Joseph P. Kennedy, Robert W. Bingham, Andrew W. Mellon, Charles G. Dawes, Frank B. Kellogg, Alanson B. Houghton; in Paris, William C. Bullitt, Jesse I. Straus, Walter E. Edge, Myron T. Herrick; in Rome, William Phillips, Breckinridge Long, John W. Garrett, Henry P. Fletcher.

The list does not stop with the three major European posts, for a number of very rich men have served in Berlin, Buenos Aires, Tokyo, and other capitals. A few have been career diplomats, but the majority have been appointed from private life. Some have been selected as a reward for political services or in return for substantial contributions to the campaign chest of the political party in power; several have sought to gratify social ambition and have been so incompetent that the burden of the embassy rested on the shoulders of the staff. Many, on the other hand, have been men of outstanding achievement in the fields of law, finance, literature, or politics, and have justified expectations by making important contributions to the diplomatic history of their times.

It would be a mistake, however, to assume that all ambassadors and ministers are men of wealth. Many have possessed no independent means and have had to live on their salaries. Unfortunately, several have been prevented by their limited finances from ascending higher on the ladder. Hugh S. Gibson, who recently retired as Ambassador to Belgium after a distinguished career of thirty years, is only one who found it impossible to go higher for this rea-

son. If he had had the private means, he unquestionably
would have been found in one of the great capitals.

Yet, strangely enough, this state of affairs causes little
concern in a country whose watchword is Democracy. It
disturbs neither the White House, the Department of State,
Congress, nor the people. If it did, it would have been
changed long ago. Naturally, there are reasons for this
apathy. Diplomatic tradition is not deeply rooted in the
country, and Congress is more concerned over farm relief,
national defense, and internal improvements than remedying
a condition which flows directly from inadequate salaries and
allowances granted the ambassadorial corps.

The salary of an ambassador is $17,500 a year, to which
are added a few allowances of inconsequential proportions.
Compare this with the provision made for the British
Ambassador in Washington. His salary and allowances for
conducting the Embassy home, apart from its office, and
providing entertainment, are fixed by the Cabinet and
range from $75,000 to $100,000 a year. It is a circumstance that tends to support an assertion sometimes made in
the Department of State that a United States ambassador
at a leading foreign post should have an independent income
of $100,000 a year. Necessarily this means that there are
relatively few men available for the office. In the days of
open income tax returns, the statistically minded, without
consulting an astrologer, could, with surprising accuracy,
make a list from which an administration would have to
fill these vacant posts.

Nevertheless, if Congress should make adequate provision, equal to what is granted the President, the ambassadorial posts, in view of the lack of diplomatic tradition sufficient to protect them from abuse, would be open to the
danger of becoming the victim of the spoilsman. Eventually

when there is a deeper-rooted tradition to surround and protect the diplomatic establishment this danger will pass, as it did long ago in Great Britain.

As it is, there has been an extraordinary advance in the past thirty years. A slow but definite start was made by Elihu Root and carried on by his successors toward improving the status of the mission establishments abroad. It is almost unbelievable now that when he became Secretary of State in 1905 the total annual allocation of the Department for support of its missions abroad was $90,000. Even officials going abroad were required to pay their own way, and such a thing as an allowance for necessary living expenses was undreamed of.

Although a greater improvement is fondly anticipated at some not too distant day, it is not to be wondered at that for the time being the Department of State prefers to continue under the present system as a lesser evil than being thrown open to the spoilsman through temptingly high salaries. Even though the chief posts go to political favorites or large contributors to the party in power, the post often goes to a man who has not achieved wealth merely by the fortunate accident of inheritance but by sheer ability, and can bring to his diplomatic office a capacity, force, and prestige that a career diplomat does not always possess.

President Coolidge had this in mind when he summoned Dwight W. Morrow to the White House and commissioned him to go to Mexico as Ambassador and restore good relations at a time of ill-feeling and misunderstanding. The success of Morrow in Mexico City is sufficient commentary on the wisdom of the selection. Only a few years earlier, Charles B. Warren, the Detroit lawyer, had performed valuable services as Ambassador to Mexico, and before that as Ambassador to Japan.

Joseph H. Choate as Ambassador to Great Britain thirty-five years ago is another whose counsel and judgments place him high in the records of the Department of State. By many he is ranked next to Charles F. Adams, the great Ambassador in London during the Civil War. At present Joseph P. Kennedy, also in London, offers another example of an ambassador who has succeeded in business and financial life and has the standing and personality to carry his own torch in his diplomatic office. Foreign ministers and prime ministers have a habit of listening to such a man.

Both types of ambassadors, the successful man of achievement from private life and the professional diplomat, have their advantages, and conditions abroad frequently determine which is to be selected. The Department of State has learned out of its long experience that the career diplomat carries out his instructions with a professional detachment, while the ambassador who is new from private life often will worry concerning his position with the government to which he is accredited when, acting under instructions from the Department, he presents a peremptory note.

If the career diplomat is successful in preserving good relations he does not worry over the personal element. Although this may appear a small distinction, foreign ministers with political backgrounds of their own have been known to take advantage of the ambassador from private life and play on his emotions because of the personal approach the ambassador gives to his duties. Moreover, the trained diplomat does not look so much on the government of the day as the last word in the country where he is stationed. Unlike the ambassador from private life, he realizes that problems very often are not solved in a few months or even years, and that there will be other governments with different viewpoints in due time. If he is astute, he will

discover when the change may take place and who will comprise the new government, and establish his contacts with the incoming elements far in advance.

On the other hand, the ambassador from private life, while looking at his problems from a much closer time perspective, may have capacities broader than the channel of a narrow professional career and bring to his task abilities and a forceful personality that will carry him through to his objectives. He is also less likely to be concerned with thoughts of the long future and of diplomacy as a life career, whereas the professional diplomat may be tempted to surround his suggestions and recommendations to his home government with a caution against making a mistake that might mar his future. The one has the intensive but narrower training of a specialist, the other the broader background of a man of affairs.

When a situation is delicately poised, however, it is often the career diplomat who is selected, because of his long and thorough preparation and the fact that his record shows he is sure-footed. Thus it was that President Hoover appointed Nelson T. Johnson and Joseph C. Grew to China and Japan, two veteran career diplomats with extensive technical knowledge and equipment as well as demonstrated capacity. And they were kept at their posts by President Franklin D. Roosevelt when he entered the White House. Political appointments were made elsewhere but not there.

Much the same motive actuated the selection by President Roosevelt, well along in his second administration, of Hugh R. Wilson, another veteran career diplomat, as Ambassador to Germany, after relations between the two countries had developed misunderstanding and irritation. Whatever the two governments and their peoples thought of each other,

it was the part of wisdom to have the diplomatic relations entrusted to skillful hands. Nor was it without significance that Germany at approximately the same time sent as Ambassador to the United States an equally skillful and veteran diplomat in Hans H. Dieckhoff.

If the Department of State had been at liberty to express its private view, it probably would have confessed keen disappointment that these excellent purposes were defeated by the acute turn in German-American relations growing out of Jewish persecutions and a long record of disagreement over Germany's discriminatory economic policies. For in 1938, only a few months after receiving their appointments, Ambassadors Wilson and Dieckhoff were summoned home by their governments as a mark of official displeasure. This represented a virtual severance of diplomatic relations. Such it was in nearly all but technical form.

The Embassy in Berlin is one of twenty such now maintained by the United States. Strangely enough from today's point of view, we had not a single ambassador until 1893. It was only then, more than a hundred years after the organization of the Department of State, that the rank was created by Congress. Even then it was confined to the few major European posts.

Actually there is little distinction between the service performed by an ambassador and a minister, and the distinction has been tending to narrow more and more. Technically an ambassador represents the sovereign or head of the state, and so may request at any time to confer with the head of the country in which he is serving. The request can not be refused. A minister, on the other hand, represents his government and may ask only to be received by the foreign minister. The practical differences between the offices, however, are in prestige and remuneration. The salary of an American

minister is $10,000 a year as compared with the $17,500 of an ambassador.

The country was content for many years to be represented abroad by the more modest office of minister. However, when it was emerging into the status of a world power, national pride demanded the prestige that goes with maximum representation abroad. The Department of State was more than willing, for the lesser rank had long been a source of irritation, if not humiliation.

It was a strain on the urbanity, patriotism, and sense of humor of a minister who had waited his turn in a reception room of the foreign office for half an hour, to have an ambassador arrive and immediately claim his right of diplomatic precedence in being received by the foreign minister. It was galling to the minister from his place in the rear ranks of a coronation procession to see the ambassador of a fifth-rate power on his prancing horse near the head of the line.

Congress not only changed all this, but has gradually been increasing the number of ambassadors abroad. There are now embassies in the capitals of the principal European states—London, Paris, Rome, Berlin, Brussels, Warsaw, Madrid, Istanbul (with an office also at Ankara), and Moscow. In the Far East, ambassadors are appointed to Japan and China, while, in view of the significance to the United States of pan-American relations, there are nine in Latin America, the same number as in Europe. There are ambassadors, naturally, in the A B C countries—Argentina, Brazil, and Chile; in Cuba and Mexico, whose relations are always of great importance to this country; in Peru, and most recently, in Colombia, Venezuela, and Panama.

In addition, because of particular situations, there are from time to time what might be termed floating or roving

ambassadors. The title is more or less honorary, for these officers are designated without confirmation of the Senate, and are paid out of a contingent fund of the Department of State. Their services are terminated at the will of the President or when their duties have been discharged. In fact, they are special agents and have been appointed from time to time throughout American history, from the days of the Continental Congress to President Franklin D. Roosevelt's selection of Norman H. Davis to represent the United States at various European conferences on disarmament and other questions. Davis, however, was known not as a special agent but by the unofficial title of Ambassador-at-large, generously given him by the President.

John Lind performed the services of a special agent in Mexico for President Wilson early in his administration. Of course, the most noted in this category was Colonel Edward M. House.

Throughout the history of the government, the office of ambassador has been filled exclusively by men, but times are changing and already two women have served in a ministerial capacity. The first was Mrs. Ruth Bryan Owen, daughter of the former Secretary of State and Great Commoner, who for four years was Minister to Denmark, and now (1939) Mrs. Florence Jaffray Harriman is Minister to Norway. It does not require a prophet to predict that before long a woman will be designated to take charge of an embassy.

There have been many types of ambassadors and ministers. There have been businessmen like Charles G. Dawes and Andrew W. Mellon, both of whom served as Ambassador to Great Britain; politicians like Martin Van Buren and James Buchanan, both of whom became Secretary of State and

President, and at a much later time, in the Harding adminis-
tration, Colonel George Harvey. These three served in
London also. There have been educators like Andrew D.
White, Ambassador to Germany, and Edward Everett,
Minister in London, and humanitarians like Oscar Straus,
who thrice served in Constantinople. There have been men of
letters such as James Russell Lowell, Minister to Spain and to
Great Britain; Lewis Wallace, Minister to Turkey; Washington Irving, Minister to Spain; Thomas Nelson Page,
Ambassador to Italy; Bayard Taylor, Minister to Germany;
and John Bigelow, Minister to France. J. Lothrop Motley,
Minister to Austria and to Great Britain, and George Ban-
croft, who also was Minister to Great Britain, were historians.

A special niche is reserved in the memories of the Department of State for the heroic envoys. Elihu B. Washburne,
who was Minister to France during the Franco-Prussian
War, was the only minister to remain in Paris during the
Commune and give aid and protection to all nationalities,
including Germans. There was Myron T. Herrick, who as
Ambassador to France at the outbreak of the World War
refused to leave his post before the German advance, and
there was Brand Whitlock, the record of whose services as
Minister in Belgium during the World War is treasured on
two continents. Nor could James W. Gerard be frightened
during the hectic war years he served as Ambassador in
Berlin.

In Japan, Cyrus E. Woods is remembered gratefully for
his refusal to leave his ambassadorial post during the devas-
tating earthquake of 1923. He disregarded personal safety to
take charge of American Red Cross relief and reconstruction activities. To the Japanese he became one of the great
heroes of the disaster.

In the long line of able diplomatic representatives, however, the prize of the greatest is given unhesitatingly to him who by one of the odd tricks of history was the first to serve. Benjamin Franklin, Minister to France during the American Revolution, is generally pronounced in the Department of State to be not only the first but the ablest of them all. Inadequately supported at home and confronted with seemingly insuperable difficulties, his mission was crowned with success when the French government decided to intervene on the side of the struggling colonies. Franklin was not the only factor in the decision, but the combination of his rare abilities, tact, and persuasive personality facilitated the alliance.

Unquestionably his attainments in many fields and the comprehensive sweep of his mind contributed to his success, because of the appeal he personally made to all classes. Like many American diplomats in the early history of the government, he had a liberally educated mind and was spiritually and intellectually closer to Europe than Americans of later years. His scientific achievements commanded respect, even as did his political and diplomatic skill. His many-sided character captured and held the imagination of Europeans.

Franklin was followed by Thomas Jefferson; and in the early years of the Republic a succession of leading Americans was sent to the great European capitals—James Monroe and John Quincy Adams, who both returned to become Secretary of State and then President; Albert Gallatin, the great Secretary of the Treasury; Henry Wheaton, the international lawyer who when Chargé d' Affaires in Denmark and Minister to Prussia a hundred years ago made a wide appeal to all of Europe by reason of his learning; and many others.

In comparatively recent times there have been ambassadors of widely recognized abilities: John Hay, Whitelaw Reid, and Joseph H. Choate, to name only a few. But, as Presidents and Secretaries of State often have remarked in private discussions, the early list contains the preeminent names and stands as a challenge today to a country infinitely greater in numbers and educational resources.

CHAPTER VII

INFLUENCES IN THE SHAPING
OF POLICY

FOR all its elaborate organization, the Department of State does not operate as a free agent. It has its home office and Foreign Service, its embassies, legations, and consulates, and the Secretary of State with his general staff of official aides; but its operations are affected by influences as numerous and diverse as human interests and emotions can make them. There are other agencies of the government which touch foreign policy at many points. There is Congress with an eye ever alert to foreign affairs; and, although insofar as the activities of the Department are concerned the President is over all, public opinion is under all. On great issues it is decisive. It constantly challenges the political acumen of the Secretary of State and the President in adjusting policy to the national temper.

This is illustrated every day in the life of the Department, but it never was brought home more amusingly to the writer than by President Coolidge. For all his reputation as "Silent Cal," Coolidge could talk freely, and almost volubly when he was in the mood. When he did talk, his discussion of serious matters was often touched with the dry Yankee humor for which he was famous.

The writer found Coolidge in this conversational mood one afternoon early in 1927 when the government was confronted with a full-fledged revolution in Nicaragua. Marines and

bluejackets had been landed in force to protect American lives and property, and a situation which was embarrassing at the outset was becoming more serious. The position of the administration was the more difficult because of a rising chorus of criticism at home charging imperialism and bungling.

That afternoon Coolidge appeared unaware of all this. Secretary of State Kellogg had just returned to his office across West Executive Avenue from a long conference with the President, who now sat relaxed in the Executive Office with one foot against the top of his desk, chair tilted back, and a newspaper in his hand. He glanced leisurely over flaring headlines telling of a drum fire attack in the Senate on his Nicaraguan policy, mentioned other subjects, and presently turned the conversation to the Central American crisis. Then with the twang for which he was famous, he said casually, "We always have plenty of free advice on how to conduct foreign affairs."

No one enjoys that remark as much as harassed officials in the Department of State.

Yet the indifference of President Coolidge was only on the surface. He was deeply disturbed. This was revealed when he soon commissioned Henry L. Stimson to proceed to Nicaragua and bring about an adjustment. Stimson accomplished his mission with such striking success that it prepared the way for him to become Secretary of State in the next administration.

Coolidge's attitude was that of a hard-headed politician. The political type, it may be remarked, is usually to be found in the White House and at the head of the Department of State. After all, foreign affairs are seldom conducted without regard to public opinion. In fact, most Presidents and Secretaries of State endeavor to win popular support for

their policies and are careful not to get so far in advance of the people as to forfeit their support.

As one Secretary of State said to the writer during a discussion of his foreign policy in the quiet of his office, "I am attacked by some for going too fast, by others for not going rapidly enough, but I cannot move in a way that will lose the support of the American people generally. That is my problem."

Occasionally some have taken the view that a program should be advanced on its own merits. This school of statesmen argues that popular support should be encouraged but that the program should be advanced with or without this public backing. This was the attitude taken by President Wilson in his fight for the League of Nations. The result is well known. He lost the fight and brought his own authority and prestige into question abroad to such an extent that the Department of State could only mark time until a new administration assumed control of the government. Then, and then only, could the Department again proceed vigorously, with the world knowing that it represented not only the government but the people as well.

The experience illustrated vividly that the Department is not only responsible to the administration but also accountable to the people. With the constantly changing and shifting play of forces, it is a kaleidoscopic picture the Department has to read. There is public opinion as it is affected by traditions and basic policies that have their roots deep in the past; the views of individuals, special groups, and organizations; the repercussions of policies of foreign governments on American diplomacy and opinion; the attitude of Congress; and finally the question of whether public opinion at home is belligerently or peacefully inclined. Much that affects the conduct of foreign affairs lies outside the narrow channels

of professional diplomacy. It should be taken into consideration in any appraisal of the Department's course.

Diplomats of long experience realize that the "free advice" of which President Coolidge spoke springs from an emotional people who do not confine their views to the territorial limits of the United States but are perennially quick to take sides over issues raised by a great foreign war. The plea of President Wilson for them to remain neutral, even in thought, when the Great War broke upon Europe in 1914 was of little avail.

Nor is a war essential to raise these problems, for a foreign government may pursue a domestic program in times of peace that will cause sufficient outcry in this country to impair good relations. The Department may caution the people that they are only complaining of the internal affairs of a friendly nation, yet this plea will be in vain if an intangible spark has been touched which ignites human emotions. Inevitably the internal policy has been converted into an external question.

This has repeatedly been illustrated in the case of Germany since Adolf Hitler became Chancellor. The repercussions from his policies in this country have provoked recriminations and denunciations even by Cabinet officers. The waters have become so muddied that it is found impossible for the two governments to take any effective measures to improve their diplomatic relations, much as this might be desired by the Department of State as a matter of general policy and undoubtedly by many officials in the German Foreign Office. Misunderstanding and resentment reached a climax in the virtual recall of their ambassadors.

The remark of President Coolidge with reference to Nicaragua revolved around the state of public opinion when agitated by events of the moment. Public opinion is also governed by traditions that have become part of the national

consciousness. Traditions may be scorned by the light-hearted; they are not ignored by Secretaries of State who are endowed with the sixth sense of politicians. The tradition of the American people against entering into foreign alliances, for example, was a factor in determining the form of that highly praised, and also much derided treaty renouncing war as an instrument of national policy, variously known as the Pact of Paris and the Kellogg-Briand Peace Treaty.

This was emphasized for the writer during a conversation with Secretary Kellogg in his office just after word had been received that all the powers would subscribe to the Pact. The Secretary of State, his shock of silver-white hair glistening in the sunlight, showed no elation as he spoke philosophically of the obstacles he had overcome. His desk was piled with papers from which he had turned a moment before, and outside officials and messengers hurried along the corridor. With him were Robert E. Olds, the Under Secretary of State, and J. Theodore Marriner, chief of the Division of Western European Affairs, who had been his principal departmental adviser in the negotiation and who nearly ten years later was to die by an assassin's bullet in Beirut.

They recalled how the proposal originally made by Aristide Briand, the French Foreign Minister, was for a treaty renouncing war as between the United States and France, and how Secretary Kellogg, at the instance of Marriner, had delayed for several months and then, with the prompting of Senator William E. Borah, chairman of the Committee on Foreign Relations, had made a counterproposal that the treaty should be multilateral.

"What M. Briand proposed," Secretary Kellogg said, "was in effect an alliance between the United States and France, and I could not accept it. Ever since the Franco-

American Alliance (of 1778) was terminated (in 1796) this government has refused to enter any alliance. However, the central idea of peace was excellent, and, if made multilateral, it would lose the character of an alliance. That was why I made my counterproposal."

What Secretary Kellogg stated has been one of the bases of American foreign policy from which no administration departs, unless it would take great political risk at home. A veteran Democratic member of the Committee on Foreign Relations, who had gone through the great League fight in the Senate on the side of the administration, told this writer years later that "stripped to its essentials the League of Nations was an alliance for joint action against an aggressor." He quickly added, "The American people rejected the League and since then it has been accepted as definitely settled that the United States will have no part in an alliance."

Closely bracketed with the policy against alliances is one of independence in the conduct of foreign affairs. Secretaries of State are careful to observe it. Nothing would arouse Congress or the country more than a departure from it. This was the germ of the advice given on foreign affairs by President Washington in his farewell address. It has often been asserted over the years, and most recently under dramatic circumstances by President Franklin D. Roosevelt in his appeal for peace in September, 1938, to the heads of the European states involved in the Central European crisis over the fate of Czechoslovakia. The President framed his plea in close collaboration with Secretary Hull and based it on humanitarian grounds. In emphasizing the political detachment of the United States from the controversy he was both exercising political caution and following precedent, for, regardless of how closely an administration may decide

to cooperate with another government in a foreign emergency, the Department of State reserves freedom of action.

Secretary Stimson did so when urging with all vigor cooperation of the powers to block Japan in her Manchurian venture in 1931 and 1932. The fact that he had assumed the leadership in that effort was not sufficient reason for him to abandon this historic position. Frequently there is parallel action in safeguarding the interests of nationals in a disturbed area or in striving for peace, but every suggestion from abroad for joint action is ruled out flatly and immediately.

Not all foreign offices are aware of this, but ambassadors resident in Washington are under no illusions.

Not so long ago the chief of mission of a great power, after many preliminary conversations, went to the Department of State on instructions of his foreign office to suggest joint action against another government because of attacks on foreign properties. His proposal was summarily rejected.

"I knew that would be your answer," the ambassador replied to the Secretary with perfect equanimity, "and I am never going to ask that question again."

The Department knew that the only reason he had broached the matter was because his government had directed him to.

One other basic policy stands out so prominently that it is sometimes referred to by diplomats as the only great policy entering into the conduct of American foreign affairs. It is the Monroe Doctrine. Sometimes challenged, often elaborated by corollaries, then redefined to its original form, frequently declared by publicists to have been abandoned by an administration, it continues to stand in undiminished force even though now subject to a pan-American interpretation which contemplates consultation among the interested

American republics in an emergency. It is safe to say that the doctrine will stand as long as the American people are prepared to fight for it and it is supported by a strong Navy.

This deep attachment to the Monroe Doctrine is what distinguishes it from so many other foreign policies which the American people gladly subscribe to and widely approve but for which they refuse to fight in an extremity. The application of the Open Door policy in China for forty years has had great popular support in the United States, but Secretary Hay when he promulgated it realized that the people were not prepared to go to war for it. President Theodore Roosevelt upon reviewing the policy a few years later learned the same thing, and Secretary Stimson in pressing his diplomatic policy against Japan in Manchuria was also aware of this situation. Yet through the years it has retained an extraordinary vitality.

In the field of Latin-American relations there is a deep well of pan-Americanism which is apparent to every Secretary of State who plumbs deeply enough. There the United States presses ardently policies of peace. Nevertheless, beyond this there is no too clearly defined fundamental policy. James G. Blaine as Secretary of State gave leadership to pan-Americanism, yet Richard Olney a few years later made his famous declaration that the word of the United States was fiat on this continent. More than three decades passed, and President Franklin D. Roosevelt announced the Doctrine of the Good Neighbor and gave it the greatest application in Latin America but admitted that events beyond his control might force a modification. One thing does appear clear in this area, that an appreciation of a community of interest among the American republics is gradually developing. In this lies the real hope of enduring peace and good relations in the Western Hemisphere.

The public's attitude toward a foreign question may be based in the tenseness of the moment or in more deep-seated causes, but whatever the occasion the Department of State seeks to appraise it. Frequently when officials in the Department are asked what the next step in a situation is to be or the possibility is suggested of action along a certain line, they reply, "What do you think the country would feel about that; don't you think Congress would become aroused and counteract by violent debate the good effects that otherwise might flow from such a course?"

On a few occasions when war has been at issue public opinion has been so overwhelming that it has left the Department powerless. During the early years of the Republic violent partisan controversy over the issues of the French Revolution led to *de facto* naval hostilities with France. A few years later, in 1812, when the country was divided over disputes with Great Britain, President Madison yielded to pressure of the West and Southwest and submitted the question to Congress, which declared war. Public opinion, however, is not always for war; it is often for peace.

The sinking of the battleship *Maine* in Havana Harbor in 1898 meant war, and the sinking of the gunboat *Panay* on the Yangtze river in 1937 did not. In 1898 the American Legation in Madrid was striving earnestly for peace and with some prospect of success if it had been permitted to proceed undisturbed, but there was an indignant public opinion aroused at home over conditions in Cuba which President McKinley decided he could not ignore. He yielded and referred the issue to Congress, where he and everyone else knew the decision would be for but one thing.

In 1937 there was no intensely aroused public opinion against Japan. There was resentment, but there was at the same time an overwhelming desire to avoid war. The loss of

[119]

the *Panay*, therefore, did not mean war. The Department in framing its demand for redress and remuneration proceeded from that premise and Japan, equally desirous of avoiding a conflict, apologized and paid promptly all the indemnity that was asked.

A less dramatic but significant example of the influence of public opinion on foreign problems, and to the exclusion of any effective influence of the Department of State, occurred in the case of the Philippines. When the issue arose of retaining or relinquishing the islands after the War with Spain, President McKinley responded to a demand from the farm regions of the West for the retention on the grounds that a great market for agricultural exports would be opened. Years later when this expectation had not been realized, Western sentiment changed, and in the meantime the American people generally had come to feel that the retention of the islands had been a costly experiment. By 1934 there was no difficulty in having Congress pass the Independence Act.

To a certain extent in 1898 and in all respects in 1934, the issue was decided without the consideration that the Department of State would have given to the diplomatic and political consequences of disturbing the balance of power in the western Pacific.

The occasions when the Department of State is left powerless, however, are infrequent. Ordinarily it can exercise a guiding and determining hand, especially if it attunes itself to public opinion. The "free advice" concerning which President Coolidge spoke is wide open to it. Nor is he the only one who has recognized this fact.

J. Reuben Clark, Jr., when he was Under Secretary of State, commented on it during a conversation with the writer in 1929 concerning the responsibility of newspaper

correspondents assigned to the Department of State. They were bent upon obtaining information, he said, and did not realize the influence they exerted on the public.

"We in the Department are aware of it," he declared. "We get the reaction of the country immediately to everything that is written. We feel it every day."

A similar observation had been made only two years earlier by Nelson T. Johnson, the present Ambassador to China, who at the time was an assistant secretary of state.

"The ability to read," he said, "is accepted as the accomplishment of everyone over the age of twelve. The average citizen is a voracious and rapid reader of the press and on every opportunity asserts his right to an independent opinion as to the interpretation which shall be placed upon the news. Thus whereas in earlier days a Secretary of State had to reckon with but a few informed men, today he has to reckon with a potential Secretary of State in each citizen and must at once justify his own interpretation of the facts."

The editorial and news columns of the newspapers, magazine articles, and the radio constantly give a cross section of public opinion, present the attitudes of organizations and groups of citizens who register their views through resolutions and public meetings, and set forth the individual opinions of publicists and experts. The Department of State makes a close study of these reports and expressions through an elaborate system of clipping, summarization, and filing in order to be informed of popular reactions.

Congress is equally important in indicating what the country is thinking, for Senators and Representatives are in close touch with their constituents, and the Senate and House of Representatives are sounding boards of public opinion. The *Congressional Record* is read as closely in the Department as the newspapers.

Then there are organizations and private citizens who deluge the Department with letters, telegrams, and petitions. Whenever there is an organized campaign being waged to influence the Department in its decisions these appeals are given to the press, so that an elaborate propaganda is built up. It is for the Secretary of State to decide with his political powers of analysis to what extent these views represent only a few individuals or organizations, or how far they reflect the attitude of the American people as a whole. When an especially controversial issue arises—and often it revolves around a program of peace—delegations of citizens from near and distant cities come to Washington to present their views to the Secretary of State. The Secretary greets them individually and cordially, and listens attentively to their appeals. He replies usually by telling them that their views will be taken under consideration. They are given attention along with all other factors in the case.

Paradoxically, it is not always necessary for petitioners to represent a widespread public opinion for their suggestions to be adopted. Special groups occasionally exert influence far out of proportion to their numbers. If they are intensely interested, are well informed, and their cause has merit, they frequently are supported by the sympathy of the country. This is often the case with reference to moral and humanitarian questions, toward which the Department, to be sure, is naturally sympathetic.

Much of the progress made under the leadership of the United States for world suppression of the traffic in opium and other drugs springs from the high purpose and initiative of groups which originally focused the attention of the Department of State on this problem. The influence of church and missionary organizations is likewise pronounced.

Missionaries are always on the frontiers of civilization where revolutions and wars of imperialism are epidemic, and are reluctant to leave. If they go to a safer place temporarily, they are soon anxious to return, and in the meantime their property often has been destroyed or confiscated. Should the Department obtain permission through diplomatic channels for them to return to their posts, and should it proceed forthwith to insist upon the return of the confiscated properties, or file claims for damages? It never decides these questions before consulting the chief representatives of the church or mission organizations in this country and is guided to an extent by their wishes in exercising the responsibility of the government in these special cases.

Similarly, representatives of religious and racial minorities exert an influence that cannot be measured by numbers. When their members are persecuted abroad, genuine sympathy is aroused and is supported by the tradition that America is an asylum for political refugees, as well as by a knowledge that many of the oppressed have relatives in this country. It is not to be wondered at that the Department of State has a fixed policy of deploring ill treatment of human beings anywhere and a long record of interceding with foreign governments on behalf of unfortunates. At present it is taking the lead in a world movement for facilitating the emigration of political refugees from Germany, a movement in which it has active support and cooperation from minority and social groups throughout the country.

There is, of course, a business and a labor public. Each is given opportunity to be heard when reciprocal trade agreements are negotiated, and each makes its influence felt in other special situations which directly affect it. Long and difficult diplomatic negotiations over North Atlantic and Alaskan fisheries with Great Britain and Japan are two of

the most notable instances when pressure of these groups spurred the Department to energetic action.

The variety of ways American public opinion makes itself felt are numerous enough to tax the keenest political judgment, yet there are many more forces continually beating upon the Department of State. A sharp shift in foreign policy by another great power may react to discourage the Department from further efforts along a chosen path, or divert policy into new channels.

Secretary Stimson had one such experience when his hopes to dissuade Japan from her Manchurian venture in 1932 by exerting stronger diplomatic pressure were dashed by Great Britain's refusal to assure him the degree of cooperation he sought. Thus checked, he defined the position of the United States by refusing to recognize the occupied territory as Japanese, and refrained from a stronger policy during the rest of his administration of the Department.

American policy is also affected by official and unofficial suggestions from abroad. In a few instances they have had epochal results. The Monroe Doctrine had its genesis in part in a proposal of the British Foreign Office which was directed against the Holy Alliance in Europe and turned on the status of the former Spanish colonies in South America. Secretary Hay applied the policy of the Open Door in China after having received suggestions from a British subject who had served in the Maritime Customs in China.

The less known circumstances surrounding the creation of the Dawes Reparation Commission in 1923 are worth describing in some detail to illustrate an interaction of government policies and public opinion between the two countries.

The United States was not a party to reparations but was deeply interested in the preservation of peace, and as early

as the summer of 1922 was apprehensive lest France might complicate the situation by occupying the Ruhr. Germany was in a serious economic and financial plight and was drifting lower. Great Britain was anxious. France was obdurate. In these circumstances Secretary Hughes felt that the United States should not be open to a charge of having stood idly by and done nothing for peace. He believed that a solution should be found by forming a nonpartisan commission of experts to determine Germany's capacity to pay reparations.

Furthermore, he believed that the most satisfactory approach was for France to offer the plan herself as her own, and then have other interested powers pledge their support. Accordingly, in the summer of 1922 he instructed Ambassador Herrick, who was returning to his post in Paris from a leave of absence in the United States, to make the suggestion to Raymond Poincaré, the Premier. But Poincaré would have none of it. He was adamant.

Nothing discouraged, Secretary Hughes continued his efforts through conversations with Ambassador Jusserand, but to no avail. In this situation, late in the year he made the proposals himself to the disinterested powers for a determination of Germany's capacity to pay. The question then was how to make the plan public. The consent of France was necessary for publication of the diplomatic correspondence, and obviously that could not be obtained. So Secretary Hughes found the way through a speech he delivered before the American Historical Association at New Haven, Connecticut, on December 29, 1922.

The speech had been prepared and printed and he was leaving for New Haven in a few hours, when he decided to add the proposals to the address, even though by their dramatic quality they destroyed the effect of the rest of the

[125]

speech. At an early morning conference with President Harding he obtained permission to proceed on this basis. Hurrying to the Department of State, he quickly wrote the reparation plan into the address, and thus got before the world the substance of his diplomatic communications which were held in strict confidence.

However, France not only was unmoved but marched into the Ruhr a few days later to enforce reparation payments. Secretary Hughes then knew he had to bide his time until France realized the occupation of the Ruhr was a mistake. He held occasional diplomatic conversations with representatives of interested powers, but nothing significant developed, and months passed. Then, on August 2, 1923, President Harding died and President Coolidge secluded himself in the White House to study pending and prospective questions. This made it more than ever incumbent on Secretary Hughes to maintain silence, and he meticulously avoided discussing reparations in public.

This was still the situation when, on October 5th, David Lloyd George, always picturesque, forceful, and dramatic, arrived in New York for a tour of the United States and Canada. When he left New York for Montreal he appeared to the writer, who was accompanying him, to have no other political object than to urge close understanding between the English-speaking peoples. Less than an hour out of New York, however, he received the correspondents in his private car and when he inquired whether there was any news from Germany it was quickly discovered that he was deeply concerned over that situation and feared it might lead to chaos in Central Europe. Searching questions were directed to ascertain his attitude on reparations. While making clear that he did not want to be put in the position of giving free advice to this country, he replied with an emphatic endorse-

ment of the Hughes proposals and urged immediate action on them by Great Britain and France with all the fire of his vivid personality and love of action.

The public reaction in this country was so encouraging that Lloyd George conducted a campaign through oral and written statements prepared in his most effective style for an examination of Germany's capacity to pay. Reports from Washington indicated a favorable attitude, and when President Coolidge a few days later, on October 10th, broke his silence and announced that the Hughes proposals still stood, Lloyd George, learning of it by radio on his special train in Canada, immediately called a press conference and declared that this amounted to a re-offer of the proposals, and that London and Paris should accept them without a moment's delay. Three days later Great Britain in a note to the United States expressed a sympathetic attitude and promised cooperation if European powers would accept the proposals. There the matter rested for a little more than a week, until Lloyd George arrived in Washington. He at once requested a conference with Secretary Hughes at his residence an hour before a dinner was being given there in honor of the former Prime Minister. The two discussed the whole situation.

The first question Lloyd George asked as he sat on a sofa with Secretary Hughes concerned the attitude of the British government. When he was told that it was not completely definite, the former Prime Minister, although no longer a member of the government, promised to get in touch with London immediately and endeavor to have the proposals accepted.

That was accomplished, and then Lloyd George, in expressing his pleasure and relief, turned to the writer and said:

"You remember the questions concerning Germany when we were leaving New York? The ball was started rolling on all this right there."

But that was not the end. The proposals had been accepted; the Plan had yet to be negotiated and signed. In a few weeks Charles G. Dawes went to Europe as the chief American delegate to the Reparation Conference and was elected chairman of the Conference. Yet even when the negotiations were concluded after months of effort it was not certain that the Dawes Plan would be signed. By that time the summer of 1924 had arrived and Secretary Hughes was in London with the American Bar Association.

He at once took vigorous action. He went to Paris, talked emphatically to Poincaré, Edouard Herriot, and other French leaders, and told them that they should put domestic political considerations aside and sign. The French government leaders with frenzied gestures refused at first but finally yielded. Then Secretary Hughes went to Berlin where there were doubts. There he told the German leaders the same thing.

They did sign, but only after Secretary Hughes had told both the French and the Germans that if they did not, they could not expect anything more from the United States in the way of cooperation. That resolved their doubts. Secretary Hughes was thus enabled to telegraph Frank B. Kellogg, Ambassador in London, that both the German and the French delegates would sign the reparation agreement at the final meeting in London.

Long afterward, officials in the Department of State, dropping the language of diplomacy for the vernacular, remarked that at the critical stage "Lloyd George carried the ball." To which should be added the observation that it was

Charles Evans Hughes who carried the ball across the goal line.

It was a notable case of Anglo-American cooperation for peace.

British policy probably affects the United States more often than that of any other country, for not only is there a common heritage, but the influence of Great Britain as the dominant world power, notwithstanding her troubles with the continental powers after the World War, is naturally the most widely felt. It is felt even in small ways.

During an Empire-wide holiday an impatient official in the Department of State one day exclaimed, "You might know the British Empire was taking a day off, everything is so quiet."

"Does this always happen?" the writer asked.

"Oh, yes. Every time the British relax, the volume of cable messages slows down from all over the world."

This was perfectly true. The greatest single galvanizing force in the world was idle, and all capitals felt the reaction. There was just less business being transacted. However, this is far from saying that the United States and Great Britain always see eye to eye.

On the other hand, there is a long tradition of almost unbroken friendship between America and France that is reflected in a sympathy and understanding running through all their diplomatic relations. There is an almost equally long line of friendship with China, and even in the years of diplomatic disputes with Japan it has never been forgotten that the Island Empire of the Far East was reopened to the Western world through the initiative and good offices of an American naval officer.

[129]

CHAPTER VIII

THE PRESS CONFERENCE SYSTEM

IT is impossible to consider outside influences on foreign policy and ignore the influences which the Department of State exerts in the opposite direction. It is not a one-way street. For this purpose the daily press conference of the Secretary of State has become a powerful weapon. Obviously it is of service to newspapers bent solely upon obtaining the news and ascertaining the point of view of the Secretary of State as spokesman of the government on foreign affairs but with an eye watchful in separating news from sheer propaganda. Not that all Secretaries descend to partisan appeal. If they would give the press conference its greatest effectiveness, they avoid half truths and one-sided presentation. The most responsible minded distinctly have used it as a means of honestly informing the country and the world of their position. The conference, however, is employed not merely to inform the public. On occasion it is used to address foreign chancelleries.

This was never more impressively shown than on a hot day late in June, 1923, when Secretary Hughes utilized it as his medium for attempting to convince the British Foreign Secretary of the unsoundness of his position in a treaty negotiation. Secretary Hughes was always masterful in handling press conferences, but never more so than on that summer day when he brought into play all the force of his intellect, his legal equipment, and his persuasive logic. His

immediate audience was a group of nine newspaper correspondents; his real audience not the correspondents, nor
even the American public, but one man seated at his desk
three thousand miles away in the Foreign Office in London.
The objective was a series of ship liquor treaties, the first
effort being directed to Great Britain. If she agreed, other
powers would fall in line.

The issue was an incident of America's experiment with
prohibition. Foreign ships laden with liquor were hovering
off the American coast and landing their cargoes surrepti-
tiously. At the same time British liners could not bring their
liquor stores into United States ports, even under lock and
key. They had to dispose of them before entering the three-
mile limit. What Secretary Hughes proposed was a treaty
granting the liners the right to bring the liquor in under
bond, and, on the other hand, the right for American
enforcement officers to search ships up to twelve miles off
shore. This double-barreled arrangement would dispose of
two embarrassing problems. But Britain was cool to the
proposal because of principles of international law which
flowed in many directions beyond the relatively narrow
questions posed by prohibition.

After weeks of consideration, Lord Curzon, the British
Foreign Secretary, in a long statement before the House of
Lords indicated that the treaty would be rejected. His statement was published in full in the American newspapers, and
when Secretary Hughes met the correspondents that day
he had both barrels loaded for a reply. He scarcely could wait
for the door of the reception room to be closed so that the
conference might begin. He had read the statement, he said,
and would be glad to state his views on condition that his
remarks should not be attributed directly to him. This was
necessary because Lord Curzon's exposition was in the form

of a domestic utterance, inasmuch as it had been addressed to a parliamentary body, and, therefore, the American government could not with propriety take official notice of it.

Secretary Hughes plunged into his argument. For three-quarters of an hour he shouted and pounded the table, his voice resounding through the closed door and far down the corridor. It was one of the most forceful and able speeches he ever delivered. The small size of his audience meant nothing to him. When he had concluded the correspondents rushed to the telegraph wires and cables. It was a graphic illustration of how statesmen in these modern times can speak over the heads of their audiences to each other. Curzon in addressing the House of Lords was actually addressing Secretary Hughes; and Secretary Hughes in speaking to the press conference was directing his remarks to Curzon.

Not that Curzon was completely convinced, but there was immediately noticeable a change in the London atmosphere. The Foreign Secretary weakened, though not completely. Negotiations through diplomatic channels were pressed. Then Secretary Hughes in August found another opportunity to drive home his argument. When attending the annual meeting of the American Bar Association in Minneapolis he talked privately with Lord Birkenhead of Great Britain, who was a guest of the Association. The Secretary followed this with more conversations a few days later with Birkenhead at a meeting of the Canadian Bar Association in Montreal. Birkenhead was a close friend of Curzon and promised to exert his influence with the Foreign Secretary. It was another illustration of the fact that foreign affairs are conducted from many fronts and not exclusively through formal diplomatic channels. Birkenhead returned to England and in September Curzon agreed to negotiate the treaty. This was done and the pact was signed.

Naturally, the press conference is a convenient channel for informing and influencing the American public, as every reader learns from his newspaper at the breakfast table. Day in and day out the reader has before him a running report from the Secretary of State on various aspects of the conduct of foreign affairs. In the direct accessibility of the Secretary of State the United States is unique among governments, for in no other world capital does the foreign minister make himself so available to the press.

While no tickets can be purchased and the immediate audience is small, usually numbering from ten to forty, the real but invisible audience numbers millions in this country and abroad. It is a forum on current events in which the principal speaks with high authority, and the direct audience of correspondents accredited through their membership in the Press Gallery consists of a group of specialists who are alert to catch the portent of the slightest intimation. The Secretary of State makes announcements, submits to questioning that takes on the character of cross-examination, explains and defends, frankly reveals, or feints with his inquisitors to avoid a premature disclosure of plans. The sessions run from a few minutes to three-quarters of an hour or an hour, depending upon the importance and number of subjects raised. The Secretary always waits for the correspondents to terminate the conference. He never takes that initiative himself.

Promptly at the appointed time, every day, usually the noon hour, the Secretary of State enters the reception room of his office suite, where correspondents are gathered representing press associations and the leading newspapers of this country as well as of London, Paris, Berlin, Rome, Tokyo, and other foreign capitals. The correspondents are seated around the long table in the center of the room or on chairs

and sofas that line the walls, from which look down the portraits of former Secretaries of State. But when the Secretary of State appears they rise and remain standing with him throughout the conference. There is an exchange of greetings, a few pleasantries, and then the business of the conference gets seriously under way.

The Secretary of State, at times aggressive, at other times leaning easily on the back of a chair at the head of the long table, makes such announcements as he has to give out voluntarily—of the progress of a diplomatic negotiation, the appointment of a delegation to an international conference, or he may read a statement defining the attitude of the United States toward an international question. Having concluded this part of the conference, he asks, "Are there any questions?" There always are. They come thick and fast, but only from American correspondents, for it is an unwritten rule that the foreign representatives shall not subject the Secretary to examination. That would savor too much of quizzing from a foreign country. They stand passive listeners but are free to use the same information as the Americans.

The questioning is sharp and pressing, although invariably in good humor; and the replies are in the same spirit. The correspondents endeavor to ascertain the details and significance of policies and receive light on new developments that have arisen in various corners of the world, and they then ask a variety of questions out of the background of their general knowledge in an effort to determine whether new policy, as yet unrevealed, is yeasting.

The business of the Secretary of State is to enlighten them as far as he considers compatible with the public interest. Moreover, if he is alive to his opportunity, he will utilize the conference to expound and defend his policies for its

effect upon public opinion at home and the information of foreign governments. The conference also affords opportunity for him to say things informally but effectively that it might not be wise for the time being to set forth in a state paper. Frequently he considers that a statement made in the conference, either orally or in writing, is sufficient notice to the world of his position and renders unnecessary a formal note. Many times it happens that when he has read an announcement of his attitude and the correspondents inquire if he intends to communicate the views formally to the interested governments, he replies that the statement is of itself sufficient notice to the world.

If further evidence is needed to indicate the importance attached to the conference, it may be found in the fact that the Department regularly sends official reports of it, with full accounts of the running fire of questions and answers, to its missions abroad for their information in keeping abreast of affairs.

Taken in conjunction with the White House press conference, where the President from time to time discusses foreign affairs, the daily press conference of the Secretary of State has become a powerful instrument of politics and diplomacy. It is now a well-established government institution. Politically it is an effective substitute for the system of interpellation of Cabinet ministers in parliamentary governments, since Cabinet officers are not subjected to that ordeal in the American form of government with its separated powers among the legislative, executive, and judicial branches. Diplomatically, it affords a flexible medium for conveying views abroad or registering protests that can be even more emphatic than a formal note.

This was never more dramatically illustrated than by President Franklin D. Roosevelt when he and Secretary

Hull decided to protest with all the force at their command the persecution of Jews and Catholics in Germany. Sufficient reports were not at hand to show whether American nationals had been directly affected. And, while ample humanitarian grounds existed for a sharp rebuke to Chancellor Hitler, in accordance with fixed American policy, a clear diplomatic basis was lacking. For the events in Germany technically were of a domestic nature, even though they had shocked the world and provided the intangible spark which transforms internal incidents into external questions. President Roosevelt and Secretary Hull consulted, and agreed that the White House rather than the Department of State should be the sounding board. Having indicated their concern by summoning the American Ambassador from Berlin for the technically phrased purpose of reporting and consulting, President Roosevelt lashed out at his next press conference with an emphatic expression of disapproval of the persecutions in Germany. In the sensational and dramatic circumstances his utterance had far more force than a diplomatic note.

Just what the medium meant to him may be appreciated more easily by comparing it with conditions before the press conference system existed in its present development. There have been several like occasions but none more compelling than those which confronted John Hay. When in 1902 Jewish minorities were being oppressed in Rumania, Hay and Theodore Roosevelt wanted to speak out, but there was no diplomatic ground on which to base a humanitarian appeal, any more than in 1938 when the second Roosevelt acted so promptly. It required the skill of A. A. Adee to find a way. He moved craftily and indirectly. First, he drafted a confidential instruction on a naturalization question to the American Chargé d'Affaires in

Bucharest, taking occasion to frame a humanitarian appeal for oppressed minorities; next he incorporated this instruction in a note appealing for distressed minorities to the signatories of the Berlin Treaty of 1878, which had declared for full and equal rights for Jews in the Balkans, and then he registered the protest of the United States by making this note public.

The same question arose a year later, in 1903, as a result of the Kisheneff massacre of Jews in Russia. Again there was no technical ground for a diplomatic protest. After much thought the Department of State encouraged the circulation of a petition of protest among Americans with a view to having it transmitted to Russia. It never was delivered, but information was published concerning the petition and in this way the opinion of the United States was registered.

In both cases, in 1902 and 1903, Hay felt that he could not explain the views of the government to the newspapers, for that might have been considered an indiscretion. Thirty-five years later it was no indiscretion, for the President, as was customary, was merely informing the correspondents of his opinions as was always the case when he met them twice each week. But everyone realized he was employing a powerful diplomatic weapon that was ready and at hand. The Secretary of State would have spoken as promptly in his press conference but deferred to the President because of the greater carrying power of the White House. For purposes of diplomacy both are merged to a great extent, but ordinarily the President will not discuss foreign affairs with the press except by prearrangement with his Secretary of State.

On the other hand, the primary purpose of the daily press conference of the Secretary of State is to consider foreign affairs. It often throws interesting light on a developing international negotiation. It was thus that the first real infor-

mation was obtained concerning the effort Secretary Kellogg had undertaken in December, 1927, to negotiate his famous treaty. Information that some such negotiation, connected somehow with discussions looking to the replacement of an expiring arbitration treaty, was under consideration had reached the correspondents from Paris.

When Kellogg greeted the group that day a correspondent referred to reports from Paris that negotiations for a treaty outlawing war were either under way or would be considered in the near future in connection with the negotiation of a new arbitration convention to take the place of one negotiated twenty years before by Elihu Root with France. Kellogg replied that he could not say definitely what form the treaty would take. He had had several talks with the French Ambassador. The logical thing would be to negotiate a new arbitration treaty, in view of the expiration soon of the present one, but he could not predict definitely what would be finally agreed on.

A correspondent suggested that an arbitration treaty to replace the Root Treaty might obviate the necessity of another treaty to outlaw war. The Secretary said in reply that he did not want to say that, as he did not know how far he could go. It was impossible for him to discuss steps in the negotiation of a treaty. It would not do any good and it could do a lot of harm. All he could say was that the matter was under discussion.

A correspondent inquired how, if the treaty was to deal with specific questions with France, it would be possible to embody the same questions in treaties with other countries. Kellogg answered that there were no unsettled issues with France to put into a treaty and, of course, a treaty that could be made with France could be made with any other country.

Another correspondent then inquired whether the subject of defining an aggressor had arisen in the negotiations with France. The Secretary replied that he did not know how anybody would ever define an aggressor, and he must absolutely refuse to get into the speculative field of what an aggressor is or is not.

With that the conference ended, but it is pertinent to observe that the final question was one that has dogged the Peace Pact ever since.

The press conference is not always devoted to serious subjects. It has its lighter moments. When the term *agenda* was used for the program of the Washington Conference of 1921, classically minded correspondents indulged in bantering argument with Secretary Hughes as to whether it should not be *agendum*, the singular pronounced with the hard *g* of the Latin, rather than the plural pronounced with the soft *g* of the English. No one enjoyed the argument more than the Secretary of State.

Another incident equally enjoyed concerned a note Secretary Hughes sent to Japan on the status of the mandated island of Yap. When the text was made public Secretary Hughes insisted that it was not a sharp note. Many correspondents felt it severe but were willing to take the Secretary of State at his word. If it were not sharp, well and good but obviously, they reasoned, if it were not sharp, then it must be blunt. They so described it in their despatches and thus sustained their own interpretation, and technically that of the Secretary of State.

The lighter touch often marked press conferences when they were held during absences of Secretary Stimson by Joseph P. Cotton, an Under Secretary of State who prided himself on his informality and directness. Ramsay Mac-Donald, it should be explained, was Prime Minister, Charles

G. Dawes was Ambassador to Great Britain, and revision of the Young Plan on German reparations was being agitated in Europe, when the following discussion took place at one of Cotton's press conferences:

CORRESPONDENT.—Is there any informal report indicating the way Germany will jump in the controversy?

COTTON.—I don't know any more than you do, probably not as much. Everybody's knowledge started from scratch at about 7:30 or 8:00 this morning.

Q.—Is there anything on the submarine question with Great Britain?

A.—The progress of any conversations between Dawes and MacDonald my mouth is simply shut on. I said I didn't think it helpful toward an agreement to have the steps generally a matter of public comment.

Q.—Did you know the American Ambassador to Great Britain got lost in Dublin?

A.—I don't know how he could. That's suspicious if he got lost there. All taxicabs go to Phoenix Park and nobody goes anywhere else.

Q.—Who won?

A.—It is bound to be a new one. There are nothing but new horses there that have never raced before.

The correspondents did not obtain any information but they were entertained.

While the press conference is the principal everyday medium for informing the American public and the world at large of unfolding foreign policy, it is not the only one. The Secretary of State is the only Cabinet officer who does not submit an annual report to Congress, for the affairs of the Department of State are too confidential and delicate to lend themselves to this treatment. For that reason, every year when the President delivers his annual message to

Congress on the state of the union he includes a discussion of foreign affairs. As circumstances warrant he also transmits special messages from time to time to Congress on foreign problems. Nor does the record stop here, for the President and the Secretary of State deliver public addresses on the subject, and the Department of State constantly issues announcements and explanations in formal statements.

Nevertheless, the most convenient vehicle for explaining and defending policies and encouraging public support of them is found in the press conference of the Secretary of State, supplemented now and then by announcements of the President in his semiweekly conferences with newspaper correspondents.

Its origins trace back to the days when John Hay received regularly a small group of four or five of the most experienced and trusted correspondents who were assigned to the Department of State, and informally explained policies and revealed latest advices received by the Department. He was the first to undertake the experiment and much, although not all, that he said was in confidence. Only once was his confidence violated and then through an inadvertence arising out of an honest misunderstanding. It ended happily, however, because of Hay's delight in a jest.

When he received the correspondents the next day he was prepared for battle. He cast a reproving eye on the offending correspondent who represented one of the many *Journals* in the country, and demanded an explanation.

"Why, Mr. Secretary," the correspondent said in explaining that he had arrived late the day before and so had missed the injunction to secrecy, "I would not have done that for the world."

"No," Hay rejoined, "you would not have done it for the *World* but you would for the *Journal*."

He forgot his displeasure in the roar of laughter.

Elihu Root, who followed Hay as Secretary of State, continued the custom of receiving a few trusted correspondents daily, but Philander C. Knox, his successor, abandoned it. Knox occasionally received an individual correspondent evenings at his home, but no groups.

In the meantime, William H. Taft as Secretary of War under Theodore Roosevelt had adopted a press conference system of his own. He was jovial and obliging, and liked the newspaper men; also he discovered that he could learn the latest news from them. So he developed the habit of receiving them daily. The arrangement was mutually satisfactory. Yet several years passed before the system became definitely rooted in the government. Theodore Roosevelt would receive a few favorite correspondents occasionally for interviews when he was being shaved, a satisfactory expedient, although the newspaper men watching the animated, spluttering face were subjected to mixed emotions of fascination and apprehension of severe laceration. Taft also after becoming President held occasional press conferences for groups.

Many newspapermen in those years, however, could not see the Secretary of State at any time and were dependent upon the generosity of the favored few. In this small group the most trusted by officials and the most generous with his colleagues was Edwin M. Hood of the Associated Press, who spanned a period of forty years, from William M. Evarts to Charles Evans Hughes. The door was always open to Hood.

John Hay offered him the post of an assistant secretary of state, but he declined for personal reasons. When Hay was seeking a striking phrase for its dramatic effect in the presidential campaign of 1904, it was Hood who suggested to him "Perdicaris alive or Raisuli dead" in the peremptory note

which grew out of the Moroccan bandit's kidnaping of Perdicaris, who claimed to be an American.

His association with high officials was unusual. When President Cleveland ordered regular army troops into Chicago during the railway strike riots of 1894 he wrote Hood describing the reasons and feelings which prompted the act. During the stress of the Republican national convention of 1896 it was to Hood that Speaker Thomas B. Reed made the exclamation that became famous in American political history, "God Almighty hates a quitter." Viscount Bryce from the time he retired as British Ambassador to the United States in 1912 until death intervened corresponded with Hood regularly. Fifteen years after Hood's death, President Franklin D. Roosevelt, who as Assistant Secretary of the Navy had known him, described him in an address as "one of the grandest men who ever lived."

When President Wilson decided to make public the note of Dr. Alfred Zimmermann, the German Secretary for Foreign Affairs, proposing a German-Mexican alliance aimed at the United States shortly before this country entered the World War, he gave it to Hood. This is common knowledge in diplomatic circles, although Hood would never admit it. He guarded confidences out of a nice sense of the proprieties and destroyed all personal correspondence, even as did A. A. Adee, his friend of many years in the Department of State.

Hood represented the personal era, although he lived to see the more general and more equable press conference system firmly established. While its outlines were traced earlier, it took definite form with the administration of Woodrow Wilson. The Democrats in 1913 had been out of power for sixteen years and came into office with liberal ideas. They

[143]

were determined that the business of government should be conducted openly. Doors were thrown wide open and press conferences for all correspondents arranged at regular intervals in the White House and the government departments. Secretary Bryan undertook to receive the press every day in the Department of State.

Nevertheless, the arrangement which augured so well did not at first move smoothly. Bryan learned that he could not speak as freely as he had from the public platform in the years he was out of office, for there were painful experiences when he spoke incautiously. Inevitably, there were repercussions from abroad. Never equipped by temperament or training to conduct foreign affairs as a seasoned diplomat, he became more and more secretive until his press conferences were more important for his comments on the success of his Chautauqua appearances than for his illuminating discussion of foreign affairs. When he was succeeded in 1915 by Robert Lansing the conferences began to have their first real importance. Lansing was always helpful to the correspondents, although required to be very discreet on account of the delicate problems raised by the World War. Yet the beginning of President Wilson's lack of confidence in him can be traced to an intimation he gave in a press conference in 1916 that the United States might be drawn into the World War.

With President Wilson the White House conferences began hopefully, but he felt that questions on foreign affairs were out of place. Even though he should refuse to answer questions on foreign affairs, he explained, he might indicate something by his manner, by the bat of an eyelash, as he phrased it. Consequently after a time the White House press conferences were abandoned, but they were continued in the Department of State throughout the War and thereafter.

The conferences with the President were not resumed until Warren G. Harding entered the White House. In fact, it was during the Harding administration that the system was given its greatest impetus. Harding was in no small degree responsible, because he was sympathetic out of his own past as a newspaperman, while in the Department of State Secretary Hughes immediately grasped the advantage to which the conferences had already been put there in directing foreign policy.

Harding, however, learned very soon in the hard school of experience that the press conferences at the White House cannot be divorced from the Department of State. As in so many other respects, the White House and the Department merge in this field. Ordinarily the President refers questions on foreign affairs from the correspondents to the Department, but from time to time he makes statements on this subject. When he does, in any important degree apart from a side remark or an incidental observation, it usually is by prearrangement with the Secretary of State for the calculated purpose of giving greater emphasis than would be conveyed by the Secretary of State. If the President in an unguarded moment speaks without sufficient preparation, there may be complications. No President has a perfect record in this respect.

Harding learned his lesson under special circumstances. It was during the Washington Conference on Armament Limitation and Pacific Questions at a time when the Four Power Treaty concerning the islands of the Pacific was under negotiation that he was asked at a press conference if the Treaty would cover the islands of Japan proper. Harding in all innocence and good faith replied in the affirmative. His announcement struck the conference like a bombshell, for unhappily for him he was wrong.

The damage was repaired as much as possible through a prompt statement by Secretary Hughes, but there were two direct consequences. One was that the international conference, in order to allay suspicions of Japan, was required to adopt a protocol specifying that the islands of Japan proper were not covered by the Four Power Treaty. The other was that Harding changed the method of questioning at his press conferences from oral to written form. Presidents ever since Harding's experience have stipulated that there shall be no cross-examination, although Franklin D. Roosevelt, with this reservation, restored the oral method.

In the Department of State the press conference has been used by Secretaries of State in varying degrees, depending upon their personalities and personal inclinations. Secretaries Kellogg and Stimson used it powerfully, the former in pressing his multilateral treaty renouncing war as an instrument of national policy when his objective was to swing foreign governments into line, and the latter in pursuing his diplomacy in the Far East in a broad action to mobilize world public opinion for peace after Japan invaded Manchuria in 1931. Secretary Hull has employed it regularly and often to impress other governments with his views on peace and liberal economic policies, but he has utilized it less as a day-to-day medium for defending and explaining than some of his predecessors.

Secretary Stimson was earnest and conscientious in his approach to the press conference. He discussed his policies at length and in a spirit of cooperation, striving to enlighten the newspapermen as far as possible without complicating his tasks by premature disclosures. More than that, often when an American ambassador had returned from his post for a periodic consultation with the Department and the White House, Secretary Stimson would invite him to his

press conference, introduce him and turn him over to the correspondents for examination. At other times, when the chairman of an American delegation to an international conference had been appointed and had received his instructions, Secretary Stimson would present him to the press conference. And Kellogg, signifying his attachment to the system, often upon returning to the Department for a visit after he had left office would attend the press conference and renew old ties.

Secretary Hughes was so active in the Department that the press was received twice each day, although the Under Secretary of State often appeared for one of the meetings. The principal announcements, though, were made by Secretary Hughes. He declared at the outset that he would make the announcements himself and sought to discourage correspondents from conferring individually with other officials in the Department. This raised such a storm of protest that the rule was relaxed, but the correspondents found the press conferences so productive of news that they largely forgot their dissatisfaction.

It was a tribute, too, to Secretary Hughes that his conferences were attended regularly by the chief correspondents in Washington of the metropolitan newspapers who specialize in national politics rather than foreign affairs. Of course the correspondents who were regularly assigned to the Department also were present. Never since have the chief correspondents regularly attended, although Secretary Stimson frequently would invite them to his home for an explanation of foreign policy and would confide in them the various steps he was taking. And daily he supplemented these contacts by designating James G. Rogers, an assistant secretary of state who had forsaken newspaper work for the law and who was closely in his confidence, to be an informal spokes-

man with the press. Because of his early newspaper background, Rogers could explain and clarify policies through conversations in his office with a frankness that has never been exceeded in the history of the Department.

In many respects Secretary Hughes led the way for Secretaries of State in the method of conducting the conferences. Always keenly sensitive of the proprieties, he would not discuss matters that did not directly concern the United States. As he once explained, this would only tend to build up a situation involving the government, whereas an attitude of prudence and wise abstention from comment would avoid this danger. In first taking this position he gave another illustration of his extraordinary memory and, incidentally, of how thoroughly the Foreign Service keeps the Department informed.

During a dispute between France and Germany over the Rhineland, Secretary Hughes was pressed by the correspondents to make some comment. He steadfastly refused. The question was repeated in various forms half a dozen times, Secretary Hughes always replying tersely, "No comment." Finally, he volunteered to tell the correspondents in confidence why he would not comment.

The situation, he explained, did not concern this country directly, yet if he should make observations, they might be misconstrued in Paris or Berlin, provoke replies that would lead to retorts from the Department of State, and thus very speedily a situation would be built up quite needlessly involving this country. Then proceeding further with his explanation, he told the correspondents that he could inform them for their own background of the facts at various stages in the developing situation between France and Germany, because some unofficial reports from Europe had been inaccurate. Without reference to notes, he recounted the

various moves and steps in detail, day by day, with dates. It was a complete and comprehensive account, the result of accurate and full reporting by the Foreign Service and of close reading of despatches by the Secretary of State—and all on a situation that did not directly concern this government. It was a case only of information received and digested in ordinary course.

Cross-examining Secretary Hughes on foreign affairs was a stimulating experience. As could be expected, before a question was completed, he had seen ahead to the end and what was behind it. Once Matthew F. Tighe, a veteran correspondent, asked an involved question of an hypothecated type that he dearly liked.

"There must be something behind that question," Secretary Hughes said. "What is it?"

Tighe hesitated and then said faintly, "Mexico."

"I thought so," Secretary Hughes replied. "No comment."

Tighe was a personality, and not the less interesting because he bore a striking physical resemblance to Mark Twain. He was well educated in the classics and was much liked by Secretary Hughes, who would address him, with a wave of the hand, as "my learned friend."

Once Tighe saw Colonel George Harvey, Ambassador to Great Britain, come from Secretary Hughes' office after a conference and sent the Secretary of State a written inquiry as to its purport. He wrote the message in Latin. In a few minutes a reply was received from Secretary Hughes saying that the conference was of no news importance or interest— also written in Latin. Such incidents enlivened departmental routine.

In general the Department's relations with the press are governed through the Division of Current Information, which was established by Philander C. Knox thirty years

ago. It supervises the press conferences, issues statements authorized by the Secretary of State, and maintains constant contact with correspondents, news photographers, and representatives of magazines and radio companies. In charge of Michael J. McDermott, one of the most experienced and competent of press relations officers in the government, its staff answers inquiries, provides a speedy channel of information throughout the Department when the inquirer does not have time for personal interviews, and is available for service at all hours. Telephone calls that rout McDermott and his aides out of bed in the small hours of the morning are customary and accepted as a matter of course. For the Secretary of State with an eye and ear sensitive to public reactions, it is one of the most important divisions in the Department. Its chief is constantly at the Secretary's right hand, prepared to advise him concerning the state of public opinion. And its personnel is on duty subject to call twenty-four hours in the day.

It does not know the meaning of such modern shibboleths as the forty-hour week.

CHAPTER IX

COMMUNICATIONS

THE press conference system would die of dry rot without the aid of its most valuable ally, modern communications. They bring to the correspondents latest information from London, Tokyo, and other world capitals as a basis of questioning the Secretary of State and provide the avenue for his views to be communicated instantly to the farthest corners of the civilized world. Without them the press conference would be futile, and there would be no diplomacy of dynamics. Foreign affairs would still be conducted in slow motion.

There are many who feel it would be better for the world if there were more of the older order remaining, but the fact stands out that modern inventions have speeded up all life, and the Department of State must take advantage of them just as business does. They accomplish what would be miracles to a former generation, as when President Roosevelt, who was cruising in Lower California Bay in October, 1935 issued through the Department of State his proclamation of neutrality in the Italo-Ethiopian War. Hundreds of words were exchanged by radio before the text was completed and approved, but that was only an incidental detail. Three years later, Secretary Hull thought nothing of telephoning the Department from the Pan-American Conference in Lima, Peru, for an exchange of views on current business.

Swift action at times may mean the difference between life and death. It did when the American Legation was in

imminent danger of being overrun by the panic-stricken native mob in its headlong rush from Addis Ababa before the approach of Italian troops in May, 1936. The legation was insufficiently manned to withstand the horde beating at the gates of the compound, even though Cornelius Van H. Engert, the Minister Resident, had armed his little staff and they had taken position to stand off the natives. It was obvious that the effort would soon fail unless reinforcements arrived. The one chance lay with the strong force of guards at the British Legation three miles away. Yet telephone lines had been cut and a runner could not have made the distance and survived.

In the emergency Engert turned to the short-wave radio equipment that had been sent to him from Washington in charge of navy experts to maintain contact with the United States if commercial communications failed. The British had no such equipment, so he could not send the message direct. But Engert was resourceful. He sent his appeal for reinforcements by short wave to the United States naval wireless station at Cavite in the Philippines. It was immediately relayed to Washington for transmission to London. The British government promptly forwarded it to Cairo from whence it was sent to the British Legation in Addis Ababa. An hour and a half after Engert sent his appeal, troops from the British Legation drove up to the compound in trucks just in the nick of time.

That was an instance of the unusual, which can be repeated whenever circumstances demand. Yet even when confronted only with the commonplace the telegraph room in the Department of State building knows no office hours, for the sun does not set upon the field of the Department's labors. The keys of the telegraph operators are rarely quiet at any time throughout the twenty-four hours of the day. As a

result a continuous stream of messages passes over the desk of the Secretary of State keeping him in hourly touch with the state of the government's relations with the remotest parts of the world.

Part of this is information. A great part of it, however, consists of requests for decisions to enable a representative of the government to act within a very short time from the moment the message falls under the eyes of the Secretary. It has produced a need for brief but careful, immediate instructions covering incidents as they occur.

At the same time the modern system of communications has brought into closer and more intimate cooperation the Department and the Foreign Service, which together are responsible for carrying on foreign relations. Policies are still formulated in the Department as of old, but the Foreign Service can cooperate as never before in shaping them through providing complete and up-to-date information and contributing mature judgment of experienced officers abroad in the field.

In contrast to the diplomatic formality of the second floor of the Department of State building where the offices of the Secretary of State and his chief aides are located, the telegraph and cable room of the Division of Communications and Records on the fourth floor might easily be mistaken for a busy newspaper office. Much the same atmosphere prevades it, with telegraph keys, printing machines, and all the equipment of an up-to-date message center. Nine operators are on duty sending and receiving over facilities leased from commercial companies and connecting directly with cable offices in New York or through ready adjustments with commercial wire points in the United States.

Among the instruments are two telegraph printing machines which operate over combined telegraph and cable

circuits directly into the American Embassy in London. They are manipulated like typewriters. When the operator presses the keyboard the corresponding letters are printed on the other end three thousand miles away. It is instantaneous, as though the correspondence were being conducted in the same room. Yet the circuits are far apart, one running across the Atlantic by the northern and the other by the southern route. One is used for incoming, the other for outgoing messages.

Adjoining the telegraph and cable room are other offices for encoding and decoding messages in secret cipher, for administrative officials, and for statistical recording of the flow of business day in and day out. One large room is given over to telephone communications with a large switch board staffed by women operators. Calls are made through it to all parts of the United States and the Western Hemisphere and by radio to far places overseas.

The suite of rooms is one of the most secluded and at the same time one of the most active in the entire building, with David A. Salmon, veteran expert and executive, in charge. History runs through the hands of Salmon and his trusted subordinates, but they must forget much of it when they leave the office for their homes. Eventually most of it will be revealed, for the Department of State publishes regularly volumes of foreign relations under an order requiring them to be "substantially complete," up to the point that foreign governments concerned will consent to their publication. Because that consent is sometimes difficult to obtain it will in some cases be many years before all is revealed of what has been carried over throbbing wires, vaulting radio waves, and in bulging diplomatic pouches; but, as far as the Department can, it makes the record public to within the past fifteen years. Foreign governments have refused permission

for publication of their correspondence for a more recent period.

Nearly 5,000,000 words a year are sent and received over the telegraph and cable facilities. The number of messages exceeds 65,000, a volume that has trebled in the past twelve years, reflecting the increase of activity of the Department in that short time. Naturally the flow of incoming reports far exceeds the outgoing, because of the activity of the Foreign Service in keeping the Department informed of events abroad. The incoming volume is three and a half times the outgoing.

The number of words sent and received daily runs up to 27,000 and the messages to over 200. In a time of international strain the volume, of course, increases. During the Central European crisis of 1938 there were sometimes 400 messages in a single day. During that fateful September when the crisis reached its peak there were over 6,200 messages sent and received, and the total number of words was over 500,000. The experience was repeated during the European crises of March and April, 1939, although not in the exceptional volume of the previous September. Not since the months when the Versailles Treaty was being framed in 1919 had there been such a load. At the peak of the September crisis the Division of Communications and Records was handling between 45,000 and 50,000 words and code symbols a day, counting incoming and outgoing messages. Since code symbols may be expanded by as much as 20 percent when they are turned into standard words and sentences, the actual number of words sent and received was somewhat greater than this.

When a code message arrives it is taken down by typewriter on special sheets which are ruled off into blocks for convenience in deciphering. If the message is long, it is cut

[155]

into sections and distributed among decoders. When it has been decoded it is assembled, gone over by master decoders for possible errors, and then sent in a sealed envelope to the official to whom it is addressed. If of special importance it may reach only the Secretary of State and the President; otherwise it finds its way into a departmental filing system, divided according to geographical regions.

Including mail service, the volume of all forms of communications totals nearly 1,000,000 items annually. If special messages and correspondence transmitted for other departments and agencies of the government because of some connection with foreign affairs are taken into account, the aggregate is 1,500,000 annually. Mail from Europe still moves slowly, but three-quarters of the letters from Latin-American countries come north by air.

Correspondence is not confined to emergencies or diplomatic questions, for the Foreign Service is constantly active in gathering trade and commercial information and forwarding it to the Department for the benefit of American businessmen. It appears regularly in governmental publications that have a wide distribution. The Department receives by mail and telegraph from the Foreign Service a stream of information of this sort. It includes reports on economic and trade factors, opportunities for new outlets for American goods, export programs, sales methods and credit terms of competitors in the foreign market. In a single year these reports and letters number more than 110,000.

While mail facilities have greatly expanded in the past quarter of a century, electrical communications of themselves have accomplished a revolution, although not in a day. It required years and was accompanied by lamentations from the older school of diplomats. First came the telephone on a limited scale, then the typewriter, the wireless telegraph,

and years later the radio telephone for overseas conversations. The conservative Department of State did not like the change.

When the typewriter was installed, veterans in the Department complained that it meant the passing of classical diplomacy—which it did—and the days when diplomatic notes were written in elegantly formed letters by longhand. The Department resisted this innovation to the last. Other agencies of the government in Washington and even foreign offices abroad had already accepted the change, and the Department of State could not resist indefinitely.

In the early nineties typewriters were introduced but not precipitately. At first they were used only for domestic correspondence. Then, becoming somewhat accustomed to the innovation, the Department relaxed slightly and employed the typewriter for mailed instructions to missions abroad. But it would not be so crude as to use it for diplomatic notes. Finally, the resistance was broken suddenly and from an unexpected quarter when one day the Department received a typewritten diplomatic note from the British Embassy. That was the last straw. Thereafter the typewriter was used for the Department's own diplomatic correspondence. At last the time had passed when one of the first requirements for employment in the Department was the ability to write a good hand.

The Department turned slowly to the use of even the telephone. In 1881 there was one in the building. It was located in a room adjoining the office of the Chief Clerk. One day it rang and Sydney Y. Smith, who was beginning his long service as a diplomatic and treaty expert, answered it. A voice crackled and Smith turned hurriedly to the Chief Clerk to say he believed the White House was attempting to tell them that President Garfield had been shot. The Chief

Clerk excitedly took the receiver and confirmed the tragic fact.

A number of years passed, but by 1895 there were still only two telephones in the Department; one in the outer office of the Secretary of State and the second in the corridor outside for the use of all other officials and employes. Thereafter, however, progress was more rapid, and today, in addition to an interoffice dictaphone system, there are over 500 telephones in the Department of State building. They are employed to communicate with far places, even on the other side of the world. So much for progress, slow as it was at first, in the space of the adult life of one man, for Sydney Y. Smith is still in active service.

Oddly enough, suggestions went to the opposite extreme when the radio had developed commercial efficiency and overseas telephone conversations were an immediate prospect. Some of the serious questions this produced in Congress seem amusing now. Secretary Hughes, for example, in 1924 was required to refute suggestions by members of the Committee on Foreign Affairs of the House of Representatives that diplomatic missions abroad were no longer necessary. He had to remind them that mechanical perfection was no substitute for the human element.

"We cannot rely on paper; we cannot rely on direct messages," he said. "We need the man in the personal contact with other men transacting the business of their government."

Secretary Hughes gave that advice seven years before the trans-Atlantic telephone was used by the Department to an appreciable extent, when Secretary Stimson in 1931 turned to it for conversations with London and Paris in pressing his Manchurian diplomacy. Yet ideas are sometimes stubborn and several years later, in 1938, Secretary Hull felt called

upon in discussing the influence of communications on diplomacy to utter a reminder similar to the one given nearly fifteen years earlier by Secretary Hughes. It was far from an accurate statement, he declared, to say that the perfection and rapidity of communications has reduced the role of the Foreign Service to one of merely carrying out instructions.

Anyone who has glimpsed the inner workings of the machine appreciates the soundness of that observation.

The evolution of rapid communications, however, has worked marvelous changes. Most of them represent an extraordinary improvement over former methods, but there are handicaps arising out of the very volume of information to be sifted and weighed from which the older system did not suffer. Obviously, the wireless telegraph and telephone, the airplane carrying fast diplomatic mail and envoys on emergency duties, and the radio have facilitated the meeting of crises. Prompt information and quick decisions are possible as never before to isolate and treat a danger spot, and to mobilize world public opinion.

A weakness in this situation is that it presents a temptation to act hastily. It requires a cool-headed Secretary of State who will resolve to think things over, to sleep on a subject, and not act until second thought has had time to exert a seasoning influence. It is sometimes remarked in the Department of State in this connection that, if Thomas Jefferson had had modern communications at his command, he probably would have decided against the purchase of Louisiana from France, one of the most forward steps ever taken by an administration. His first disposition was to reject the French offer to sell, and if he had had electrical communications and felt required to make a fairly prompt decision, in all likelihood he would have decided against the purchase. As it was, he had time to consider thoroughly

before replying, and after long thought decided to proceed with the purchase.

The same assets and liabilities exist with reference to communications in the domestic as in the foreign field. The Department of State can readily obtain information concerning the state of public opinion from the newspapers and the radio, but the picture is often confusing because of its volume and diversity. In consequence, officials are often left in a state of wondering doubt. Naturally, it places a premium upon the powers of discernment and political sagacity of the Secretary of State.

The influence of modern communications is felt in other ways. If they are of service to the Department of State for conveying its views to the American people and to foreign governments, they are equally at the service of individuals and organizations seeking to affect foreign policy. In this respect the radio is of supreme importance. Nor is its use confined to Americans. When a foreign official, a member of a cabinet or of a parliament in Europe, takes to the air to expound his views for the enlightenment of the American public, he is exercising an influence which can react significantly on the conduct of foreign affairs in Washington. He is addressing an appeal to the sentiments and intelligence of a public whose attitude must always be of first concern to the Department of State.

When this occurs the public is not only a witness but a participant in the conduct of foreign affairs at grass roots, for an appeal is being made to influence the opinion of Americans and through them the policies of their government. It is international politics in the open and at bedrock.

If the appeal is in line with the position of the Department of State, well and good. If out of line, no censorship is imposed because of the tradition of free speech in this

country. Therefore, if the circumstances are of sufficient importance, countermeasures are adopted to offset the effects of the appeal through radio addresses or statements to the press, or inspired utterances of administration supporters on the floor of Congress.

The commercial radio, however, is a distinct advantage to the Department of State as a channel of information when it broadcasts a speech of the head of a foreign government announcing his position in a matter of grave concern to the United States. Work stops in the Department when that happens. Officials gather around radio sets in various offices, while the Secretary of State, surrounded by assistant secretaries of state and other aides whom he has invited to his office, is among the most attentive listeners. If the address is in a language he does not understand, an interpreter, readily found in the Department for almost any tongue, gives a running English translation.

This was the setting when Chancellor Adolf Hitler delivered his momentous speech during the Central European crisis of September, 1938. A few days later when Prime Minister Neville Chamberlain spoke, the Cabinet was in session in the White House and paused in its deliberations to listen with President Roosevelt and Secretary Hull. The direct impressions received were far more valuable than the resumé the American Ambassadors in Berlin and London otherwise would have been called upon to give by telephone for the information of their government.

Yet the trans-Atlantic telephone has been used much less in diplomacy than might be supposed since Secretary Stimson employed it. When he was to speak with the Embassy in London or Paris he would summon a dozen or more departmental officials and experts to his office and have them listen in with head telephone receivers. If a question arose that

[161]

he could not readily answer, he would find the information among some one of his group of specialists. During the height of the Manchurian crisis of 1931 and 1932, however, he conducted conversations this way on an average of not more than three or four times a week. Sometimes it was to the annoyance of a distinguished ambassador who, because of the difference in time between Washington and Paris, was routed out of bed in his nightshirt.

Secretary Stimson was the greatest user of the overseas telephone, but his distance record was set on an unofficial call from a Batavia newspaper editor in the Dutch East Indies who wanted to interview him on his Far Eastern policy. Secretary Stimson was so impressed with journalistic enterprise that would call him up from the opposite side of the earth that he granted the request. The transmission, it may be remarked, was excellent.

Experience has shown that, while valuable for a quick exchange of views, the telephone does not always solve problems. Sometimes it complicates matters needlessly by causing a misinterpretation of previous general instructions. There is a natural tendency to use the telephone for detailed directions when it would be wiser to stand on earlier broad orders and let the envoy use his own discretion. In another way it has fallen short of expectations as a vehicle of diplomacy in spite of the fact that stenographic reports are made of the conversations. It encourages snap decisions when it would be better for officials to take second thought and proceed with less haste. It is primarily for this reason that Secretary Hull has used the overseas telephone relatively little, except during a crisis to receive instant, factual reports from ambassadors in the principal capitals.

The White House, as in so many other directions, supplements the Department of State in receiving direct messages from ambassadors. During a crisis the President's telephone

will ring and an ambassador in London, Paris, or some other capital will give him the latest information. However, unlike the telephone calls to the Secretary of State, these are on a personal rather than an official basis. The average ambassador does not approach the President this way, nor would a Foreign Service officer think of it. Only ambassadors who are on close terms of personal friendship with the President call him on the telephone, and to emphasize the personal character of their conversations no record is kept. No stenographer is on an extension line, as in the case of the Secretary of State.

During a crisis there may be as many as three of these conversations a day, but ordinarily there is not more than one a month. The President relies primarily upon the Department of State for his information on foreign affairs. Ninety-five percent of his information comes through the Department, which is his vehicle for the handling of foreign affairs. He is careful, as a rule, not to confuse matters by crossing wires.

After all, the telegraph has been found to provide sufficient speed for most situations, and has the advantage of the protection of secret diplomatic code. The Department of State tested it thoroughly to determine its value and found that to Geneva, for example, it was nearly as swift as the telephone, due, perhaps, to the priority the Department could obtain. Once it required just one minute to get through to Geneva. Contacts are established speedily with most European capitals. However, where land telephones are available on the American continent they are used to transact a great deal of business with the Legation in Ottawa, and the Embassies in Mexico City and Havana.

With Asia the situation is different. Telephone service to that continent is still awaiting further development before it will be on a basis satisfactory to the Department. More-

over, land communications to interior points in Asia are slow and troublesome. Consequently, the Department of State utilizes not only commercial communication facilities but the United States naval radio to a considerable extent in the Far East. Ships of the Asiatic fleet are available for this service, while the focal point is the powerful naval radio station at Cavite. Ordinarily it requires from six to twenty-four hours for messages to come through from distant Far Eastern points to the Department, although by demanding priority in important cases it can obtain more rapid service. But even then there are chances of delay, if not in actual transmission, in checking uncertain or garbled messages.

In order to preserve diplomatic secrecy, telegraph messages are sent in code that is frequently changed to guard against leaks. This is one of the reasons the telephone is not used more often, for secrecy there is not always possible. Even though the voice is scrambled in its flight through the ether, the scrambling does not take place on the land lines leading to the wireless station. Foreign Service officers are keenly aware that the land lines in Europe are not inviolate. They guard themselves accordingly, and do not engage in too important conversations over them.

Sometimes they find amusement at the expense of foreign listeners tapped into the lines. In telephoning from one embassy to another they will caution the speaker on the other end of the line to "go slow so they can be sure to get it," a joke, at the expense of the unseen listeners.

Because of this state of affairs communications are often slowed down greatly in the cases of messages which must be guarded with the utmost caution. Diplomatic code is not sufficient. For a certain distance it can be used with assurance, but beyond that doubts arise and precautionary measures are taken. An important diplomatic instruction in-

tended for an American ambassador in the Far East, for instance, may be sent by cable to Manila and thence to Shanghai, but from that point forwarded to its destination by boat.

In Europe the Paris Embassy is used as the focal point in this type of communication. The Embassy regularly sends out couriers with diplomatic pouches containing highly confidential messages to other European capitals. There are two services of this character. One courier goes south into Italy and thence into the Balkans as far as Istanbul. The other goes east into Germany and thence north into the Baltic states. It is all in the business day, accepted as a matter of course, and regarded as nothing unusual by officials who have become accustomed to the ways of diplomacy in this modern age.

Notwithstanding these limitations, electrical communications have transformed the conduct of foreign affairs, with far-reaching diplomatic consequences. No longer is it necessary to vest an envoy with merely broad authority—although general instructions are still essential—and to trust largely to his discretion, wisdom, and tact. No longer is there an excuse for a chief of mission to exceed his instructions, as has happened in the past to the discomfiture of his government.

Furthermore, the Department of State does not have to wait for a foreign war to be over before building its case for Americans and their interests where rights have been infringed and property damaged, or lives lost. Now the case is built as events unfold. Reports are received and active measures taken without delay through the ambassador or minister accredited to the offending government. This diplomatic chief of mission calls on the foreign minister as frequently as occasion requires, to make representations

and perfect the record for demanding indemnification, official regrets, and assurances that American rights will be respected in the future.

Then, from time to time, the case of the United States is set forth in a formal note. Months may be taken in the preparation of this document and hundreds of cable messages exchanged in checking every point of fact and policy with Foreign Service officers in the field for exact information and their views on points at issue. Often thousands of words of these exchanges will be concentrated in a single paragraph of a note that, when given to the press and published, is read rapidly and even casually by the American citizen at his breakfast table.

He may not realize that the note is intended as much for his information as for the foreign minister to whom it is addressed. After all, the foreign minister has been informed of the position of the United States right along by the American ambassador. The note from his standpoint amounts to a grouping and recapitulation of many incidents that have been called to his official attention as they have occurred, and presented with an emphasis that a formal and comprehensive communication inevitably conveys.

But for the American reader, the note is news in a very real sense. He has not known before the details of representations made by his government. Through the note published in his morning newspaper he is brought abreast of the official record and his views are influenced for or against the foreign policy being pursued by his government. As in so many other cases, this is again a matter of instructing and appealing to public opinion at home, which must be behind the government to render its diplomacy potent.

CHAPTER X

MAINTAINING CONTACT ABROAD

ALTHOUGH constant contact is now possible as never before between the Department of State and diplomatic officers abroad, modern communications have not abolished distance entirely. Discretion and judgment must still be exercised in the field, regardless of the telephone, the cable, and the telegraph. General instructions are as necessary as ever. They have been used down through the years and as great care is taken in drafting them as at any time.

There are high marks of excellence to shoot at that have been provided in the course of the long life of the Department and in the contributions of successive Secretaries of State. The standard was set early; in fact, the neatest example to be found in the files of the Department is in the first instruction ever issued. It was sent by the Continental Congress in 1775 to Arthur Lee, its secret agent in London. A member of the distinguished Virginia family of that name and a stanch friend of the colonies, Lee was practicing law and was active in English politics. Largely through personal friendship with Samuel Adams he had been appointed in 1770 London representative of the Massachusetts Bay Colony, so the Continental Congress had every confidence in him. Nevertheless it had to be circumspect in drafting his instructions. It accomplished a masterpiece in denoting the unlimited scope of his assignment and in brevity and precision of phraseology.

"It would be agreeable to Congress," the instructions read, "to know the disposition of foreign powers toward us, and we hope this object will engage your attention. We need not hint that great circumspection and impenetrable secrecy are necessary."

The purity and totality of the expression "impenetrable secrecy" command admiration at this distance of over a century and a half.

The practice of giving general instructions to envoys probably will persist as long as there are diplomats. Once an ambassador or minister has taken the oath of office he spends two or three weeks in an office assigned him in the Department of State familiarizing himself with the duties before him, obtaining information from officials and from the files of what has gone before, and learning at first hand from the Secretary of State and the President the policies of the administration. When he is thus equipped, broad orders are issued concerning his responsibilities for promoting friendly relations; safeguarding American lives, properties, and interests; and such other matters as are of special concern in the relations of the two governments. Then he leaves to take up his diplomatic residence abroad.

From time to time special instructions are sent him by telegraph for meeting situations as they arise. With this assistance and the collaboration of Foreign Service officers on his staff he carries on as the chief representative of his government. He makes his contacts and reports frequently to the Department of State. If he is to make a prepared address on a public occasion, he submits the text in advance to the Department for approval. He quickly discovers that his duties are not limited to brushing off his silk hat and going to a tea every day. If he is worth his salt he must keep in touch with diverse interests so that he may interpret the

country in every aspect to his government. He cannot confine his observations to the official life, important as that is, nor can he restrict his activities to the Foreign Office and the American colony. He must know the whole country as well as the policies of its government.

His is a delicate task of personal adjustment. He must be sympathetic enough to the country of his official residence to interpret it, but he must not become so enamored of it as to lose perspective, if his usefulness is to continue. If he is thrown off balance, he is encouraged to resign or he is ignored by his own government, depending upon which course is more convenient for the authorities in Washington. Periodic trips home help him to maintain a proper balance and to freshen his viewpoint of public opinion in his own country.

Thus safeguarded, he can be of the utmost service to the Department of State. The opportunities before him are limitless. He, of course, tries to be on cordial terms with the prime minister and the foreign minister, but his efforts do not cease at that point, for there are many other contacts to be established and maintained. This is not always easy, for in many countries where there is native reserve in the national character, connections can be established only in the course of long residence. Even then a trained intelligence and a sixth sense of perception are required to detect the difference between accurate information and false impressions or cleverly disguised propaganda. There are so many sources of information that without the assistance of his staff the task would be a physical impossibility.

Contacts are of the essence of relations, and they can be as diverse as official and human interests. What this means for an alert diplomat may be appreciated by considering the case of the Ambassador in London. Naturally he endeavors

to maintain close relations with the Prime Minister and the Foreign Minister. He also consults the President of the Board of Trade and officials of the Home Office. He knows the parliamentary leaders and members of the Cabinet. His acquaintance in the Foreign Office is not confined to the Foreign Minister, but extends to other officials of that ministry. At the same time his Embassy staff have their friends in the Foreign Office and in other sections of official life. Yet this accounts for only a part of his responsibility to the Department of State, for it relates only to governmental activities and policies. There is much more.

The Ambassador forms friendships in financial, industrial, and professional circles in England. He comes to know and meets frequently bankers, manufacturers, exporters and importers, shipping men, lawyers, physicians, educators, in fact leaders in the cross section of the life of the entire country. Obviously, he can not do it all alone, and so directs his staff in the work of keeping in contact regularly with various phases of life.

He may send an Embassy secretary every day to the City for financial observations and reports, an attaché to various tradespeople, and another to professional circles. American consuls are under his direction, and he obtains periodic reports from them. He will learn of steel activities from the consul in Sheffield, cotton from the consul in Manchester, and of shipping activities through weekly reports from various consular and diplomatic officers. The information is consolidated and forwarded to the Department of State.

It requires a broad background and an expert staff to evaluate the information obtained from so wide a front. Unless the observing officials know something of industrial life they cannot appreciate the meaning of business reports and their own observations in the industrial sections of the

[170]

country. With this in mind, the Department of State regularly details Foreign Service officers upon their return to the United States for periodic visits to go to industrial regions and learn what American manufacturers and businessmen are doing. The secretary of an embassy will speak before chambers of commerce, confer with industrialists, inspect plants to keep abreast of industrial progress, ascertain the needs of American manufacturers, and increase his own information so that he will be better equipped to interpret the corresponding life in the country of his official residence.

When he returns to the embassy and resumes his reporting, his information is distributed swiftly to the American public. His reports are sent by the Department of State to the Department of Commerce to supplement the service of its commercial attachés and distributed to American businessmen in trade letters. If the matter is urgent, as in the case of an opportunity for a construction or commercial contract abroad, the word is telegraphed to the branch offices of the Department of Commerce throughout the United States and relayed from those points.

Then there is the general information supplied by an embassy. Some of its reports to the Department of State merely duplicate what is available to readers of the newspapers; some would not be popularly recognized as news, although they may help in the determination of policy. A great deal is so confidential that it is sent in code and will not be published until years later. And regularly, every day, there is sent a comprehensive summary of press comment on affairs of the moment. It makes a broad picture for the benefit of the Department, one that is constantly changing and that is always abreast of affairs.

These reports find their way into the files of the Department and to the officials and divisions directly concerned

with the subject matter. But there are also reports that do not find their way into the official files. An ambassador often will supplement his official reports by personal correspondence with the Secretary of State, an assistant secretary of state, or, if he is on close terms of personal friendship, with the President. The unofficial letters contain informal expressions of viewpoints that would not properly be for the files of the Department of State. Although these are supposed to be incidental side lights, the memoirs and biographies of ambassadors and ministers whose personal correspondence has been made available contain as interesting information and observations as are to be found in their official reports.

Joseph H. Choate, one of the ablest of all Ambassadors to Great Britain, engaged in an illuminating personal correspondence with John Hay and Theodore Roosevelt, in the course of which instructions were sometimes explained or modified. George von L. Meyer, when Ambassador in St. Petersburg during the Russo-Japanese War, wrote exceedingly informative letters to President Roosevelt. This happens in every administration and usually the letters come into the light of day through the personal files of the President, Secretary of State, or the ambassador himself.

The custom is still followed. Envoys write personally to officials with whom they feel on intimate terms and so contribute to the store of information that is constantly being amassed for use in the conduct of foreign affairs. And in these days, personal letters are supplemented by telephone conversations. Furthermore, when ambassadors and ministers return periodically to this country on leaves of absence they spend considerable time in Washington conferring with the President, the Secretary of State, and other officials of the Department of State. Offices are assigned them in the Department and they utilize the time to orient themselves

to American public opinion and governmental policy. This practice is of the greatest value, for even though they are kept under close instruction abroad, gaps inevitably appear in their information that personal contacts at home will fill.

The benefits flow in the other direction also, for they can report much more illuminatingly to officials by personal conversation than by a despatch or a letter. Often when several ambassadors have returned to Washington simultaneously the President will take advantage of their presence to summon them and the Secretary of State to his office for round-table discussions. The primary purpose is to give the President and the Secretary of State a better and closer understanding of world conditions upon which at any time they may be called to make important decisions.

In exceptional circumstances ambassadors will be summoned to Washington for a report. President Franklin D. Roosevelt resorted to this expedient in the closing months of 1938 and early in 1939. Not only did he request Hugh R. Wilson, Ambassador to Germany, to return for an indefinite stay in the Department of State as a sign of displeasure over Germany's internal and external policies; but he also had Nelson T. Johnson, Ambassador to China, return for a special report on the war in the Far East in order that American policy could be weighed carefully in the light of the best information obtainable. Both Ambassadors Wilson and Johnson are career diplomats with many years of experience and are, therefore, the type to furnish seasoned judgment, and counsel that would discourage insufficiently considered action.

Some have exercised special influence through personal discussions, notably William C. Bullitt in the administration of the second Roosevelt, who when Ambassador, first to Russia and then to France, made a number of trips to

Washington and held long conferences with the President. His presence at the White House or with the President at Warm Springs, Georgia, came to be regarded in diplomatic circles as a prelude to possible administrative changes in the Department of State, shifts of ambassadors and ministers in the field to other posts, or a sharpening of diplomatic policy toward Central Europe or the Far East at times when aggressive actions of dictator states were causing grave apprehension.

The ambassador appointed from political life often has the advantage of being close personally to the President and the Secretary of State; the diplomat selected from the career ranks may not have this personal entrée, but his expert and trained judgment has a solid value in the direction of foreign policy.

It is scarcely necessary to recall that these frequent contacts were not possible before the modern age of electrical communications and rapid travel. Formerly a diplomat when he went abroad was given general instructions, to be sure, but once out of the country he could not be reached readily. His government had to trust largely to his abilities and judgment. In this respect Charles F. Adams was a particularly fortunate selection for the London Legation during the Civil War. He had many other attributes to recommend him, a clear head, courage, and decision, but one of his greatest faculties was an ability to interpret skillfully the instructions of Secretary Seward.

Some choices have not been so fortunate. There was Nicholas P. Trist, who was vested with considerable discretionary power to negotiate the treaty with Mexico at the close of the War of 1846–1847. He engaged in violent controversy with General Winfield Scott, exceeded his instructions, and returned to Washington discredited, although his

treaty was accepted with slight change. At other times the Department of State has been embarrassed by the zeal of an envoy who never would have been permitted to precipitate a crisis, if close communication had been possible. It was thus, for example, that soon after the experience with Trist the Department faced another embarrassing situation. It grew out of the efforts of E. G. Squier, as diplomatic agent to the Central American states, to negotiate rights for a Nicaraguan canal.

Great Britain controlled the Atlantic seaboard of Central America and Tigre Island on the Pacific side. Squier in 1849 signed a treaty with Honduras for the cession of Tigre Island for eight months and part of the shore of the Gulf of Fonseca for a naval station, but almost immediately a British squadron appeared in defense of Tigre Island. Squier gave the squadron six days to leave and it yielded possession of the island, which remained under United States authority until the Clayton-Bulwer Treaty restored it to Honduras. The Department of State was exceedingly embarrassed for it did not want war, but under the circumstances had to support Squier.

Such an experience now would be inconceivable. Before the situation became acute the envoy would be recalled. The problem now is not how to get in touch with an ambassador but how to instruct him intelligently and at the same time guard against confusion by sending so many detailed orders as to render uncertain the meaning of his original general instructions. Many diplomats, while welcoming detailed instructions, are convinced that efficiency is promoted by still leaving them with a considerable measure of discretion.

Naturally many methods are open to an envoy for keeping in contact with the government to which he is accredited. There is the formal conversation with the foreign minister

[175]

when carefully circumscribed discussions are conducted, reinforced by memorandums of each other's position. Human nature being what it is, the formal meeting may have many gradations, depending upon the subject matter and the training, temperament, and personal friendship of the principals. Sometimes they are stiff; at other times free and easy when the envoy may even be addressed by his nickname—if he has one. Experience knows no fixed rule but ordinarily the conversations are frank, whatever form they take.

A few years ago when a military officer was appointed foreign minister in a certain country and the American ambassador made his first call upon him, the foreign minister, more used to the ways of military than diplomatic life, said bluntly that, lacking as he did experience in diplomacy and being unused to the intricacies of that profession, he intended always to speak frankly. The ambassador, a true diplomat, replied in the same spirit, saying that with many years of experience in diplomacy he had "become steadily more convinced of the stupidity of indirection" and the foreign minister could "always count on complete frankness" from him. At least this has the advantage of saving time usually consumed in diplomatic conversations of the traditional type when the question at issue is approached gradually through references to incidental matters and then, when reached, is clothed in fine words that of themselves could give no offense. Neither side is deceived. Each knows exactly what the other means.

Indirection is also often absent from informal discussions. A minister and a chief of division in a foreign office may be discussing the framework of a commercial treaty, involving a multiplicity of preliminary details and requiring months for consideration, with sharp trading proceeding on each side.

Yet the two officials may be good friends and their hardness will not extend beyond professional limits. As they negotiate and bicker and fight for advantage, they smoke their pipes, address each other by their Christian names, and indulge in language not associated in the public mind with diplomacy.

The minister or ambassador abroad, of course, keeps in frequent touch with the foreign minister and may be on sufficiently good terms to be able to call the prime minister on the telephone. But this is not always sufficient, for a foreign minister and a prime minister for reasons of policy may not feel free to inform him completely. It is here that relations with other embassies and legations are of particular importance. Official and personal contacts have been established as a matter of course, there is social life when diplomats of many governments meet, indulge in golf games, week-end parties, dining out, and other social diversions that offer opportunities for quiet professional talks when views and information are freely exchanged. What one hasn't heard perhaps someone else has.

If there is an international conference to which the United States is not a party but in which it is interested, various delegates may tell part of the story and together the combined testimony will present the true picture. On the other hand, the task of acquiring information is simplified when the foreign government feels in especially close relations with the United States and out of a broad policy of cementing those relations voluntarily informs the American ambassador of steps that are being taken in an emergency not directly involving the United States. The ambassador is received regularly by the foreign minister and told of the situation in detail for the confidential information of his government. The Foreign Secretary in London and the Foreign Minister in Paris may summon the American

ambassadors at frequent intervals and disclose moves being made on the European chessboard. At other times, the ambassadors may request appointments for the purpose of obtaining information, and promptly be accorded interviews.

It also is not unusual for a foreign minister to inform the American ambassador well in advance of policies adopted by his government in areas that hold concern for the United States. This has been the case even in the Far East where the information has been given in confidence as much as a month in advance of its announcement to the nation and the press.

If an emergency arises threatening American rights, the ambassador will make inquiries and submit such representations as are required at the outset for protective purposes and then with his staff will turn to the task of ascertaining exactly all the facts. He will report promptly to the Department of State that he has taken up the matter at the foreign office and is investigating. He knows that correspondents of American newspapers are filing despatches and that the Department of State will see them. For the present he himself could do no more. The Secretary of State is looking to him for a complete and accurate report but is expecting him to take sufficient time to ascertain the details beyond question.

Several days may elapse before the investigation is completed. Then the ambassador will send an extensive report, giving facts, figures, and dates, and on that his government will base its case in any action it may decide to take. But whatever it finally does, the Secretary of State expects the report to be as complete as possible and proof against any charge of inaccuracy.

Apart from the collection of information, the envoys and their staffs in the capitals of the world are a medium through whom formal communications are exchanged with foreign

governments. Although the Department of State will send a note through an embassy in Washington, the communication as often goes through the American embassy in the foreign capital to the foreign office. Frequently it is written by the ambassador upon instruction of the Department but with details left to the discretion of the envoy in the light of his more intimate knowledge of the situation. Then, having delivered the note, he cables the text to the Department.

The formal note is the standard form of registering a representation or protest but there are less formal ways. An ambassador may conduct oral conversations on a subject with the foreign minister and conclude that phase of the discussions with a formal note. At other times a memorandum will be submitted, or *aide-mémoire* to confirm in writing the substance of oral conversations. There are also more indirect ways of conveying the attitude of the Department of State, as in announcements or comment of the Secretary of State at his daily press conference.

From the standpoint of general policy one of the most emphatic means of defining the position of the government is through the discussion of foreign affairs by the President in his annual message to Congress. A special message to Congress on a foreign issue will carry the greatest weight, while strong emphasis can also be given through a public address by the President or Secretary of State from a platform or over the radio.

Occasionally more dramatic methods are employed for impressing a foreign government. Some convenient means will be used in the knowledge that foreign offices and diplomats who work so much under a code will catch the true significance. The means can convey a more emphatic protest than a note no matter how strongly it might be phrased.

As we have already seen, it was for the purpose of impressing Germany with the displeasure of the United States over a long series of incidents that marred diplomatic relations and also because of attacks on Jews and Catholics in the Reich that President Franklin D. Roosevelt in 1938 summoned Ambassador Wilson to Washington. The circumstances were sensational and the object was served of expressing an emphatic protest.

Resorting to a dramatic method to register the attitude of the government is not at all unusual. There have been many instances over the years. When, for example, President Hoover ordered the Thirty-first Infantry from Manila to Shanghai during the Japanese attack on Shanghai in 1932 he intended to convey a definite meaning. On the surface it was a reinforcing of American troops in the International Settlement which was in danger of being overrun. Actually, it was a message through the Chief of Staff of the United States Army to the Chief of Staff of the Japanese Army to be careful not to trespass on American rights. This significance might not be grasped by civilians but it was clear to military minds. In issuing the order, which was undramatically tapped out by the Deputy Chief of Staff with one finger on a typewriter in the office adjoining that of the Chief of Staff (it was a Sunday afternoon and the clerks were off duty), President Hoover knew that the Japanese Chief of Staff would grasp the meaning and report it to his government.

The military is used for conveying information in many ways. Both the Army and Navy maintain attachés in embassies and legations and, if circumstances justify, can drop hints to military officers of the country in which they are stationed. They may suggest that bombing civilians and unfortified cities would create a precedent from which the

aggressor might suffer in turn in the course of time. Admirals in high command overseas can define the position of the United States in blunt statements that might be resented if they came from a diplomat but are accepted as the customary language of a seadog. More than once the Commander-in-chief of the Asiatic Fleet during the warfare in China has announced that the United States would never abandon her nationals but would go to their rescue in case of danger.

Information that the Army and Navy obtain is available to the Department of State. Sometimes the services combine this function in a single individual. A former diplomat who was a reserve officer of the Army and therefore familiar with military affairs might have been going to Europe for a vacation and might have arranged to be the guest of an old friend who was a general in the field in the Spanish Civil War. He would see all that was going on with the knowledge and consent of his old friend and upon returning would give the benefit of his observations to the proper officials, perhaps even dropping quietly into the White House for a conversation with the President. This is one of the informal ways of maintaining contact and acquiring information without which the Department of State would grope blindly in the dark.

Ways of accumulating this informal information are as wide as human activities can make them. Prominent Americans in business or professional life upon return from business or pleasure trips abroad may call at the Department of State when they are next in Washington and give the benefit of their observations and views to official friends. Former officials of foreign governments who have served in cabinets or parliaments or foreign offices and have friends in the Department of State will spend hours with one or more of

the ranking officials in the Department who are personal friends or to whom they have letters of introduction, discussing the trend of world affairs.

Then there are former officials of the United States who during their years in public office have developed friendships in foreign government circles, entered into correspondence, and continued it after leaving office. Often their correspondents have also left office, but each side is in touch with men in office. Their letters contain information and valuable viewpoints, the substance of which find their way in easy course to the Department of State.

At the opposite extreme from these informal exchanges stand the official visits of heads of state, of sovereigns, presidents, prime ministers, and foreign ministers. They attract wide public interest, often lead to rumors of important events impending, and sometimes raise false hopes that some great forward step is to be taken in international relations. Regardless of the basis or lack of basis for these expectations, the occasions are marked by full ceremonial, escorting troops, and state dinners. At times they are made for the purpose of a negotiation, or to smooth the path to an international conference on disarmament, economics, or a similar subject of world-wide interest. More often they have no other object than the important—to be sure—but general one of cementing good relations by contributing to better understanding.

It was for this broad purpose that King George VI of Great Britain accepted an invitation from President Roosevelt to be his guest in the White House in June, 1939. Other royalty had preceded him to Washington—King Albert of the Belgians soon after the World War, Queen Marie of Rumania in 1926, and five years later, in 1931, the King of Siam. All the customary ritual for the visit of a head of a state was accorded them, but there was nothing behind the

scenes other then general conversations with the President, the Secretary of State, and other officials.

Relations between the United States and Canada have been marked by an exchange of visits between President Franklin D. Roosevelt and Lord Tweedsmuir, the Governor General, while on numerous occasions prime ministers and Secretaries of State have also exchanged visits. Usually these have been for the broad purpose of contributing to mutual understanding, although on one occasion Prime Minister W. L. Mackenzie King came to Washington and was a guest at the White House for the express purpose of completing the negotiation of the reciprocal trade agreement of 1935. Again in 1938 he came to Washington to sign a second and enlarged trade agreement.

Prime Minister Ramsay MacDonald of Great Britain twice came to Washington for special purposes. Upon his first visit to President Hoover in 1929 they sat on a log at the President's Rapidan camp and discussed naval disarmament. Personal relations were established at that time between MacDonald and Secretary Stimson which were continued in visits Secretary Stimson made to Europe for observation and consultation in various capitals and at Geneva, headquarters of the League of Nations. These visits were of the greatest value in Anglo-American relations of that period. Nor did Secretary Stimson limit his consultation to MacDonald. He conferred with leaders of many European governments during his European visits and during his attendance at the London Naval Conference of 1930.

It was in the period when efforts were made to find the basis of a stabilized world order supported by a world public opinion for peace that Pierre Laval, Premier of France, made an official visit to Washington. That was in 1931, two years after MacDonald had discussed naval limitation and

INSIDE THE DEPARTMENT OF STATE

the significance of the Kellogg-Briand peace pact to outlaw war. Laval gave his attention to economic questions and good understanding between his country and the United States.

MacDonald made his second visit to the United States in the first year of the administration of Franklin D. Roosevelt and was again a White House guest. He conferred over plans for the forthcoming World Economic Conference in London, a conference doomed to failure. It was during this visit that by way of emphasizing the good relations between the two countries, the Prime Minister conducted a press conference from the President's desk in the Executive Offices of the White House.

One visit that did not appear specially important at the time took on an interesting significance more than two years later. It was unofficial. It did not call for blaring bands and escorting troops. It was the personal visit made to this country in October, 1936 by Eugenio Cardinal Pacelli, Papal Secretary of State, who in March, 1939 was elected Pope Pius XII. He was received personally by President Roosevelt at his Hyde Park estate and was the guest of the President at luncheon. There they talked freely and established a personal friendship which made for more complete understanding and sympathy between the American government and the Vatican during the remaining service of the Cardinal as Secretary of State and after his elevation to the highest office of his church.

Two years later, in 1938, Anthony Eden, who had retired as British Foreign Secretary, made an official visit to Washington in his capacity as a member of the House of Commons and was received with as much warmth as though he were still in the British Cabinet. He held conversations with President Roosevelt, Sumner Welles, Acting Secretary of State, and at a luncheon spoke before an audience that included the entire American Cabinet.

Visits of foreign ministers are fairly frequent, especially from Latin America. And Presidents and Secretaries of State have made their contributions to good relations by visits to the countries to the south. In fact, ever since President Theodore Roosevelt inspected the Panama Canal during its construction and Woodrow Wilson went to the Paris Peace Conference, Presidents have not hesitated to leave the country. Thus freed from the restraining force of one tradition, President Franklin D. Roosevelt went to the Inter-American Peace Conference at Buenos Aires and touched at several capitals and cities on the East coast of South America where he was received with highest official honors. He urged the cause of peace and mutual understanding in the Western Hemisphere.

Similarly, President Coolidge attended the opening of the Pan-American Conference in Havana, Cuba, in 1928. And, after being elected President but before entering the White House, Herbert Hoover made the circuit of South America on a battleship, stopping at important ports to spread the message of good will and common understanding.

Much earlier Secretary of State Elihu Root made the South American tour for the same purpose and was followed in that course by his successor, Philander C. Knox, and a decade still later, in 1922, by Secretary Hughes. Secretary Hull has continued this effort through his attendance at pan-American conferences in Montevideo, Buenos Aires, and Lima and his calls en route at various capitals and ports where his presence and good words contributed to better feeling.

Direct diplomatic negotiations are indispensable and have a direct purpose, but it is doubtful if the cause of good relations is served better than by these official visits. In the long run they are one of the most valuable forms of official contact open to the nations.

CHAPTER XI

MAINTAINING CONTACT AT HOME

WHEN Japan began her invasion of Manchuria in September, 1931 her Ambassador to the United States, Katsuji Debuchi, was preparing to return to Tokyo for an overdue leave of absence of several weeks. Instead, he was summoned to the Department of State where Secretary Stimson, in view of the potentialities, requested him to remain in Washington. The Ambassador had anticipated the request and so could inform the Secretary of State that he had already canceled his plans and would remain at his post indefinitely. Through the months that followed and until Japan had completed her conquest of Manchuria, he was an almost daily caller at the Department while the United States sought to mobilize world opinion for peace and to discourage Japan from her venture.

Those were days of polite but plain talking. Secretary Stimson was vigorous; Ambassador Debuchi pleasant but firm in carrying out the instructions of his Foreign Office. Notwithstanding the disagreement of the two governments, he retained the personal esteem in which he had long been held in Washington. One reason he was asked to remain was because of the confidence Secretary Stimson reposed in him. Only after the Manchurian conquest was completed and diplomacy of the Far East entered a new phase did he return to Tokyo, retiring from the diplomatic service after a long and distinguished career.

[186]

The last few months of his residence in Washington were the most important of his life because the relations of the United States toward Japan were directed through him. Not only did the Department of State prefer to move through him, but Secretary Stimson, because of his intense interest and concern, desired to direct American diplomacy himself at first hand in the Far East at that delicate juncture. Otherwise he might well have moved primarily through the American Embassy in Tokyo. For the Department of State in directing its attention to a particular area may act through its embassy abroad or the embassy in Washington of the foreign government concerned. Whichever course is followed depends upon circumstances of the moment. Both points are utilized, but the major effort is made through one or the other. In the same way, a foreign government in initiating policies may move through its Washington embassy or the American embassy in its own capital.

Because the embassies and legations in Washington often become the focal points, contacts the Department of State maintains with them are as important as those it has abroad. Its relations with foreign offices cannot be considered solely from the standpoint of the work of its diplomatic missions abroad. In fact, so many world problems constantly arise that the Washington post is to many governments their most important diplomatic mission. And with fifty-four foreign embassies and legations, Washington ranks with London as a great diplomatic capital of the world.

The life of most ambassadors and ministers is active from the moment of their arrival. All the ceremonial required by protocol is accorded the arrival of the newly designated envoy. Upon stepping from the train at Union Station, almost in the shadow of the Capitol, he is greeted by the full staff of his embassy or legation, and by officials of the

[187]

Department of State—the Chief of Protocol, a political adviser of the Secretary of State, the chief of the geographical division in the Department under which his country falls, and an aide of the President. Introductions are made, greetings exchanged, news cameras flash, and it often happens that old friendships are renewed. Then the envoy is escorted to a White House automobile which takes him to his embassy or legation. The next few days are spent in establishing his official status.

The day after his arrival he calls on the Secretary of State in order to pay his respects and request an appointment to present his letter of credence from the head of his state to the President. To facilitate this formality, he gives to the Secretary of State copies of his letter of credence and of the remarks he intends to make when he is received by the President. These are taken in hand and a draft made, in the Department's geographical division concerned, of the reply the President will make to the envoy's remarks. The draft is sent to the White House and the President makes such changes as he desires before adopting it as his own. A time is next set for the ceremony at the White House. Usually it is late in the afternoon after the President has completed his routine conferences of the day.

Shortly before the hour set, the Chief of Protocol of the Department goes to the embassy or legation in a White House automobile and, with as many more automobiles as are necessary to accomodate the envoy's staff, returns with them to the White House. The envoy and his staff are in brilliant uniform, or if none is prescribed for their service, in formal dress, as are the Chief of Protocol and the President.

Upon entering the White House they are met by junior military and naval aides of the President in full-dress uniform. Introductions are made all around, and then when

word is given that the President is ready to receive the envoy he is escorted by the aides into the oval Blue Room directly beyond the main entrance and overlooking the south grounds. The President is standing with his chief military and naval aides on either side, and the presentation is made. The President then presents his chief aides and there are introductions of the envoy's staff. After these formalities, the President invites the envoy to be seated and they converse for several minutes. Ordinarily their conversation is personal and incidental but occasionally, if grave problems exist, the President will plunge immediately into a discussion of them.

After five or more minutes of this conversation he refers to the fact that he and the envoy have some papers to exchange. The envoy, accordingly, gives the President his letter of credence and the document containing the remarks he is to deliver. The President in turn gives the envoy the text of his reply. Both sets of remarks are supposed to be read, but this ritual is omitted as unnecessary. Farewells are then said, and the envoy and his staff take their departure and return to the embassy or legation in the White House automobiles. The envoy is thus duly accredited to the government and authorized to conduct official business.

The chief of mission and the Department of State maintain constant contact. Ambassadors and ministers go to the Department frequently, if not to call on the Secretary of State or the Under Secretary, to confer with assistant secretaries of state, chiefs of division, or other officials. The nature of their business determines whom they will see. No formal appointment is necessary except in the case of the Secretary of State or the Under Secretary. For many years the Secretary of State to facilitate these contacts, set aside his forenoons every Thursday as a time for receiving

[189]

ambassadors and ministers without the formality of an appointment. This became known as "Diplomatic Day." Secretary Hull, however, after he had been in office a few years decided that this was unnecessary and discarded the arrangement. He informed the foreign envoys that they had merely to telephone for an appointment any day in the week and they would be promptly received. So what had become a firmly intrenched custom passed into the realm of outmoded things. The present method has worked very satisfactorily for the Department and the diplomats.

While ambassadors and ministers do not hesitate to seek immediate appointments with the Secretary of State, others who are not confronted with pressing problems form the habit of calling regularly once a week on the Under Secretary of State, a political adviser to the Secretary, or the chief of a division for general conversations during which they will canvass the world situation and exchange information. It keeps them up to date. Many representatives of smaller countries whose governments are chary of telegraph and cable tolls do not receive much official information themselves and so find this a convenient way of obtaining latest authoritative news of world events, since the United States does not economize in such matters and consequently, there is an abundance of information in the Department.

If the subject is sufficiently important, an ambassador and the Secretary of State at the conclusion of a conversation will agree upon a joint memorandum summarizing their discussion for the official files of the Department and the embassy. If this is not necessary, the Secretary of State immediately after the ambassador has taken his departure will call a confidential stenographer and dictate a memorandum of the conversation for the information of other officials in the Department and for the departmental files.

Secretaries of State are meticulous on this point. They never omit this service for the records. On the other hand, it is a practice never followed by the President when he receives an ambassador. Unlike a minister, who represents only his government, an ambassador is the representative of the head of his state and so may request at any time through the Department of State an appointment with the President himself. When the request is made, diplomatic courtesy requires that it shall never be refused. The ambassador is supposed to make the request only on urgent matters, or to take up some subject of immediate personal as well as official interest to the President. However, some who have obtained their appointments by impressing their governments with their close personal acquaintance with the President will ask at intervals to be received, and for no purpose other than a general conversation. The object is well known in the White House and the Department of State, but the request is invariably granted, and in good humor.

Nevertheless, whatever the circumstances, the President does not make a record of the conversation. In the first place, he relies upon the Department of State as the real source of information on foreign affairs. In the second place, he prefers to foster the greatest freedom of conversation and not discourage it by making a record, a fact well known to his diplomatic callers. It is the same principle that governs in Cabinet meetings, where no records are made, in order that the freest discussion may be encouraged.

Ambassadors and ministers, however, do not themselves conduct the greater part of their governments' business with the Department of State. They attend to the weighty questions, but much of the other work is carried on, especially in the preliminary stages, by counselors and secretaries of

their missions with chiefs of division and experts in the Department. This means that there is a meeting of trained civil servants.

If, for example, a European government is contemplating sending a communication to the United States, the Counselor may call on the chief of the European division in the Department. Often these men are acquaintances of long standing from service in other capitals at the same time, a quite normal experience for diplomats as for naval officers, to whom the world is a checkerboard. They are always encountering friends all over the world. The Counselor informs the division chief in a general way of what his government is contemplating, seeks his advice as to the best way to proceed, and, incidentally, endeavors to learn how it might be received.

The division chief listens carefully, expresses some tentative views, but asks for a little time in which to consider various aspects of it. At the first opportunity he discusses it with his superiors, obtains their reactions, and, if he considers it important enough, may take it up informally with the Under Secretary or the Secretary of State. He then has the Counselor come to the Department and imparts to him as much as he considers advisable at this stage. Later, having received a report from the embassy, the European government decides whether to proceed with the matter by sending a formal note. If so, the embassy is notified and the Counselor and division chief discuss the best manner and time for its presentation, whether it should be made public, and other details. This not only oils the wheels of diplomacy but it may prevent a too abrupt presentation of a matter of some importance. It is all in the day's work for the professional diplomat.

There are occasions when an ambassador or minister will present a question himself when to Americans it would

appear to be of only slight significance. They can see no reason why a foreign government should take any official notice of it. Protests by foreign diplomats against attacks made on heads of their governments by American newspapers and magazines enter this category. Such protests are embarrassing to the Department of State because of its concern for good relations and mutual understanding. But in view of the doctrine of freedom of the press the Department can do little but counsel patience. The ambassador himself may appreciate the American tradition of freedom of the press but has to make a protest because his government does not understand it. Not only the printed word but pictures prompt these representations.

About all the Department can do is to express informally to the ambassador its regret and a hope that it won't happen again. If resentment is acute, the Secretary of State may issue an official expression of regret, equivalent to an apology to the aggrieved government. It is a matter of concern because small incidents can complicate relations. They have more than once led to retaliation through vicious attacks on the President and the Secretary of State in the inspired press of the offended country. There have been times when a foreign government has kept the offending newspaper or magazine out of its country in order to avoid having its people become aroused against the United States and thus embitter relations between the two countries. More than once a Secretary of State in making an appeal for fair play in a speech has had such situations in mind, although he does not actually mention them in view of the firmly intrenched tradition of a free press in America.

However, patience can be exhausted. Thus attacks of the German press on President Franklin D. Roosevelt and his Cabinet officers became so outrageous late in 1938 that when Dr. Hans Thomsen, the German Chargé d'Affaires in Wash-

ington, sought on instructions of his government to protest an attack by Harold L. Ickes, the Secretary of the Interior, on the Nazi regime, the protest was abruptly rejected. At the same time Sumner Welles, the Acting Secretary of State, bluntly informed the Chargé d'Affaires that as long as the attacks of the German press continued, Germany could expect a continuance of criticism in the United States. His remarks on this occasion were broad enough to take in both official and press utterances. He let it be known in the most emphatic terms that the Department of State would not lift a finger in an effort to encourage a less inflammatory tone in American newspapers. The incident was unusual in diplomatic history; so were all the circumstances.

While foreign envoys work under the diplomatic code that governs their profession the world over, they readily adapt themselves to American ways. After presenting their letters of credence to the President many hold press conferences at which they speak frankly of the relations of their governments and the United States, and answer questions. Thereafter they are readily available to newspaper correspondents in person and by telephone. Their principal point of contact with the government, of course, is the Department of State; but they confer with officials in other government departments as circumstances require, although never without obtaining permission of the Department of State. They also form friendships with members of Congress and especially with members of the Committee on Foreign Relations of the Senate and the Committee on Foreign Affairs of the House of Representatives. This is all in the course of their duties in keeping informed of governmental and political affairs as they bear directly or indirectly on foreign relations.

All of them make trips throughout the country as a matter of self-education. If an ambassador is a live wire, he will form

the acquaintance of leading men in the business, social, and professional life of the country. He will know the presidents of large corporations, financiers, and leaders in the social, cultural, and educational life. Many of them speak before college and university audiences and groups representing a diversity of interests in principal cities. In these ways they come to know the country, and at the same time are enabled to interpret their own country to Americans.

The diplomatic establishments in Washington have the same status as the corresponding ones of the United States abroad. This is arranged by mutual agreement. An embassy in Washington is matched by an embassy abroad, and a legation by a legation. If the United States for any reason is over-deliberate about sending an envoy abroad, the foreign government concerned may be equally slow about accrediting a chief of mission in Washington. Parity is closely observed as a matter of diplomatic nicety.

As in the case of the United States diplomatic service, there is no fixed period that ambassadors and ministers serve in Washington. Domestic or international circumstances decide this. Some governments plan to change their envoys every three or four years, but many have remained nine or ten years. Jules J. Jusserand, the distinguished French Ambassador who began his career in Washington as a member of President Theodore Roosevelt's famous tennis Cabinet, was in charge of his Embassy for over twenty years. Ministers of smaller countries have remained for long periods, and Viscount d'Alte, Minister of Portugal, who also arrived early in the Theodore Roosevelt administration, remained for over thirty years, until his retirement for age.

As in other capitals, the foreign diplomatic corps is organized under a dean who invariably is the senior ambassador in point of service in Washington. Any questions

arising of joint concern on matters of diplomatic procedure or etiquette but apart from separate governmental policies are considered by the corps at meetings presided over by their dean.

The ambassadors of the great powers have a constant flow of business to take up with the Department of State, while relations of Latin-American governments with the United States are always important. But there are a number of smaller nations maintaining legations in Washington whose business is slight. Their contacts with the Department are infrequent, except on incidental matters that could be disposed of by telephone. They maintain their legations principally for national prestige. Nearly all of them, from the greatest to the smallest, are housed in palatial residences on Massachusetts Avenue, Sixteenth Street, and other thoroughfares in the exclusive residential sections.

Great Britain and her Dominions are represented several times over, for not only does the Empire have the great Embassy on Massachusetts Avenue but Legations are maintained by Canada and the Union of South Africa. Ireland also maintains a legation in Washington. Before many years they may be joined by a Legation of Australia. The Dominion legations conduct the foreign affairs of their own governments but maintain close liaison with the British Embassy in Washington, one of the most important posts in the diplomatic service of the Empire. Some consider it the most important, as once was pointed out to the writer by a former member of the government in London. Paris would be, in his opinion, he said, except that the Foreign Office can reach the Ambassador at that post readily by telephone. This instrument is not so convenient for extended confidential conversations with Washington, he explained, and so the Ambassador to the United States must

be entrusted to a greater extent with general instructions and less reliance placed on specific, detailed orders.

Under international law and comity the envoys enjoy diplomatic immunity, while their embassies and legations legally are sovereign soil of their countries and so inviolate against intrusion of local authorities. Immunity runs to the person of the diplomat and because of it he enjoys freedom of customs and other privileges. During the prohibition era he was protected in the serving of liquors; in fact, his supplies were brought from abroad by ship to Baltimore and thence to Washington in trucks under escort of motorcycle police. Nevertheless, the use of liquors proved embarrassing when newspapers gave publicity to the arrival of the trucks, and Sir Esme Howard, the British Ambassador, finally issued an order to his staff prohibiting importations. Repeal brought peace of mind at last to the diplomats.

While a foreign envoy may not be arrested, his immunity does not imply license. He must be meticulous, and the Department of State keeps a jealous eye on his conduct. If he flagrantly violates traffic rules, he will hear from it, quietly but emphatically; and if his wife disregards them too often, he may also hear from it. More than once the wife of a diplomatic secretary has disregarded them to the extent that it has inspired a quiet word to his foreign office and he has been transferred to another post. And diplomats themselves on occasion have conducted themselves so outrageously when stopped by traffic officers that they have found it convenient to return to their own countries.

Of course, there is an inflexible rule against a foreign diplomat abusing the hospitality of the United States by mixing in domestic politics. Such cases have been infrequent. When they have occurred ways have usually been found to get word quietly to the diplomat's foreign office so that he

could be recalled without publicity, thus avoiding a diplomatic incident. At other times an envoy has read the writing on the wall and left voluntarily. Years have sometimes elapsed before the true circumstances have been learned.

It has never been disclosed previously, for instance, that Vittorio Rolandi Ricci, the Italian Ambassador, left Washington in 1922 after a rebuke by Secretary Hughes for political activity in the United States. Published official records of the time contain no reference to the incident. The issue was precipitated when Senator James E. Watson of Indiana, an administration stalwart and close personal friend of President Harding, charged in a speech on the floor of the Senate that Sir Auckland Geddes, the British Ambassador, and Ambassador Ricci in speeches around the country had endeavored to influence American public opinion on the tariff, immigration, and other questions. It was in June, and Congress was at that time debating the Fordney-McCumber Tariff Bill, a measure which was causing concern abroad because of its high rates.

Sir Auckland made no public reply to the attack but went to the Department of State and conferred with Secretary Hughes. Nothing was divulged concerning their conversation, but evidently the Ambassador's explanation was satisfactory, for his status remained undisturbed. Ambassador Ricci, however, issued a statement which, while denying that he had discussed immigration, frankly admitted that he had expressed his views on the tariff. He defended this in emphatic, even belligerent terms, on the ground that the tariff was an international question.

Secretary Hughes promptly summoned him. He greeted the Ambassador warmly, spoke of his personal esteem but then reproved him sternly. The tariff might have international aspects, he said, but if foreign governments ob-

[198]

jected, they should confine the statement of their position to diplomatic channels. If representations were made in this way, he would receive them. But an ambassador seeking to influence American public opinion on the subject, he declared, was engaging in domestic political activity, and this would not be countenanced. Ricci, in reply, expressed his personal friendship for the Secretary of State but stood his ground and insisted that the tariff was an international question. He then said that he was leaving in two days for his summer vacation in Italy and would be away for two months. He never returned to his post. In time another Ambassador was sent in his place. This was explained in Rome and Washington as a normal change and it is still a question whether Ricci was recalled by his government or decided for himself that his usefulness in Washington was at an end. At least he was not dismissed by the United States. Only rarely has such abrupt action as dismissal been taken. The dismissal of Dr. Dumba, the Ambassador of Austria-Hungary, occurred during the World War under exceptional conditions.

An equally noted case was that of Lord Sackville-West, the British Minister, who fell into a trap during the presidential campaign of 1888. Replying to a letter from what he understood was a naturalized Englishman, he wrote that the continuance of the Cleveland administration in office would be best for British interests. Republicans published the letter on the eve of the election. It aroused a storm of controversy, stiff diplomatic correspondence with Great Britain, and dismissal of the Minister.

Nearly twenty years earlier, in 1871, Count Constantin de Catacazy, the Russian Minister, had given offense by interfering in claims negotiations, public abuse of President Grant, and in general apparently pursued a wily and

deceitful course in his official relations. Secretary Fish did not want to impair American friendship with Russia by dismissing the Minister, and tactfully secured his recall by having the facts placed before the Grand Duke Alexis upon his arrival in this country for a hunting trip in the West. The most famous case involved the plottings against the neutrality of the United States during the French Revolution by Edmond Charles Genêt, representative of France. His efforts broke down and his recall followed.

Embassies and legations cannot be used as bases for plotting against the United States, but it is within the proprieties for them to spread good cheer and friendliness through their social life. Not only is it within the proprieties but it is welcomed by the rest of official Washington. Invitations are gladly accepted to luncheons, teas, dinners, receptions, and musicales. They contribute brilliantly to official social life in the national capital during the winter season.

The diplomatic corps not only gives but receives, for its members are invited to many functions by American officials. The Secretary of State gives one diplomatic dinner for the corps during the season, and his wife is "at home" to the diplomatic corps and members of political and residential society one or more times. They also entertain at luncheons and dinners for distinguished foreign visitors. What further hospitality they extend depends on their personal inclinations and private resources. Some Secretaries of State have entertained freely and frequently; others not at all beyond the minimum requirements.

The high spot in the diplomatic life is the annual dinner given by the President and the First Lady in honor of the chiefs of mission in the state dining room of the Executive Mansion. The great horseshoe table is adorned with the gold

service, and afterward there is a musicale to which additional guests are invited.

The nearest approach to a gathering of a court society in America is the annual diplomatic reception at the White House to which are invited the chiefs of mission and their staffs, members of the Cabinet, and others of highest social rank and distinction in Washington. Although a White House function, the details are planned and supervised by protocol and ceremonial officers of the Department of State. It is the most brilliant of the state receptions given during the year. The picture is one of contrasts—foreign diplomats in their resplendent uniforms with gold braid, cockades, plumes, swords and decorations, admirals and generals in full-dress uniforms, and, marking the democratic tradition of America, diplomats of the United States in plain evening dress.

It is not a simple costume party where the first to arrive are the first to be received by the President and his wife in the Blue Room. Everything moves in a pattern that has been painstakingly prearranged by the Department of State in strict accordance with rank and seniority. The diplomats are more than individuals; they are representatives of their governments. And the knowing observer can attach significance to so simple an act as a cordial or tempered greeting, or who dances with whom. Yet, if the President in receiving an envoy says cordially, "You must come and see me," the diplomat is more often than not left in doubt. He does not know whether to accept it as a pleasantry or literally. Frequently he resolves his uncertainty as he would wish, and in a few days asks for an appointment to call on the President.

Thus these people go about their activities, with the Department of State as the mainspring of their contacts with American life.

CHAPTER XII

ONE DAY IN THE DEPARTMENT

ANYONE who considers life in the Department of State
exclusively one of gaiety, of watching with cynical
amusement aspirants for official favor, and of quiet daily
routine would have been shaken out of preconceived ideas
had he been in the Department late on the Sunday evening
of December 12, 1937, and shared the shock that officials
experienced from a brief emergency despatch sent by
Nelson T. Johnson, American Ambassador to China, conveying the alarming information that the United States
gunboat *Panay* had been sunk by Japanese airplanes on the
Yangtze river. That was all the despatch said. It did not
mention survivors, but it required no stretch of imagination
for officials to realize that a major crisis confronted the
government; that more and probably worse news would follow speedily, and that a severe test confronted the Department. Once more the placid atmosphere that surrounds the
Department when the international waters are unruffled was
swept aside.

Detailed reports telling exactly what had happened, the
scope of the disaster, the number of dead and wounded,
would surge through the ether or under the waves in a constant stream, and these, together with the skill with which
the crisis was met, would determine its underlying gravity.
No one was thinking in terms of war, but the seeds of war
might be there.

All this and much more shot through official brains when that first despatch was received. At once the machinery of the Department, and of the rest of the government that was directly concerned, the White House and the Navy, swung into operation. The fact that the crisis broke on a Sunday was incidental, not even unusual, for serious international events are no respecter of quiet weekends. And when that first official despatch was received no one could know that the crisis would be disposed of to all essential purposes in the span of a hectic twenty-four hours.

Four hours before that first alarming word was received, events on the Yangtze had summoned Maxwell M. Hamilton, chief of the Division of Far Eastern Affairs, and his assistants to the Department of State. Reports were piling up telling of fighting along the great river and they required immediate consideration. The Japanese military machine had been grinding ruthlessly for months in China and was no respecter of persons, foreign or Chinese. Disregard of American rights had prompted a series of protests from the Department of State.

Ambassador Johnson was at Hankow with the Chinese government, but several members of his staff and American nationals who had remained in Nanking had been evacuated only that day by the *Panay*, which had headed toward Hankow for greater safety. Still no major disaster was expected, even though at 5:53 P.M. Hamilton read a despatch from Ambassador Johnson that the *Panay*, after anchoring upstream, had been forced to move because of artillery fire directed at Chinese from Japanese batteries on shore.

More despatches concerning the situation on the river continued to be received as the evening wore along. They were delivered to Hamilton on the third floor by messengers from the code room on the floor above, when at 10:06 P.M.

the code room excitedly telephoned down that a despatch received from Ambassador Johnson said the *Panay* had been sunk by Japanese airplanes. There were no details.

Reaching for his outside telephone, Hamilton called Secretary Hull, who was in his apartment at the Carlton Hotel a few blocks away and read him the despatch. He next notified Hugh R. Wilson, Assistant Secretary of State and close diplomatic adviser of the Secretary, and Stanley K. Hornbeck, political adviser to the Secretary of State on the Far East. These three hurried to the Carlton to be with Secretary Hull as more details were received. They were promptly joined by Admiral William D. Leahy, Chief of Naval Operations.

During the next few hours the group of high officials, faced with grave responsibilities, read incoming despatches that were relayed from the Department of State and the Navy. Secretary Hull talked with the President by telephone from time to time, to report and consult on the situation, and Admiral Leahy kept in touch with the Navy for technical information. It was clear that they had to act promptly and decisively, but before acting they had to know in some detail what had happened. For the present their discussions could be only general.

On board the small gunboat were diplomats, army officers, newspaper correspondents, photographers, and foreign refugees. They knew this from earlier routine reports, but they did not know at first that there had been loss of life, and that the commanding officer, Lieutenant Commander J. J. Hughes, and many others had been wounded under most aggravating circumstances.

The *Panay* was a river gunboat of the Yangtze Patrol that has been maintained by the United States since 1858 on the great river of central China under treaty rights for the protection of Americans and their interests, commercial and

missionary. Inasmuch as Japan had not declared war on China, treaty rights stood unimpaired by the warfare that was proceeding. The gunboat had every right to be where it was, and Japan had repeatedly pledged herself in response to American representations to respect the rights of third parties in China.

Retreating before the Japanese advance, the Chinese government had moved from Nanking far up the river to Hankow and had been followed there by Ambassador Johnson and certain members of his staff under the protection of the gunboat *Luzon* of the Yangtze patrol. The *Panay* had remained at Nanking for the protection of a few members of the Embassy staff remaining to care for Americans in the city, and to assist in their evacuation if it should be found absolutely necessary for all to leave. Passage down the river was impossible because of obstructions placed by the Japanese, so when the *Panay* took on the Americans it could only proceed with safety up the river to Hankow. There were on board George Atcheson, Jr., and J. Hall Paxton, second secretaries of the American Embassy, Captain Frank N. Roberts, assistant military attaché, newspaper correspondents, and a few foreign noncombatants. Three vessels of the Socony Vacuum Oil Company accompanied the gunboat.

The *Panay* moved up the river with its nationality clearly marked by large flags. The weather was clear, and visibility excellent. After several miles it anchored, but, finding itself near the range of Japanese artillery that was firing from shore, it moved a few miles farther and anchored in a broad stretch of the river twenty-eight miles above Nanking. The accompanying vessels anchored near by.

This was the situation when shortly after noon, without warning, Japanese airplanes attacked, bombing and machine-gunning the ship. The attack continued without interruption

[205]

through repeated power dives of the fighting airplanes and in the face of machine gun resistance from the gunboat until the *Panay* had to be abandoned. Even then the motor boats taking the crew and passengers ashore were machine-gunned by the airplanes, and the refugees had to conceal themselves among the reeds on the bank to escape detection.

After nightfall they got to a near-by Chinese village where they were hospitably received. There they managed to telephone a message briefly and by relays from place to place to Ambassador Johnson at Hankow. The *Panay* had meanwhile sunk, and the accompanying oil vessels been beached or sunk, with loss of life. Ambassador Johnson and naval officers with him immediately sent reports to Shanghai for transmission to Washington, and American and British gunboats hurried to the scene.

During this time the Japanese, alarmed over the consequences of the attack, sent rescue vessels, and the dead, wounded, and uninjured from the *Panay* were taken on the international fleet of small ships that had rushed there, and thence to Shanghai. There a naval court of inquiry sat on the case for days, received and analyzed the testimony of the survivors, and forwarded a report to Washington that became the accepted official United States version of the attack. It was one of the most provoking and grave affronts that had confronted the United States for many years.

This was what was learned in due time, but few details were known that first night in Washington. By midnight Secretary Hull realized that he would have to wait until the next day before definite action could be taken, but enough was known for him to send a preliminary instruction to Ambassador Grew in Tokyo to make representations to the Japanese Foreign Office, impress upon Koki Hirota, the Foreign Minister, the gravity of the situation, and demand

that means be taken to guard against further attacks. At midnight Hamilton and his associates left Secretary Hull and went to the Department of State, where they despatched this message, and made an announcement for Secretary Hull through the Division of Current Information. This division of the Department had promptly thrown open its doors when the first report was received. The announcement stated that necessary measures would be taken as soon as the facts were assembled. They then retired for a few hours' sleep and returned to their posts early in the morning, prepared for what all knew would be a day of intense activity and high tension.

Secretary Hull had left instructions to be informed of any graver turn in the situation during the night and was at his office in the Department Monday morning well in advance of the customary 9:00 A.M. hour. The Division of Far Eastern Affairs was in action early, and the Division of Current Information was open, giving and receiving information from the press. Overnight cable reports from Ambassadors Johnson and Grew and naval officers of the Asiatic Fleet were read carefully, and then Secretary Hull called a staff conference in his office to consider the situation, piece together the facts, and discuss what measures to adopt.

Grouped around the great desk in his office, with the Secretary of State presiding from the center position, were the Under Secretary of State, Sumner Welles; the Counselor for the Department, R. Walton Moore; Assistant Secretary of State Wilson; the Legal Adviser, Green H. Hackworth; Dr. Hornbeck; and Hamilton. They considered all aspects of the situation in a running debate of what measures it would be advisable to take. As circumstances required they consulted the Navy Department on technical questions. There was no attempt to reach final decisions, but policy

[207]

was rapidly being crystallized and would be agreed upon before many more hours had elapsed. This conference lasted two and a half hours, when Secretary Hull was summoned to the White House by President Roosevelt, who had subordinated all other government business to concentrate upon the crisis.

In the meantime things had been happening along the diplomatic front in the Far East. Ambassador Johnson at Hankow had instructed Clarence E. Gauss, American consul general in Shanghai, to present all the information to the appropriate Japanese authorities there. This Gauss did, calling upon the Japanese consul general, who assured him that the Japanese military and naval authorities had ordered all operations to be stopped in the vicinity of the attack. In Tokyo, Ambassador Grew, as was to be expected, also reacted like a trained diplomat of long experience, for he took the initiative before Secretary Hull's preliminary instruction of the night before had reached him. He went to the Foreign Office where he made representations along the lines of what proved to be the instructions that soon afterward reached him from Washington.

Foreign Minister Hirota also moved promptly to give adequate assurances on behalf of his government. Not content with standing on the conference Ambassador Grew had sought, he did the unusual in calling on the Ambassador in his chancery before an official Japanese report of the incident had been received from China, and expressed the profound apology of his government. He said that Hirosi Saito, Japanese Ambassador in Washington, had been directed to make a similar apology to Secretary Hull in person.

The Foreign Minister went further and said that his government accepted full responsibility for what he de-

scribed at that time as the "accident." After he had received the official report from Japanese authorities in China, he changed this description and referred to it thereafter as an "incident," one, he maintained, due to a mistake when the airplanes were pursuing Chinese forces. Ambassador Saito had obtained an appointment with Secretary Hull for 1:00 P.M. to carry out the instructions, but before receiving him, the Secretary of State was called to the White House.

There President Roosevelt gave Secretary Hull a memorandum of what to say to the Japanese Ambassador at 1:00 P.M. He was to inform the Ambassador that the President was deeply shocked and requested that Emperor Hirohito be so advised. Further, he was to say that the facts were being assembled and would shortly be presented to the Japanese government, that in the meantime the Japanese government should be considering extending full expressions of regret and proffering full compensation as well as giving assurances guaranteeing that there would not be any similar attack on Americans in the future.

All this Secretary Hull communicated to Ambassador Saito at a grave conference. The appeal of the President to the Emperor was as dramatic and effective as it was unusual. More than anything else it impressed upon the Japanese the seriousness with which the attack was regarded in the United States, for the Emperor is considered by his subjects as above politics and one to whom a direct appeal would be warranted in only the most exceptional circumstances.

For his part, Ambassador Saito, speaking for his government, extended full regrets and apologies. It was "a very grave blunder," he said, and the Japanese forces in the field were attempting to give relief to the survivors of the attack.

That was the situation up to early afternoon on Monday, December 13th. In the meantime, Sir Ronald Lindsay, the

British Ambassador, and Jules Henry, Chargé d'Affaires of the French Embassy, had called at the Department of State and sought information concerning the attitude of the United States for communication to their governments. And when Congress met at noon, sharp debate broke out, deploring the incident, expressing indignation but, significantly, without any manifestation of war spirit.

This attitude, taken in conjunction with the prompt expressions from Japan, carried every assurance that an adjustment would be reached and that no armed retaliation would follow. Furthermore, in order to emphasize the attitude in Tokyo, the Japanese naval and military attachés in Washington called at the Navy and War Departments during the afternoon in uniform and with all other formality to express the regrets of their branches of the service to the appropriate officials.

The situation was rapidly crystallizing, and after Secretary Hull returned to the Department from lunch he resumed his conferences with official advisers. They had before them the results of the morning deliberations, the activities in Tokyo, the message of the President to the Emperor, and the conference between the Secretary of State and the Japanese Ambassador. It was now a question of reviewing these developments, assessing latest advices from the Far East, for messages were continuing to pour in from all sectors in that area, and of giving definite consideration to the position that the government would formally adopt.

Various additional suggestions were made by the advisory group, and then several of the officials were directed to make drafts of a note for communication to Japan. When the several drafts were completed late in the afternoon, there was another general discussion, points were strengthened, and a few additional ones made to incorporate the consensus

of ideas that had developed out of the day-long deliberations. Then the note was reduced to final form. During the evening it was encoded and placed on the cables to Ambassador Grew with instructions to present it the next day, Tuesday, December 14th.

The note declared that the American government and people were deeply shocked, that the ships of the Yangtze patrol were on the river by every right, that the *Panay* was flying the American flag conspicuously, was engaged in legitimate business, and had official and private personnel on board. The *Panay*, the note pointed out, had been moving so as to avoid danger when it was attacked. It pointed out that the Japanese government had previously promised on many occasions to respect the rights and interests of other powers during the Sino-Japanese warfare, yet there had been several cases when American rights were violated, Americans endangered, and their property destroyed. In several instances the Japanese government had admitted the facts, expressed regrets, and given assurances that precautions would be taken against a recurrence.

In the case of the *Panay*, the note asserted, there had been a "complete disregard" of American rights, American life had been taken, and American property, public and private, had been destroyed. In these circumstances, it declared that the United States requested and expected of the Japanese government a formally recorded expression of regret, complete and comprehensive indemnification, and definite and specific assurances against a repetition of such an experience.

That was the position taken. It was reached and the case to all practical purposes disposed of within twenty-four hours of the time that the first word was received of the attack. It closed an intense period of activity in the Department, and provided another instance of the way general

[211]

policy is adjusted to specific situations. The machinery for dealing with the crisis was there, and was used.

What happened later in regard to the *Panay* was routine. Not that the crisis was necessarily past. Events were to show that it was, but until time had elapsed that fact was not certain. The situation was watched vigilantly and proper measures taken as the record was completed.

The next day, Tuesday, December 14th, the Japanese Foreign Minister delivered a note to Ambassador Grew based upon what had taken place during the previous twenty-four hours and his own official advices which had by that time been received. This referred to the attack as an "incident" and blamed poor visibility for the "mistake." What was more to the point, it expressed regret, offered "sincere apologies," promised indemnification for all losses, and stated that those responsible for the "incident" would be dealt with appropriately. In addition, the note said that strict orders had been issued against a recurrence. It closed with fervent hope that relations between the two countries would not be affected by the "incident."

Still that was not a reply to the formal note of the American government. It was a statement of the case in response to the initial representations. The United States awaited the formal reply. That day, Tuesday, Secretary Hull again conferred with President Roosevelt to bring him up to date on the situation, but he had nothing new to say and stood on the position already taken.

Ten days passed, and on December 24th Foreign Minister Hirota delivered the note of reply to Ambassador Grew. This contended that the attack was a mistake and was unintentional. It stated that strict orders had been issued against a recurrence and for the exercise of greater care by Japanese forces in China in regard to American rights and interests.

The commander of the flying force that made the attack, it said, had been removed from his post, and staff members of the Japanese fleet and the commander of the flying squadron and all others responsible had been dealt with "according to law."

Ambassador Grew cabled this note to Secretary Hull who the next day, Christmas Day, instructed him to deliver a note expressing satisfaction over what had been done but refusing to accept the Japanese version of the circumstances. The note closed with the hope that what had been promised and what had been done would prove effective in preventing any further attacks or unlawful interference with Americans and their interests and property in China.

All that now remained was an adjustment of costs, and that required time. The Department of State in the following weeks obtained all information possible for submitting an indemnification demand, appraised the damage, and on March 19, 1938, instructed Ambassador Grew to present a statement to the Foreign Office covering indemnification for the deaths and personal injuries and for property losses. This statement was delivered three days later, on March 22nd. It asked payment of $1,945,670.01 for property losses, and $268,337.35 for deaths and personal injuries, a total of $2,214,007.36. It then added, as an expression of basic good feeling toward Japan, that no punitive damages were being demanded. Had a sum been included for these, the total might have reached any amount, and probably Japan would have felt it incumbent to pay.

The Japanese government did not haggle. One month later, on April 22nd, it presented to Ambassador Grew a check in full payment of the entire amount demanded.

That closed the case. It marked the end of a crisis which for twenty-four hours had given the Department of State

an exciting and anxious experience, one that called for its utmost exertion and one, except for the state of public opinion in both countries and the indefensible position in which the Japanese government found itself, that might have led to far more serious consequences. It gave to the Department a day of activity that through its years of experience it has found may confront it at any time, and does more often than it would wish.

CHAPTER XIII

OTHER LARGE SCALE OPERATIONS

T HE *Panay* incident was only one of many that have
swept aside the quiet atmosphere of routine life in the
Department of State. Even though it did not hold the germs
of war it was a real crisis while it lasted, and the Department
was a hive of activity. It is always so during an emergency.
Diplomats come and go, newspaper correspondents congre-
gate in the press room and the corridors, officials hasten
from conference to conference in the offices of the Secretary
of State and his chief assistants. Messages burn the cables
and surge through the ether, the overseas telephone comes
into use, and the President enters the situation to take direct
control with the Secretary of State at his elbow.

Day merges into night; weekends are ignored as the eyes
of the country turn to Washington. There are no holidays
for the Department at such times. During the Christmas
holiday of 1926 and the New Year's Day that followed, the
Department was called upon to throw all its energies into
the emergency of the Nicaraguan Revolution with American
bluejackets and marines landing at danger points. And in
later years Chancellor Hitler has had a way of using weekends for his thrusts for power in Central Europe. While
these have not directly involved the United States, they
have raised questions of serious concern for the peace of
Europe, which if destroyed would pose problems of the
greatest gravity for the entire world.

During the Central European crisis of September, 1938, all sense of time was lost in the Department, where days ran into each other, weekends were forgotten, and day and night became as one. Lights burned all night as offices remained open with officials on duty throughout the twenty-four hours of each day. Secretary Hull caught only such cat naps as he could at his hotel residence near the Department. Even in those periods of irregular rest he was aroused by telephone calls and messengers arriving with urgent official despatches from his office.

His mind was delicately attuned to the crisis, and he did not permit it to be encumbered with inconsequential details. When, for example, Chancellor Hitler and Prime Minister Chamberlain had their first night conference he issued orders to be informed of the result at his hotel, but he was not interested in speculative deductions. He wanted to be informed of two things only: first, the text of the *communiqué*, and, second, the length of time the two officials were in conference. Those two facts would tell him more than hundreds of words of assumptions by persons on the scene but not participating in the deliberations.

That conference happened in the midst of exciting events when the machinery of foreign affairs ground ceaselessly. The final plea for peace delivered by President Roosevelt to Chancellor Hitler was the culminating step in a complicated series of events, of despatching and receiving messages from foreign capitals and of trans-Atlantic telephone calls. The White House, as is invariably the case in an international crisis, was merged into this activity, with President Roosevelt constantly on call and in a rapid-fire series of conferences with Secretary Hull and Under Secretary Welles.

Should the United States raise her voice for peace by throwing her weight in the balance? If she did, would this

arouse in this country fears of becoming involved in European politics and cause so great a storm of protest at home as to undo any good effects of a direct move? If steps were taken, would they be of any avail? As is often the case when a close question is posed, there was not complete unanimity within the Department of State. Some felt that action was warranted; others believed that it would do no good, that the crisis was beyond the control of diplomacy from a distance of three thousand miles and would be decided on the basis of power politics by governments close to the scene. But once the decision was reached by the President to exert the influence of the United States for peace, these doubts were put aside and all joined in the supreme effort that was then made.

Secretary Hull and Under Secretary Welles were in their offices or conferring with President Roosevelt at all hours. R. Walton Moore, the elderly Counselor for the Department; Assistant Secretaries of State, George S. Messersmith and A. A. Berle, Jr.; James Clement Dunn, political adviser to the Secretary of State on European affairs; Jay Pierrepont Moffat, chief of the Division of European Affairs, and Green H. Hackworth, Legal Adviser of the Department, were constantly on duty or on call.

Secretary Hull's office was in charge of Harry A. McBride, assistant to the Secretary and a veteran career diplomat who had occupied that post under Secretary Stimson and had been retained by Secretary Hull because of his experience and abilities. The Division of Current Information, which maintains contact with the press and the radio under the direction of Michael J. McDermott, worked eighteen and twenty hours a day. In the few hours given to sleep its staff was available by telephone. The text of President Roosevelt's first appeal, to the heads of the principal states

involved in the controversy, was issued at 3:00 A.M., but the newspaper correspondents were at the Department waiting for it.

The period of greatest activity was from September 24th, a Saturday, until late the following Tuesday evening. Secretary Hull on that Saturday afternoon was in constant consultation with his chief departmental assistants and with President Roosevelt. They had before them the latest advices from American embassies and legations in London, Berlin, Prague, Paris, and Rome. The next day, Sunday, Secretary Hull was in his office from 9:00 A.M. to 1:00 P.M. but then went to his hotel subject to instant call, while despatches and reports were frequently sent him. Other officials worked at the Department throughout the day receiving and studying diplomatic messages and preparing information for the Secretary of State and the President. The Division of Current Information was open all day and far into the night.

Secretary Hull and Under Secretary Welles went to the White House at 6:00 P.M. for a two-hour conference with President Roosevelt, and at 10:00 P.M. Under Secretary Welles returned to his office in the Department of State. At midnight Secretary Hull and Under Secretary Welles again entered the White House for a conference, but at 12:25 A.M. the Under Secretary was back at his office in the Department, this time with the message appealing for peace which the President addressed to the heads of the principal states involved. The telegrams were encoded and placed on the cables, and the Division of Current Information then called scores of newspaper correspondents to inform them that an important statement would be available in an hour or more. The message was given them shortly before 3:00 A.M.

Monday was a day of trans-Atlantic telephone calls for the Secretary of State with ambassadors at the important

European posts, of listening by radio to Chancellor Hitler's speech, of receiving hundreds of cabled reports, of frequent departmental consultations, and of conferences at the White House. Secretary Hull conferred with President Roosevelt repeatedly, while that evening Assistant Secretary of State Messersmith, an expert on Central European affairs who formerly had been Minister to Austria, went to the White House for late deliberations during which he maintained contact with Secretary Hull. He retired at 3:30 A.M.

Tuesday was a day of similar intense activity. Secretary Hull conferred at length with his assistants in the morning and in the meantime kept the President informed of developments by telephone. At noon he and Under Secretary Welles went to the White House for a conference of an hour and a half with the President; and a few minutes after this was concluded, the President and the Secretary of State took their places with the Cabinet at a special meeting called to consider the crisis.

Again, from 6:00 P.M. to 8:00 P.M. the Secretary and Under Secretary conferred with the President, and then it was that President Roosevelt decided to send his final peace plea, this time to Chancellor Hitler alone. He dictated the message, and Under Secretary Welles brought it to the Department of State and placed it on the cable at 9:55 P.M. Meanwhile the newspaper correspondents, notified by McDermott that an important statement was to be issued soon after 10:00 P.M., arrived *en masse*. Stephen T. Early, secretary to the President, joined McDermott, and together they gave out the message, first explaining it and then opening the doors for the correspondents to make their exit in a football rush for telephones in the press room.

The correspondents had the floor at the end. It was the climax of a period of as intense activity as the Department had experienced for a long time. It was not unique, though,

[219]

for there have been other times when the machinery has been suddenly thrown into high gear to deal with an immediate emergency.

Consider, for example, the tense period of uncertainty when Japanese naval forces attacked Shanghai in 1932 and endangered American and other foreign lives and interests in the International Settlement. Ranking officials of the Department of State and of the War and Navy Departments spent long and anxious hours in consultation. Their final decisions were reached at a Sunday afternoon conference with President Hoover in the White House. At that time orders were formulated for sending military reinforcements to the danger zone for the added protection of Americans, lest United States warships already in the harbor and the regiment of marines permanently stationed there should prove inadequate.

The Department of State also operated under high pressure during the negotiation of the Hoover moratorium on war debts. That was in a peaceful atmosphere, but it called for lengthy deliberations in which the Treasury Department and the White House participated, the despatch of many notes to the principal capitals of Europe, and frequent telephone conversations with American official representatives in London and Paris. Notwithstanding that the proposal was aimed at relieving an acute financial situation which threatened to have far-reaching repercussions in Central Europe, it required elaborate negotiations and energetic treatment to produce a satisfactory arrangement.

Not all was over in the Central European crisis of 1938 with the tumbling rush of correspondents to the telephones, for President Roosevelt had despatched a message to Premier Mussolini urging his cooperation for peace. This was delivered promptly by William Phillips, Ambassador in Rome.

A similar appeal was made at about the same time by Prime Minister Chamberlain to the Italian Premier, who then conferred with the German Chancellor by telephone. The result was the summoning of the Four Power Conference at Munich. A peace agreement was reached on Thursday, September 29th.

Did American intervention do any good? Historians will ponder that question for years and the full truth may not be known until the archives of foreign offices and personal correspondence and memorandums have seen the light of day. History in time will render the verdict. As for the Department of State, it turned toward the future and other problems that before many months embraced the great European crises of March and April, 1939, over the partitioning of Czechoslovakia and the seizure of Albania. Then again its machinery was thrown into intensive operation, although not as dramatically as at the time of Munich, for by then it had become a question of determining policy at home in the face of a threatened European war rather than of appealing to the dictators for peace.

While a sudden emergency stirs the Department into intense activity, there are other types of problems standing outside the usual run of business that call for sustained but less dramatic effort. Around them are written some of its most interesting records. Programs have been put forward over the years to encourage world peace through cooperation with other governments and with the League of Nations. For the past six years there has been a constant endeavor to consolidate peace in the Western Hemisphere, and for nearly forty years a policy of encouraging stability in the Far East. True, the Department has not had an uninterrupted record with regard to the Orient. There have been deviations, but always the Department has returned to the main track,

as in the case of the Lansing-Ishii Agreement which was abrogated several years after its adoption in 1917.

Lansing seemingly believed in the Open Door policy as fervently as any of his predecessors, as strongly as John Hay, or Elihu Root who by an exchange of notes with Japan in 1908 had sought to assure the maintenance of the *status quo* in the Pacific and the Open Door in China. In concluding the long-disputed Agreement with Viscount Kikujiro Ishii, Lansing was satisfied that he had safeguarded the cardinal American policy in the Far East. To be sure, the Agreement admitted that Japan, because of territorial propinquity, had special interests in China; but in a protocol Japan stated that she would not take advantage of conditions to seek special rights in China which would abridge those of other friendly States.

However, for some unexplained reason Lansing at Japan's insistence agreed, presumably with the approval of Woodrow Wilson, the apostle of open covenants openly arrived at, to keep the protocol secret. It stands as the only known case of a secret clause in the records of American diplomacy. And, being unknown to the world, it strengthened Japan's hand toward China. It also threw the Agreement open to attack in the United States where, had all the facts been known, there might have been no attack. Succeeding Secretaries of State learned the facts from the confidential record and at the first favorable opportunity the blunder was remedied. The secret clause was entirely acceptable; the question was how to get it on public record and before the world.

The Washington Conference on Armament Limitation and Pacific Questions provided the occasion, and Japan was not in a position to object. The device was the Nine Power Treaty binding all the signatories, including Japan, to

observe the Open Door policy in China. When this pact was negotiated Elihu Root was designated by the Conference to draft it. Then it was that Secretary Hughes disclosed the secret protocol to Root, who, without saying anything to anyone, incorporated it verbatim in the Treaty. Japan signed. That killed the force of the Lansing-Ishii Agreement and soon thereafter it was abrogated through an exchange of notes.

Yet it was sixteen years later, in 1938, before the facts were revealed to the world in the routine publication by the Department of State of diplomatic correspondence of the Washington Conference. There had never been a departure in literal text by the Department from Far Eastern policy, but in all the circumstances there had been an important deviation for five years in the eyes of the world. A former Secretary of State who had been out of that office more than a decade accomplished the feat of remedying the situation easily and readily. All that was necessary was the information out of the confidential files and the occasion for using it.

What part the Division of Far Eastern Affairs of the Department played in the negotiation of the Agreement and its abrogation has not been told. The Division has furnished guidance in countless cases since its establishment more than thirty years ago, and without its steadying hand Secretaries of State might have gone astray more often. The hand of this Division was felt in the steady pressure applied by the Department on Japan, from the time of the Paris Peace Conference to the Washington Conference, to withdraw from Shantung. Finally Japan agreed to this through an understanding reached with China at the conference of 1921–1922. The Division was a tower of strength to Secretary Stimson during the Manchurian crisis of 1931 and 1932, and it has played a similar part for Secretary Hull

during the Sino-Japanese warfare that began in 1937. More than any other single factor it has assured continuity of policy in the Far East, in the administrations of successive Secretaries of State. There have been changes of tempo, a shifting of emphasis in the approach, but the general pattern remains.

The position taken by Secretary Stimson recognized that when Japan invaded Manchuria in 1931 she not only upset the Nine Power Treaty and naval and other treaties concluded at the Washington Conference but the Kellogg-Briand Pact outlawing war as an instrument of national policy. Although confronted by a crisis of such far-reaching implications, Secretary Stimson grasped its significance and moved promptly to meet it. His efforts were directed in the first instance toward having Japan moderate her course. They expanded as events unfolded to take in the world in the sweep of his operations.

There were almost daily conferences with Ambassador Debuchi of Japan; discussions with the Ambassadors of Great Britain, France, and other powers having interests in the Pacific and in Asia; conversations with the Chinese Minister; representations to the Foreign Office in Tokyo through the American Ambassador to Japan; communications with the League of Nations in Geneva; and visits there and to European capitals by the Secretary of State as he sought to mobilize the diplomacy of the world for peace and stability and the observance of plighted words. He stood on historic American policy and also had in mind the interests of the United States for far into the future.

When Japan completed her conquest of Manchuria in 1932, the Secretary of State reserved American rights under the Nine Power Treaty in identic notes to Japan and China which from the standpoint of the Open Door policy

were based on one Secretary Bryan had sent protesting the Twenty-one Demands of Japan on China in 1915. Bryan declared that the United States would never recognize Chinese acceptance of the Demands, but Secretary Stimson went further, for, unlike Bryan, he had the Kellogg-Briand Pact before him.

Accordingly, he not only refused to recognize the Manchurian conquest but brought the treaty renouncing war into the picture by seeking to have all other nations adopt the nonrecognition doctrine in view of the obligation they had accepted for peace when they signed or adhered to the Pact of Paris. It was the first world-wide effort to implement the Kellogg-Briand Treaty by putting teeth in it. Secretary Stimson even proffered American cooperation with the League of Nations for peace, but he fell short of success when Great Britain held back from a too definite projection into the Far Eastern maelstrom.

Secretary Stimson had no power to do more, not only because of the reticence of Great Britain but because of apprehensions his vigorous tactics had aroused in the United States. But as months passed and the administration of Franklin D. Roosevelt was beginning his hope was that the Far Eastern policy he had pursued would be continued. It was, although not as aggressively at first. Nevertheless, when the Manchurian conquest was followed by warfare in China proper the tone of the Roosevelt administration became more and more stern in asserting treaty rights and respect for international law and order.

At the end of 1938 after Japan had announced a "new order" for East Asia that disregarded treaty commitments, the United States in a note delivered by Joseph C. Grew, Ambassador to Japan, reserved American rights in that area under the Open Door policy and treaties and agree-

ments, even as Secretary Stimson had done in Manchuria nearly seven years before.

Except in emphasis there was little if any change between the two administrations, one Republican, the other Democratic. In terms of administrations it is a consistently sustained record; in terms of Department of State policy it comprises many chapters. More will be written and the outcome may not be decided for years.

In all this time the Far East did not occupy the exclusive attention of the Department. It gave close study simultaneously to European affairs. Efforts were constantly made to assure peace and stability. Secretary Kellogg's conspicuous contribution was not the only one. There were other efforts, marked at times by official visits of Prime Minister MacDonald of Great Britain to Washington when he discussed naval limitation and peace problems, and visits of Secretary Stimson for the same broad purposes to Europe. There was continuous perseverance over a period of nearly fifteen years, from 1921 to 1935, through both Republican and Democratic administrations for the reduction and limitation of armaments. In that task the Department of State was the negotiating agency, while its experts collaborated in the details with officials and experts of the Navy and War Departments.

The first attempt was a conspicuous success, except to those who did not want to see ships scrapped under any circumstances, for the Washington Conference of 1921–1922 not only reduced and limited naval armaments but by so doing cleared the political clouds of the Pacific for a decade. The Washington Conference, however, did not go as far as had been hoped. It did not deal conclusively with cruisers and other auxiliary ships, although it dealt decisively with capital ships, and it established the 5-5-3 ratio.

That expression, denoting the relative strength of the three major naval powers, was an inspiration that flowed from Theodore Roosevelt, although he had been in his grave nearly three years. It came about this way. Secretary Hughes at the opening session of the Conference made a detailed proposal for scrapping ships. He named them, announced what this would mean eventually in total tonnages but did not define it in terms of a ratio. Kirke L. Simpson of the Associated Press, a specialist on naval matters, noted this omission and desired to set forth in his despatches the ratio concisely and picturesquely, so that it would focus in the public mind. The total tonnages that the three major naval powers would have under the proposal would be 500,000 each for Great Britain and the United States and 300,000 for Japan. This meant 60 percent for Japan as against 100 percent for each of the other powers. In considering the formula, Simpson recalled how Colonel Roosevelt used to say to him that he always endeavored to phrase a policy in a way that would capture the imagination of the people. With this as his guide, Simpson reduced the formula to its simplest mathematical form by a process of division, and decided that the best way to describe the plan would be by calling it the 5-5-3 ratio. This pithy expression of the essence of a complex subject caught the popular fancy, stuck, and was adopted by the Conference itself.

The Washington Conference did not go so far as had been hoped, for it was unable to reach a comprehensive agreement on cruisers and other auxiliaries. That problem was one to which the Department of State and the Navy Department gave increasing thought. Their officials and experts lived with the subject month in and month out and after a few years, in 1927, the United States took the leadership and called the Tripartite Naval Conference at Geneva to deal

with auxiliaries. Participating were the United States, Great Britain, and Japan, but the admirals of the United States and Great Britain ran into headlong collision over cruisers, and the conference failed. It was the first sign of the coming deterioration of the system of naval limitation.

Efforts, however, were not abandoned. For years attention had been given to the possibility of reducing land armies and finally, during the Hoover administration, that was taken up at a general conference in Geneva under the auspices of the League of Nations. It got nowhere. In the meantime naval limitation of capital ships had been continued by the treaties of the London Naval Conference of 1930, and there at last cruisers and other auxiliaries were really limited. Events in the Far East, nevertheless, led in a few years to Japan's denunciation of the Washington Treaty of 1922, and to her refusal to enter the London Naval Conference of 1935. That conference devised a continuance of the system of naval limitation, but only a hollow shell remained.

For fifteen years the subject had been uppermost, had occupied much of the attention of the Department of State, and had served a worth-while purpose by checking naval rivalries, holding down excessive expenditures in a world straining under a load of World War debts and weary of war, but finally weakened as the World War receded into the background, new national rivalries arose, and the totalitarian states in Europe and the Far East began their lunge for a place in the sun by the use of power politics.

Through these years there were other questions that occupied the Department of State at international conferences. There was the World Economic Conference at London in 1933, in response to a movement begun during the Hoover administration and continued in the administration of Franklin D. Roosevelt before it decided to torpedo the

effort because of domestic financial policies. There were also from time to time international conferences in the Western Hemisphere. These focused the attention of Latin-American experts of the Department whose thoughts were directed to Europe and the Far East only as activities in those areas might impinge upon the western world.

Ever since pan-Americanism took organized form there have been periodic conferences of the twenty-one American republics. They are now held at five-year intervals, while special ones may be called as occasion warrants. At these conferences mutual problems of the republics are taken up and agreements reached on political, economic, social, and cultural lines. It represents a steady movement for dealing with problems of the Americas and calls for constant attention in the Department of State. Almost never dramatic, this work represents one of the progressive and solid activities of the Department.

International conferences are not the only places where treaties are concluded. Many are negotiated in the Department of State or by ambassadors and ministers abroad acting under instructions of the Department. They cover a wide range of topics—commerce, extradition, and other technical questions. The Kellogg-Briand Pact was negotiated by Secretary Kellogg after months of effort. The importance attributed to it was signalized by his going to Paris and signing it in person at an impressive ceremony in which he joined with Aristide Briand, the French Foreign Minister, in notifying the world that what they considered a milestone for peace had been reached. Later, after ratifications had been exchanged, President Hoover formally proclaimed the Pact to the world at a brilliant ceremony in the East Room of the White House with former President Coolidge and former Secretary Kellogg in attendance.

This treaty was concluded only after long and arduous effort. Scores of diplomatic conversations were held, notes exchanged, understandings reached, interpretations given, until finally the governments of the world felt warranted in proceeding with the project and affixing their signatures.

Reciprocal trade agreements are not treaties. They fall within the category of executive agreements under authority granted the President by Congress, but the manner of negotiating is the same as with a treaty. They are treaties in all but technical form. Because of the hundreds of details months of exchanges and negotiations are required. The subject is first taken up in preliminary conversations designed to explore the ground and ascertain whether an agreement is possible. Once this has been determined in the affirmative formal negotiations are arranged. Hearings are held for domestic interests to present their cases, and when these have been concluded the active international negotiations begin. Because of the technical nature of the problem, commissions of experts usually represent each side. Weeks of difficult discussion and of hard horse trading ensue, trade policies are canvassed, tariff rates studied item by item, proposals and counterproposals made, and numerous notes exchanged, until the last *t* has been crossed and the last *i* dotted. When officials of both governments are satisfied that the agreement is in acceptable and correct form it is initialed and a date set for signing. Sometimes this is a perfunctory ceremony. If unusual importance is attached to the agreement an elaborate setting is prepared.

On the day and hour set officials gather in the Department of State—the Secretary of State and his chief assistants in the negotiation, and the foreign ambassador and his principal aides. Papers are spread before them, other officials attend as guests, and the document is duly signed and sealed. Later

by formal executive proclamation it is brought into operation.

Of all the reciprocal trade agreements the most important is the one between the United States and Great Britain, together with its collateral Canadian-American agreement. When it was signed in 1938 special measures were taken to emphasize its importance to the world. As in the case of the proclamation of the Kellogg-Briand Pact, the East Room of the White House was selected, and to give greater significance, the walnut cabinet table used by President Lincoln was brought from a Washington museum and used in the ceremony. President Roosevelt was present as Secretary Hull and Sir Ronald Lindsay, the British Ambassador, affixed their signatures. Prime Minister Mackenzie King, who came from Ottawa, signed for Canada, and then addresses of felicitation were delivered.

Important as are the economic phases of the Anglo-American Agreement, a greater significance is attached to its political implications, signifying as it does an intention of the two great English-speaking nations to work in close collaboration and understanding. It was in this realization that the ceremony of signing was so highly dramatized. It represented the latest achievement in the effort of these two nations to cultivate good relations—an effort that constitutes one of the longest and most sustained of the Department of State in any field. It has extended over a long period, one that has been marked by misunderstandings from time to time but never broken by war since their great conflict of a century and a quarter ago.

CHAPTER XIV

RELATIONS WITH CONGRESS

ALTHOUGH good understanding with Great Britain has long occupied the attention of the Department of State, efforts to improve Anglo-American relations were marred for many years by Congress, which could not resist the temptation to engage in the traditional American sport of twisting the British Lion's tail. That tendency subsided when the United States entered the World War on the side of Great Britain. It never since has been resumed in its original vigor, and apprehension aroused in the democracies over power politics of totalitarian states is now making a sympathetic basis for Anglo-American relations. The prospect is clouded only by misunderstanding over war debts.

If in the course of the years of sniping at Great Britain, Congress indulged in shirt-sleeve diplomacy, it at least can be said that there have been others more sensitive to the refinements and niceties of diplomacy who have used similar tactics. When Richard Olney made his famous pronouncement of the supremacy of the United States in the Western Hemisphere he was engaging deliberately in shirt-sleeve diplomacy; and when Woodrow Wilson at a critical point in the Versailles Peace Conference ordered the *George Washington* to stand by to take him back to America, he was using the same forceful type of persuasion. Both won, as shirt-sleeve diplomacy has many times. Not that it is a type to be preferred, but even officials in the Department of State in

moments of frankness concede that there are times when its use is warranted. On occasion the classic procedure of sitting around the green baize table should be discarded.

Congress at times resorts to shirt-sleeve diplomacy; at other times, because of its preoccupation with domestic matters, it displays a deplorable ignorance of foreign questions, takes a petty attitude, or is filled with unwarranted fears and apprehensions. Yet, with all its faults, Congress stands close to the people. In the end it usually reflects their views; certainly its opposition is futile unless it has the support of the country. Even its resistance is beneficial, for it subjects policy evolved in the Department of State to the acid test. It is a stabilizer, and it can operate as a check on an overhasty Secretary of State or a reckless President. With all its shortcomings, it is a decided and even decisive force in the field of foreign affairs.

While the President has sweeping and elastic powers for conducting foreign affairs through the Department of State, he does not have exclusive jurisdiction. There is a divided responsibility—between the executive and the legislative. Small wonder that the Department of State considers that the importance of its relations with Congress cannot be overemphasized.

The past abounds in instances of the influence of the legislative branch in this field. And that influence, for several reasons is greater now than ever. For one thing, foreign relations are infinitely more complex than they were a century ago. As the country has grown, its interests abroad have widened; at the same time modern communications bring all problems as they arise swiftly to the Department of State. In consequence there has arisen a need for immediate action, which in turn requires advance preparation. Yet much of the preparation requires legislation, because so

many of the lines along which the Department must proceed have a legal base and authority must be obtained from Congress.

Thus it was that Congress was encouraged by the Department to pass neutrality legislation in 1935. It responded, but refused to give the executive branch all the powers that it desired. When finally, nearly four years later, President Roosevelt in his annual message to Congress in 1939 recommended sharp modification or repeal of the legislation because experience had shown it to be unworkable, that suggestion attracted more attention in Europe than any other part of his message. It was a convincing demonstration of the great effect the neutrality policy had had for four years on the foreign relations of the United States.

When the question arose of funding the war debts, Congress insisted upon retaining control of its financial powers and would not permit the Department of State to be the sole judge. Again, when in view of a long series of defaults Congress passed the Johnson Act shutting the doors of America to loans by defaulting governments, another element was injected into the relations of the United States with nearly all of Europe; and the Department of State was powerless to do anything effective about it. It could and did make recommendations for adjustments, but Congress ignored them.

The relations of the Department of State with Congress, however, are not confined to legislation or to the treaty powers of the Senate as defined in the Constitution. The Senate confirms diplomatic appointments. Congress as a whole passes appropriations for maintaining the Department and its agencies abroad. If a legation is to be raised to the status of an embassy, Congress must accomplish it by legislation. The President and the Department of State may go

far toward bringing the country to the verge of war, but the power to declare war is vested in Congress.

There is a wide field in which legislative action is required; and there is more, as was evidenced by the controversy early in 1939 over foreign policy implications of the arrangement for France to purchase military airplanes in the United States. If that deal involved any informal understanding, express or implied, tantamount to an alliance, the repercussions in Congress demolished it. Whatever the circumstances, once more it was demonstrated that Congress by vigorous criticism may emasculate or undermine completely a policy announced by the White House or the Department of State, for an administration may forfeit its support on foreign as well as on domestic questions. The debates of Congress are given as much attention in foreign offices abroad as the usual diplomatic notes. Foreign embassies and legations in Washington report the activities of Congress promptly to their governments. And if the objections of the House or Senate to a Department of State policy are sufficiently important, they can deprive the Department of effectiveness, because foreign governments quite naturally will come to believe that it does not have the support of the American people. The debate over the Versailles Treaty, its rejection by the Senate, and the subsequent repudiation of the Treaty by the American people in the presidential election of 1920 affected the course of foreign policy for the indefinite future. Congress can also muddy the international waters by attacks on foreign governments, thus contributing to misunderstanding and bad feeling and thereby complicating enormously the work of the Department of State.

If, as we have already seen, a foreign diplomat accredited to the United States engages in improper activities, such as attempting to influence American political opinion, adminis-

INSIDE THE DEPARTMENT OF STATE

tration Senators and Representatives will not hesitate to speak out sharply in warning, as Senator Watson did in 1922 against the British and Italian Ambassadors. If an American diplomat abroad goes beyond his province to cause offense, Congress will not hesitate to discipline him by voicing its displeasure. Although it has no direct control over an envoy, its word is salutary.

In one case the House of Representatives reacted immediately with a resolution of censure because of a speech Thomas F. Bayard, former Secretary of State, delivered in Edinburgh in 1895 while serving as Ambassador to Great Britain. In the speech Bayard assailed the protective tariff. Congress did not like it. There were rumblings of discontent and then the House took action. Having adopted the resolution, it was powerless to do more, but the resolution served its purpose of censure and warning against a repetition.

Even the word of a single influential Senator can be effective in admonishing the Department of State. This was demonstrated more than once during the years when the present Roosevelt administration had unprecedented majorities in both Houses and seemingly could ignore individuals with impunity. Yet a veteran Senator like Hiram Johnson of California could ask a critical question of only a few sentences on foreign policy and obtain an immediate reaction from the Secretary of State. Some might consider the question of only incidental interest and certainly of no political importance. Not so a Secretary of State of the political experience of Cordell Hull. He recognized Senator Johnson's influence in the Senate, realized that the Senator was probably speaking for a considerable body of political opinion in his own and neighboring states, and invariably responded promptly with assurances by word or deed. The California Senator's eye focused on no question more closely than relationships

with Great Britain, lest consultation and cooperation in the Far East by the Department of State might lead to joint action equivalent to an alliance.

For many years, especially during his service as chairman of the Committee on Foreign Relations, the voice of Senator William E. Borah of Idaho carried as far or even farther in Europe than that of the Secretary of State. His leadership of the forces of opposition in the historic fight in the Senate against the Versailles Treaty left an indelible impression in Europe and contributed to his prestige abroad perhaps as much as the quality of the views he expressed.

Individual members, acting independently of the administration, also exercise influence in other ways. Even bills they introduce bearing upon various aspects of foreign relations have their value. They may be ridiculed in the press but they are not treated lightly in the Department of State because they are considered in committee and debated on the floor and, even though rejected, they provide an opportunity for the focusing of public opinion. It is a test that helps inform the Department of the trend of national thought, often when it is seeking further light for a clearer indication of the country's views.

Obviously in all these circumstances it is essential for the Department of State to maintain close contact with Congress. Coordination is particularly desirable because so few officials of the Department have served in Congress and have had the opportunity of learning its ways from actual experience. At present there are two officials, Secretary Hull, who has been a member of both the House of Representatives and the Senate, and R. Walton Moore, Counselor for the Department, who has been a member of the House. Usually there is not more than one, when the Secretary of State has risen through the ranks of Congress. That has not hap-

pened very often in the past forty years. Besides Secretary Hull there were Secretaries Kellogg and Knox who had served in the Senate, and Secretary Bryan who had been a member of the House. The six others since the Spanish-American War, with the exception of Lansing, had had political experience, but none as members of Congress.

While this is a far different picture from that presented in parliamentary governments where cabinet officers are members of the legislative body, the Department's relations toward the legislative branch long have been growing closer. Nevertheless there is a dividing line. At one time the cleavage was considerable. John Hay considered it beneath the dignity of the Secretary of State to appear before congressional committees and was meticulous in observing that self-imposed rule of conduct, but that aloofness has long since disappeared.

Contacts are now maintained through committees when the Secretary of State and his chief assistants appear to explain policies or to go over the annual appropriation bills, for Congress keeps a jealous eye on these expenditures and insists upon knowing for what purposes the Department intends to use funds. All items entering into its ordinary costs and those of the Foreign Service and diplomatic missions abroad are scanned and explained.

Both foreign affairs committees also will invite the Secretary of State to appear and explain the position of the Department on pending measures, or the Secretary will not stand upon ceremony but ask to be heard, a request that is promptly granted. Although he will be careful not to appear to attempt to dictate, he will present his position frankly and often vigorously. How emphatic the Secretary is depends upon the urgency of the situation and the Secretary's temperament. Inasmuch as the committee sessions at these

times are executive, behind closed doors and under the seal of confidence, plain speaking is encouraged. Nor do the committee members resent it; they are accustomed to rough-and-tumble debate. Their professional veneer prevents the debate from descending to the level of personalities.

When the Committee on Foreign Affairs of the House of Representatives was first considering neutrality legislation in 1935 and Secretary Hull appeared before the Committee to discuss the administration's views, there was plain talking. The Committee was overwhelmingly Democratic, and it was a foregone conclusion that it would accept Secretary Hull's views, but that did not deter opposition members from questioning the Secretary sharply.

Several neutrality bills were before the Committee at that time, running from one to give the executive branch of the government wide discretion in imposing arms embargoes against belligerents to one at the other extreme permitting no latitude but making it mandatory when a state of war arose abroad for an embargo to be applied. Opposition members who had long fought to prevent American entanglement abroad and who feared that wide discretionary powers might be used to involve the United States in foreign wars attacked the administration's recommendations vigorously. Representative George H. Tinkham, a Republican from Massachusetts, who had taken a strong stand against the Versailles Treaty sixteen years earlier, led in the attack. Secretary Hull was equally aggressive in asserting his views. Their argument became a straight-out punching match, a duel. But that was all it was, all it amounted to, for the Committee in due course adopted the administration-favored measure with discretionary features.

That, however, was in the Committee on Foreign Affairs of the House which, when its majority is of the adminis-

tration party, is disposed to go along with the Department of State. Not so the Committee on Foreign Relations of the Senate. It is much less party-minded on foreign affairs. Issues cut across it regardless of what party is in power or dominates the committee. So it was that the Senate committee, although controlled by Democrats, approached the question from a more independent and critical standpoint and adopted the mandatory bill. As so often happens in a struggle between the two committees, the Committee on Foreign Affairs of the House eventually yielded and accepted the Senate measure.

That was the measure then passed by Congress, to the keen disappointment of the Department of State. In fact, it was considered so unworkable that President Roosevelt did not apply it against China and Japan in the war which began in July, 1937. He took advantage of a technical construction of its terms to refrain from acting as long as there was no formal declaration of war, and eighteen months later the President recommended that Congress erase the legislation from the statute books or amend it extensively.

Appearances of the Secretary of State before committees is a customary procedure, but he cannot be forced into a congressional debate and he is under no legal obligation to outline foreign policy explicitly. If either the Senate or House of Representatives adopts a resolution calling upon the Department for information, the request may be refused on the ground that to comply would be inconsistent with the public interest. Congress recognizes this and in adopting a resolution seeking information from the Department almost always does the courteous thing by adding the phrase "if not incompatible with the public interest."

Congress understands that some facts or circumstances probably should not be made public. It realizes that if the

Department should make available everything it learns concerning foreign affairs in other parts of the world it would not be on speaking terms with several countries for more than twenty-four hours. Also it would probably have to order its representatives home from abroad, for no foreign officials would talk to them on questions before they were ready for formal public announcement. The Foreign Service would be rendered futile.

So the Department can be as vague as it feels like being, and there is no constitutional or other requirement that will force an attitude of complete candor. Yet the system is more democratic in practice than in constitutional theory, for the Department cannot safely ignore the force of public opinion. If there is insistent enough demand from the country for light on a situation, common sense and practical politics will lead to adequate explanations. Legally, the Department can leave the country more or less in the dark, and let the verdict be rendered only when the people go at regular intervals to the polls; actually, it prefers not to follow such a shortsighted policy. It has found that, if sufficient demand exists, the expedient thing is to disclose the facts, or modify or abandon a policy.

A gap exists between the Department and Congress, but it is bridged, even though the Department of State has no official representative regularly at the Capitol day in and day out, as it would if the United States were a parliamentary government. Not only can resolutions be adopted and inquiries instituted at executive sessions of the Committees on Foreign Relations and on Foreign Affairs, but Secretaries of State, recognizing the importance of good relations with Congress, invite individual inquiries. Senators and Representatives take frequent advantage of this open-house invitation and call upon the Secretary of State and other officials

of the Department in person or by telephone to elicit information and discuss courses of action. When they appear in person they are never kept waiting long but are ushered as promptly as possible before the officials after being announced by the attentive messengers in the corridors.

Their inquiries are not restricted to treaties, although giving advice and consent to treaties and conventions by a two-thirds vote of those present is the most explicit duty entrusted to the Senate in regard to foreign affairs. It has ratified scores of them, defeated others, emasculated many by reservations, and placed others in pigeonholes of the Committee on Foreign Relations, where they have accumulated dust and finally died of suspended animation. Its record of obstruction gives point to the sour observation of John Hay that the Senate is the graveyard of treaties.

The Department of State is thoroughly aware of this state of affairs and brings to bear all its powers of persuasion in order to induce favorable action, although it moves warily and leans backward to avoid any appearance of dictation, lest it awaken the jealousy that has always existed between the legislative and executive branches of the government. The Secretary of State not only appears before the Committee on Foreign Relations to explain and interpret, but informal conversations are conducted with individual Senators, and administration spokesmen appeal to public opinion for support. Nevertheless, the record is dotted with failures. It is one reason that other ways have been found to reach understandings with foreign governments. There are side doors as well as a front door. Arrangements can be and are reached in other ways than by treaties and conventions.

Many understandings are embodied in protocols and in exchanges of notes that constitute little more than gentlemen's agreements. They are reached on the part of the

United States under the constitutional powers of the President for directing foreign affairs, and are as binding as the pledged word of governments can make them. Diplomatic conversations are held, the position of each government is ascertained, and understandings reached and confirmed in formal diplomatic communications. While these can be changed through subsequent negotiations more easily than a treaty can be revised, the practice has on the whole worked well.

The latest example is found in the exchange of notes of November 9 and 12, 1938, with Mexico, setting up a joint commission for adjustment of claims arising out of the expropriation by Mexico of agrarian lands owned by citizens of the United States. This could have been just as well arranged by treaty, but in that case its fate in the Senate might have been open to considerable doubt because of many controversial aspects that could have been raised in the course of debate.

While this was an understanding reached through diplomatic negotiation under the broad powers entrusted to the President to conduct foreign affairs, there are many arrangements that cannot under the Constitution be entered into without specific legislative authority delegating certain powers of Congress to the Executive for the purpose, and here the device of executive agreements based on acts or joint resolutions of Congress has been found to be a satisfactory substitute for treaties. Just where the dividing line lies is not clear, for the subject of executive agreements still awaits thorough research. Some time it may be carefully explored and a dividing line drawn by an Act of Congress between the two fields of treaties and executive agreements, but that time is not yet discernible on the horizon. Practice rather than theory, political considerations and expediency

[243]

have led to the use of executive agreements in the somewhat nebulous condition of affairs that has thus far existed. Congress as a whole, that is, the Senate and the House of Representatives together, by a legislative act or a joint resolution, delegates a certain part of its authority to the executive branch of the government to conclude bilateral agreements on specified subjects with foreign governments. Since the Department of State was established, for the practice began early, more than a thousand of these agreements have been negotiated.

Some have been of particular significance. When the annexation of Texas was taken up it was first attempted by a treaty that failed to receive the necessary two-thirds vote in the Senate. Annexation was then arranged through a joint resolution that was adopted by a majority vote of Congress. A half century later, in 1897, when it was found by a preliminary canvass that a treaty for the annexation of Hawaii would not command a two-thirds vote in the Senate, annexation was accomplished by joint resolution.

Recently, during the administration of Franklin D. Roosevelt, Congress by joint resolution authorized the President to make the United States a member of the International Labor Office at Geneva, although this organization has its basic charter in the Versailles Treaty which the Senate had rejected nearly fifteen years earlier.

The most famous instance is the Rush-Bagot Agreement which defines the peaceful relationship between the United States and Canada. This became effective in 1817—after Congress authorized the President to arrange by diplomatic negotiation for the reduction of American naval forces on the Great Lakes and Lake Champlain. Through diplomatic exchanges with Great Britain a reciprocal basis was reached whereby the American forces on the lakes were reduced to a

few small ships. Canada took equivalent action, and the international waters have ever since been on a demilitarized basis, a striking demonstration of peace between the two countries.

The reciprocal trade agreements with which Secretary Hull's name is identified fall within the same category—an authorization by Congress for their negotiation without subsequent Senate approval to make them effective. Nor is this an entirely new procedure, for Congress had previously created the flexible tariff system whereby rates might be adjusted by the executive branch, and in the Tariff Act of 1909 it set up maximum and minimum rates under which, after negotiation through the Department of State to make sure that there would be equality of treatment, the government applied more than 130 minimum tariffs in a few months.

As a matter of fact, the Department of State is confronted with the circumstance that not only is much of the action of Congress on foreign affairs by majority vote in both houses, rather than by a two-thirds vote in the Senate alone, but that a considerable influence is less formally exerted through debate and comment by members in public statements of their personal views. The results have on several occasions affected American policy for years or for the entire future.

War debts and neutrality furnish only two instances. There was the cry of "fifty-four forty or fight" over the Oregon question in the mid-nineteenth century, in the face of which the Department could not have moved otherwise, had it wished. There was the historic debate in the Senate over the Treaty of 1898 with Spain, centering upon retention of the Philippines, a debate that colored the conduct of foreign affairs for years. More than thirty years later it was followed with the congressional act by a majority vote of both Houses

providing for eventual independence of this Far Eastern possession. There were the persistent efforts of several Secretaries of State after the World War to have the Senate consent to American adherence to the World Court, efforts which ended each time in failure. There were significant debates in 1913 and again in 1920 over alien land legislation when policies pursued by the State of California complicated relations between the United States and Japan.

Again, in 1924, the Department of State was taken aback by the reception in Congress of Japanese representations over the immigration issue. The Department thought it had found an acceptable solution by proposing to grant Japan a quota status but to restrict her total immigration to 100 persons in any one year. Yet the final Japanese note on this question contained a reference to "grave consequences" if a proper adjustment was not reached. When this note reached the Senate in response to a request for the diplomatic correspondence, it was pounced upon by Senator Hiram Johnson who forced the issue with Senator Lodge, chairman of the Committee on Foreign Relations. As a result Congress rejected the arrangement and voted for Japanese exclusion, without even a nominal quota allowance. Ever since, the issue has been a sore point in relations with Japan, to the discomfiture of the Department of State.

Twelve years earlier, in 1912, Senator Lodge contributed a corollary to the Monroe Doctrine when a question arose of the naval intentions of Japan in Magdalena Bay. He postulated the rule that a naval base could not be established in the Western Hemisphere by a non-American power and not arouse the grave concern of the United States.

However, the role of the Senate or of Congress as a whole in foreign affairs is not always one of obstruction or of independence. More often it is cooperative, and especially if the

Department of State exercises wisdom in its relations with the Committees on Foreign Relations and Foreign Affairs. Their members are seasoned politicians, in touch with public opinion, and experienced in public affairs. Many of them have studied foreign affairs closely, and from time to time the Committee on Foreign Relations contains former Secretaries of State like Elihu Root and Philander C. Knox, who contribute powerfully to its deliberations, and former ministers who know the ways of diplomacy. If wisely approached and dealt with frankly, the committees can be of the utmost service to the Department. They also provide a seasoning influence. The long years of service of many of their members makes for continuity and adherence to basic policies in foreign affairs, and tends to prevent the Department of State from getting too far in advance of the people.

Much of the inspiration Secretary Kellogg received for proceeding with the negotiating of the treaty outlawing war came from Senator Borah, who was at the time chairman of the Committee on Foreign Relations and deeply interested in the peace project. Kellogg kept him informed constantly of the progress of the negotiations and sought his advice at every opportunity. He also conferred with Senator Borah on other questions, in fact so frequently that it was a common saying in Washington at the time that he could be seen every day ringing the doorbell of the Idaho Senator. Kellogg from his six years in the Senate recognized the importance of maintaining close liaison with the Committee on Foreign Relations.

Others have acted on the same impulse. The Secretary of State will have the chairman of the Committee for lunch and outline the status of pending questions; the Senate Committee chairman will drop in at the Department of State now and then to keep informed of latest developments,

and the President will invite him to lunch in order to make close cooperation even more certain.

This is a recognition of the very real place of the Senate and of Congress as a whole in the conduct of foreign affairs. Nor is recognition accorded solely through the consultations with the foreign relations and affairs committees. Often when delegations are appointed to important international conferences they will include one or more Senators. McKinley saw to this when he named Cushman K. Davis, chairman of the Committee on Foreign Relations, and Senators William P. Frye of Maine and George Gray of Delaware to the commission to negotiate peace with Spain in Paris in 1898. The treaty was approved by the Senate by a safe margin. President Wilson, however, as we have pointed out, ignored the Senate when he selected the commission for the Paris Peace Conference at the end of the World War. He may have lived to regret it, although no word of regret escaped him.

On the other hand, two Senators were appointed to the Washington Conference delegation in 1921, and the treaties negotiated at that Conference were approved by the Senate. In the same way, President Hoover named Secretary Stimson chairman and then appointed Senators to the delegation that represented the United States at the London Naval Conference of 1930. Its treaties were approved.

Influential Senators on numerous occasions have been out of step with the administration. That usually is the case when the Senate majority is of the opposite political party from the White House. Cushman K. Davis fought Cleveland's Hawaiian policy of nonannexation and, when McKinley entered the White House and Davis became chairman of the Committee on Foreign Relations, he threw his influence, consistently to be sure, for annexation. There were

also years of misunderstanding between Senator Lodge, long before he became chairman of the Committee, and Secretary Hay, misunderstandings that can be explained in terms both of policy and personal pettiness, an inability of the two to get along.

The chairman of the Committee on Foreign Relations can be of great service to the Secretary of State, if they are in sympathy, as a medium for issuing statements of policy. Often the Secretary wishes his attitude to be revealed for the information of the American people and of foreign governments, but the diplomatic situation is so delicate as to make a formal statement by him inadvisable. In these circumstances he finds it convenient to advise the chairman informally of his views and quietly inspire a statement. When the chairman issues the statement it serves the purpose of the Department of State, yet does not have the force of a direct governmental utterance. Even though there may be doubts as to whether it is inspired, it constitutes an advance warning of the position of the government. That is exactly what the Secretary of State desires.

In his relations with the chairman of the Committee on Foreign Relations the Secretary of State is dealing with no tyro. On the contrary, the list of Senators who have occupied the post, the outstanding chairmanship in the Senate since the Committee was created in 1816, is an impressive one. It includes men of broad political backgrounds, wide national influence, and diplomatic attainments. The first was James Barbour of Virginia, who later became Secretary of War, Minister to England, and, in 1839, chairman of the Whig national convention.

Rufus King of New York, who was chairman of the Committee in 1821, had previously been Minister to England, and in 1816 had been an unsuccessful candidate for Presi-

dent. John Forsyth of Georgia, who was chairman in 1832, after leaving the office became Secretary of State, a record duplicated years later, in 1897, by John Sherman of Ohio. Among the most famous who have held the chairmanship are Henry Clay of Kentucky, Thomas H. Benton of Missouri, and James Buchanan of Pennsylvania, who later became Secretary of State and President.

William R. King of Alabama, who was chairman of the Committee in 1849, previously had held important diplomatic posts abroad and later was Vice President of the United States. The present chairman, Key Pittman of Nevada, is a direct descendant of King, the only time two members of the same family have held this position in the history of the Committee.

Then there were the Virginian, James M. Mason, of Mason and Slidell fame during the Civil War; Charles Sumner of Massachusetts, Simon Cameron of Pennsylvania; Hannibal Hamlin of Maine, who previously had been Vice President in the first Lincoln administration; and Henry Cabot Lodge of Massachusetts, who in the course of a long political career during which he gave close attention to foreign affairs, was thrice chairman of Republican national conventions. Such men are not the type that the Department of State would care to trifle with or ignore.

While the Secretary of State is the chief adviser to the President in the conduct of foreign affairs, the chairman of the Committee on Foreign Relations can be termed a close second in influence, whether he is for or against the administration.

CHAPTER XV

RELATIONS WITH THE ARMY
AND NAVY

ALTHOUGH the relations of the Department of State
with Congress are of primary importance, there is an
interrelation between foreign and naval and military policies
that calls for constant collaboration. In war the Department
of State necessarily is subordinate to the armed services.
Ordinarily, in time of peace, it exercises full sway, but its
voice carries the farther because of a strong Navy, and it
employs the military establishments as instruments to aid
in carrying out programs. The Army and Navy are not
organizations exclusively for waging war. They also have
peacetime functions.

Cynics and ultrarealists may maintain that diplomatic
success depends more on the caliber of the nation's guns than
on the caliber of its diplomats. While the Department of
State would be the last to admit this, it has experienced too
many emergencies when American lives and interests were
at stake to deny for a moment that the Army and Navy have
their place in diplomacy. Without them the Department
would be paralyzed, for in the present state of civilization
there is no hope of an immediate farewell to arms.

When, during the attack of the southern armies of China
on Nanking in 1927, Americans were concentrated in dire
peril on Socony Hill, Foreign Service officers brought them
to safety on ships in the Yangtze by letting them down a
cliff to the river on ropes under the protection of a barrage

from an American destroyer. When a decade later Ambassador Johnson was ordered to leave the Embassy compound in Nanking before the approach of the Japanese and seek a safer place, he went a few hundred yards to a gunboat at the dock. And when a little later the gunboat *Panay* was bombed above Nanking, Army, Navy, and Foreign Service officers were on board and shared the dangers of the attack and the final trek to safety along shore in the next few days.

Except for the Navy, Engert would have been overrun in the Legation compound in Addis Ababa, for, as we have already noted, it was by naval wireless that he sent his globe-encircling message for the assistance that was so promptly rushed from the British Legation three miles away. Nor was this accidental. The Department of State at the outset of the Italo-Ethiopian War, realizing that an emergency requiring prompt communication might arise, was foresighted enough to request the Navy Department to send the portable wireless set in charge of expert personnel to the Legation for use if all other avenues of communication were closed. The need arose and the Navy was equal to the occasion. It not only transmitted the request for help but the bluejackets also participated in the defense of the compound until reinforcements arrived. It was one of many services the Navy has performed for the Department of State, almost as a matter of routine.

Relations of the Department of State with the Navy, however, are not limited to occasional thrilling incidents. They rest on a much broader base, one that requires constant coordination of policy. Obviously, the Navy does not make foreign policy but according to its form and size it may help to shape it. At least the policy may require the backing of a formidable fleet or depend on the Navy for implementation. If large enough, the fleet even riding at anchor will command

the respect of the world in an emergency when a diplomatic note might not produce even an echo. It is really doubtful whether the diplomatic frontier extends far beyond the military front.

From the international standpoint the nation's prosperity and security rest mainly on competent diplomacy, flourishing trade, and strong defense; and, to give them maximum effect, close coordination is necessary. There must be a nice balance between the Department of State and the armed forces. In achieving and maintaining this there is daily correlation among the three departments. As diplomats, lapsing into the vernacular of the college sport world remark, "The three are constantly throwing forward passes, from one to another."

Sometimes one is out in front, at other times another, for the Department of State can be more zealous than the armed services that are popularly supposed to crave action. As a matter of fact, the Army and Navy are often much less eager for an aggressive foreign policy than the Department of State or the White House because of a keener appreciation of a state of unpreparedness or other military factors in case precipitate diplomacy forced the issue. More than once the Chief of Staff of the Army or the Chief of Naval Operations, or both, have drafted memorandums pointing out that a foreign policy contained military hazards of which they feared the diplomats were not sufficiently cognizant. Not that the Secretary of State and his assistants were deliberately reckless, but their training simply had not equipped them to sense dangers that were discernible to the professional military mind.

It was in a realization of the value of this special equipment that Secretary Stimson, after he had pressed his vigorous Manchurian diplomacy for weeks, formed the habit of

calling into frequent consultation in his office in the Department of State the professional heads of the Army and Navy, General Douglas MacArthur, Chief of Staff, and Admiral William V. Pratt, Chief of Naval Operations. He was not plotting war, but he wished to obtain the benefit of their specially qualified judgments as military men who knew from experience both arms and the Far East.

Often Secretaries of State have called the heads of the Army and Navy into consultation when diplomatic policies involving military factors were under consideration. Many of these professional advisers have had years of experience with practical foreign problems, at posts abroad and as experts at international conferences, some for more years than the Secretary of State and the President have been in public life. Their judgments are usually swift and often intuitive. They are particularly of service in sensing policies of a foreign government from its military dispositions. The trained military mind can read these signs when they would scarcely arouse the suspicion of a diplomat reared in another profession.

When, for example, Japan was far advanced in the conquest of Manchuria, begun in 1931, word was received that Russia had quietly moved her Far Eastern military headquarters from the coast to Lake Baikal, far inland. That to the lay mind was a piece of casual information, of some interest but of no particular significance. Not so to the military mind. It spoke volumes. It meant, and at once, that Russia was preparing to reinforce heavily her Far Eastern garrison, a deduction that was conveyed to the Department of State. Russia did exactly that. The movement of additional troops to the Far East soon began and continued for months until a strong enough force was near the Manchurian border to offset the Japanese. Simultaneously work was

undertaken for double-tracking the trans-Siberian railroad. An entirely new element had been injected into the Far Eastern situation, a fact of first importance to the Department of State.

Consultations among the three departments of State, War, and Navy are not confined to discussions among the Secretary of State and the two chiefs of staff. At times the Secretaries of War and of the Navy will join in the discussions. At other times when a serious issue involving coordination is at stake the three Cabinet officers and the two chiefs of staff will go to the White House for consultation with the President. At still other times when important but less grave questions are to be decided, the Navy and Army chiefs will exchange views directly with key men in the Department of State below the Secretary. Thus, when a matter involving disposition of naval units in the Orient arises, the Chief of Naval Operations will call upon the chief of the Division of Far Eastern Affairs or the political adviser for that area in the Department of State and reach an understanding. This is a regular practice. It saves time and is perfectly satisfactory. At a convenient opportunity the Secretary of State and the President will be informed of the decision.

Similarly, there are often consultations in the field. The Commander-in-chief of the Asiatic Fleet confers constantly with the Ambassador and other diplomatic officers in China in order to coordinate activities closely. To make certain that their relations will run smoothly, the Commander-in-chief of the Asiatic Fleet is never appointed by the Navy Department until the approval of the Department of State has been obtained. The reason is obvious. He is a diplomatic official as well as a naval officer because of the conditions confronting him in the disturbed state of affairs in China.

His principal duty is not only to show the flag in ports as a matter of prestige for his country but to extend protection to Americans and their property insofar as possible. Naturally, to carry out this mission with maximum efficiency he must maintain contact with the diplomatic and consular officers at the many ports along the coast and the great inland waterways.

It is the task of affording protection to Americans during wars and revolutions abroad in which the services so often merge in practical operation. The duties being performed are essential to the pursuit of policies decided by the Department of State, with the Navy and on less frequent occasions the Army becoming arms of the Department. At these times even announcements of their operations, except for detailed movements, are left to the Department of State. It is frankly and openly their directing agent in these situations, subject, of course, to the approval of the President who is also the Commander-in-chief of the Army and Navy.

The same policy was followed with reference to the Spanish Revolution as in China. When that revolution broke out suddenly and unexpectedly, hundreds of Americans were in the fighting zones, and the Department of State was confronted with a major problem of evacuation, the first large scale transfer of nationals from an entire country since the outbreak of the World War in 1914 found Americans scattered all over the Continent. The Department could not have carried out the evacuation except for the Navy. The European Squadron that had been discontinued a few years before was reconstituted and ships sent to the various ports, bringing to safety not only Americans but nationals of other countries in the course of movements that continued for months.

[256]

Again, when revolutions have occurred in Latin America, the Navy, supplemented by marines, has been used as an arm of the Department of State in protecting Americans and their property. In response to demands for a hands-off policy and also because revolutions in that area have subsided, the ships with their bluejackets and marines have not been employed in this way for several years. When they were so used, it was in carrying out policy defined in the Department of State. Operations of this character were carried on in Nicaragua from 1912 to 1928, with only one brief interval. Finally, when the forces were withdrawn, it was in response to a policy decided by Secretary Stimson, with the approval of the President. All those years marines were used to police danger points, as they have been used in the Dominican Republic, Haiti, and other countries of that general region, and always as an arm of the Department of State, even when policing developed into active fighting and long campaigns.

At other times, the Department of State has used the armed forces on missions of peace. Thus it was that naval ships were rushed to Japan to assist in rescue operations after a hurried evening conference in the White House between President Coolidge and William Phillips, Acting Secretary of State, at the time of the great earthquake of 1923. They did not await official advices but acted on the basis of press reports describing the seriousness of the disaster. It was a work of relief in which diplomatic and consular officers and Army officers who were on the scene also played a conspicuous part.

Other peaceful missions are conducted by the Navy under policies determined in the Department of State through regularly constituted squadrons that visit foreign ports as an evidence of good will and to show the flag as a matter of diplomatic prestige. Thus it was that for years a European

[257]

squadron was maintained, steaming in Mediterranean waters and to Atlantic ports of the Continent, and that another squadron, consisting of a gunboat and two destroyers, regularly operates in Central American waters, both on the Atlantic and Pacific sides. There are also the Yangtze River and South China patrols for protective purposes in Chinese waters. And now that aviation has arrived, good-will flights are made by the armed services to countries in the Western Hemisphere at the instance of the Department of State.

Military and naval missions are also maintained in a number of Latin American countries to assist those nations in developing their own national defense services and to develop mutual understanding and foster friendship. Arrangements for these missions are always made by the Department of State through formal agreements negotiated with the countries concerned.

In conducting peacetime activities in cooperation with the Department of State naval officers visit foreign ports, exchange salutes, and occasionally have even negotiated treaties under authority of special powers given them for that express purpose. The outstanding instance was the mission of Commodore Matthew Calbraith Perry to Japan in 1853. He reopened Japan to foreign intercourse, after two centuries, on terms of equality for all nations and negotiated a treaty giving effect to the new status. That service has never been forgotten in the United States, and in Japan Perry is regarded as a national hero. The beneficent effects of his mission promise to continue through the years as an influence for understanding between the two nations even in times when they find themselves in diplomatic controversy.

Perry on that occasion was a diplomat first and a naval officer only incidentally. There have been other such examples in the course of the years. In recent times, from the

close of the World War until the United States resumed in 1927 diplomatic relations that had been severed with Turkey, the functions of diplomacy in Constantinople were conducted by Rear Admiral Mark H. Bristol as high commissioner. He operated under both the Department of State and the Navy Department, for he commanded ships in the Bosporus and maintained relations with Turkey. At the same time he shared responsibility with high commissioners of Great Britain and France for administration of the city of Constantinople. The dual nature of his status was recognized by the presence on his staff of both naval and Foreign Service officers. It was a notable instance of the merging of the two services.

Several years earlier, in 1914, the Department of State and the Army and Navy were commingled when Vera Cruz was occupied. The city was taken by bluejackets and marines, the Army entered to hold it pending negotiations, and throughout the incident was of first concern to the Department of State. Mexican questions, in fact, long called for joint exercise of responsibilities along the coast and the border during the years of revolution. The Department of State was as vitally interested as the Army when Brigadier General John J. Pershing was sent across the border in 1916 in quest of Pancho Villa. The Punitive Expedition was very much subject to Department of State policy and was withdrawn from Mexico when the Department and Army chiefs in consultation with President Wilson decided that the time had come for a halt in the chase of the guerrilla leader.

This was one of the few instances when the Army has been used on such missions, for in foreign affairs the Navy enters more often and more regularly than the War Department. Another case, however, was the participation of the United States through the military in the march to Peiping, or

Peking as it was then known, in 1900 to relieve the legations; and years later the Army was represented in the patrol by the powers of the railroad from Tientsin to Peking in order that the legations might never again be bottled up in the ancient city. This patrol duty covered more than a quarter of a century, from 1912 to 1938. It was authorized by a protocol negotiated in consequence of the experience of 1900. Other powers participated in it, although the right was not exercised until the Chinese revolution of 1911 had awakened fresh apprehensions.

The United States sent the Fifteenth Infantry to Tientsin and there it remained for twenty-six years until new conditions resulting from the breaking of the front of western powers by the World War, the sweep northward of the southern forces in the Chinese revolution of 1927, and the attack of Japan on China beginning in 1931 no longer gave point to maintaining troops there. When they were withdrawn, Japan was in occupation of the railroad and the capital city.

During these years the United States also kept Marine forces in the International Settlement at Shanghai and around the Legation in Peiping. They still remain there, performing functions which, notwithstanding their military character, are essentially carried on for the Department of State.

While Navy officers, roaming the seas and visiting the five other continents, often perform diplomatic duties because the occasion arises from the very nature of their services, Army officers are also charged with missions for the Department of State from time to time. General Tasker H. Bliss, former Chief of Staff, was a member of the commission to negotiate peace at Paris in 1919. Major General Enoch H. Crowder, who rose to be Judge Advocate General and prepared the draft of the Selective Service Act in the World

War, had a long administrative and diplomatic record in Cuba. He closed his public career as Ambassador to Cuba from 1922 to 1927.

General Pershing, at the instance of the Department of State, was appointed, in 1925, president of the plebiscite commission which attempted to solve the dispute between Chile and Peru over Tacna-Arica. Major General Blanton Winship, after an army career culminating as Adjutant General, was appointed Governor of Puerto Rico. Major General Douglas MacArthur, upon completing his service as Chief of Staff, was appointed military adviser to Manuel Quezon, President of the Commonwealth Government of the Philippines. It is a post where, because of his prestige and attainments, the fact that he sits with the insular cabinet, and his close personal friendship with President Quezon, he might be said to have more the status of a proconsul than even the High Commissioner himself. That, in fact, was why he was selected for the office, at the instance, be it said, of President Quezon himself.

But of all the soldier-diplomats of recent years unquestionably first place goes to Major General Frank R. McCoy, who has just retired after reaching the statutory age of sixty-four. He demonstrated over a period of more than thirty years that he was as resourceful in peace as in war, as distinguished in diplomacy as in fighting. He was peace commissioner in Cuba for Theodore Roosevelt, headed the military commission of the United States to Armenia after the Armistice of November 11, 1918, and in 1923 was in Tokyo helping restore normal life after the earthquake.

Recognizing his talents, the Department of State selected him in 1927 to supervise elections in Nicaragua, and two years later, in 1929, appointed him head of the settlement commission in the dispute between Bolivia and Paraguay

over the Chaco. And when in 1932 the League of Nations, with the cooperation of the United States, decided to send the Lytton Commission to Manchuria in an effort to facilitate a settlement between Japan and China, General McCoy was appointed the American representative on the Commission. In the weeks he spent in preparation for that duty he dropped his military life and established offices in the Department of State where quietly and without ostentation he made his plans and consulted with the diplomatic branch of the government. When he returned, he reported to Secretary Stimson, although unofficially, for technically he was serving on the Commission as a private citizen. It was a notable example of how a military officer can doff his uniform and appear in the habiliments of a diplomat.

Relations of the Department of State and the military services, however, are not confined to special situations. They exist constantly through consultations. When the Department negotiated a new basic treaty with Panama to replace the first one that had been concluded thirty years earlier, in 1904, many arrangements affecting the Army in the Canal Zone required consideration and consultation. But apart from these special questions there is a constant association of the peace and military departments through the operations of military and naval attachés who are stationed abroad at embassies and legations under the supervision of ambassadors and ministers.

Copies of many of their reports when received in the War and Navy Departments are routed to the Department of State. In the same way, reports to the Department of State from the Foreign Service that would be of interest are sent to the War and Navy Departments. There is a continual interchange of information. And to make more certain that there will be smooth operation of the interrelated machines,

the Chief of Staff and the Chief of Naval Operations hold periodic conferences with the Secretary or Under Secretary of State to survey the work of their representatives abroad.

Information obtained by military and naval attachés is, as we have noted, of especial value to the Department of State when a foreign problem, as so often happens, has a military background. For the professional military mind can read certain signs that would be of uncertain meaning to a diplomat. A military attaché may look out his hotel window, see troops on the march, and from that incident and other data read a train of events that his government should know. Details are supplied with exceptional care. Thus it is that during a campaign in support of a foreign policy that is causing the Department of State concern, the exact location of troops will be ascertained as well as the numerical designation of regiments and other units and even the names of their commanding officers. It provides a picture from which future prospects can be gauged more accurately than if the information were not in hand. How it is obtained is one of the mysteries in which laymen are not initiated.

However, the attachés do not report on political affairs. They limit themselves to their own professional world. If they should attempt to interest themselves in the political side of international relations, they would be quickly withdrawn by the government, for that field is reserved for Foreign Service officers.

The Navy is just as valuable as the Army as a source of reports, for it covers the world in its operations with ships in the Pacific, the Far East, the Mediterranean, and the Atlantic. Yet at no time does it engage in more intensive deliberations with the Department of State than when preparations are undertaken for an international naval conference, for foreign policies will be affected by the number

and types of ships that will be agreed upon for years to come. Naval and foreign policy are joined in the issues to be taken up in the conference. Sometimes they are not determined without a struggle between the admirals and the diplomats. When this occurs, the President decides. He is a sort of referee but not a detached one, for he, too, has his own views. Behind all these forces stands public opinion, especially as reflected through Congress.

It too frequently is forgotten that the Washington Conference of 1921 was preceded by a running series of debates in Congress the previous winter, when Senator Borah and others raised powerful voices for armament reduction and for economy which the country applauded. It was not overlooked at the time; it was a direct and forceful influence on the executive branch of the government when the project of a conference was first taken up in diplomatic channels.

When the decision was reached to call the conference, long and careful preparation on naval details was necessary. Without it Secretary Hughes could not have made his startling proposals for all around reductions on a balanced basis at the opening session. For weeks the heads of the Navy— the Secretary of the Navy, the Chief of Naval Operations, and members of the Navy General Board—appeared regularly at the Department of State for conferences with the Secretary of State and his experts on disarmament to lay plans for participation in the conference. Aspects of the American position were canvassed, the world situation studied, reports examined of positions likely to be taken by other governments, and from time to time the consultants called on the President to go over plans. Finally the position to be favored was determined and instructions drawn to guide the delegation to the conference. It was a pattern followed for all subsequent naval conferences.

Whenever these preparations are undertaken there is always a question as to whether the views of the Navy or of the Department of State will prevail. The Navy, naturally, is thinking first of its duty of being prepared for eventualities, and the Department of State more of political relations. Both are intertwined, but the Navy is thinking in terms of war operations. The Department, on the other hand, is thinking in terms of peace and is reconciled to making some sacrifices for the sake of good understanding among the nations and in a realization that, if a conference is to be a success, there must be both give and take on all sides. At times the participants are far apart; at other times quite closely in accord at the outset, so that an accommodation of views is easily reached.

When the Washington Conference was called, the country and the entire world, for that matter, were war weary, restive under wartime taxes, and earnestly hoping for peace and economy. However, the political clouds over the Pacific were dark and lowering, a circumstance of primary importance to the statesmen of Europe, America, and Japan. In this situation the Department of State, for the sake of political easement in the Pacific, favored the acceptance of a higher ratio for Japan than did the Navy chiefs. The latter insisted that a 2-to-1 ratio, in favor of the United States over Japan, was essential for purposes of defense. Secretary Hughes, however, understood that Japan under no circumstances would accept as low a ratio as 50 percent. And for the sake of good understanding that would flow from a limitation treaty and other agreements, he believed that some concession could be made.

He felt warranted in forcing the issue with President Harding by pointing out that not only a naval treaty but political pacts covering the Pacific area and the status of

China were to be considered by the Conference, and that all of them would fit into one composite project. It was more than a naval conference. In its broadest aspect it was decidedly political. Secretary Hughes won President Harding to his views, and so the Navy was overridden. It was decreed that the United States would be prepared to accept a ratio of 60 instead of 50 percent for Japan. With that understanding Japan consented to attend the conference, which even naval officers now admit was a success. It stabilized the world's armaments for a number of years and in conjunction with diplomatic and political arrangements cleared the clouds from the Pacific for a decade.

A different situation existed when the Tripartite Naval Conference was called at Geneva in 1927. The world was farther away from the Great War, the country had had relief from heavy taxation, and President Coolidge had for several years been following a policy of retrenchment that had borne fruit in lower naval and other governmental costs. However, President Coolidge, while eager for a diplomatic success, could not be swayed readily. In fact during his years in the White House he had become more and more sour toward Europe, in contrast with his sympathies toward the League of Nations and ideas of collective security when he was elected Vice President in 1920. In addition, unlike the Washington Conference, the Conference at Geneva was to take up only naval questions.

In these circumstances it was not surprising that the Department of State did not oppose the views of the Navy Department when preparations for the Conference were undertaken. If it had, it probably would have been overruled by the President. In any event, there was complete unanimity, so much so that it was a foregone conclusion that on the central issue of limitation of cruisers the Navy would

[266]

have its way. It was devoted to the cause of 10,000-ton cruisers armed with 8-inch guns. Similarly, the British Foreign Office was subordinated to the Admiralty, and the British admirals held a quite different view toward cruisers than the Americans. They wanted a large number of smaller ships of this category armed with 6- instead of 8-inch guns. Both had sound reasons from the standpoint of their own strategic positions in advocating the policies they did. That never was disputed; it was generally recognized. But the fact remains that in the conference the British and the American admirals rushed into conflict, refused to yield, and the conference collapsed, to the lasting regret of President Coolidge, who considered it his only diplomatic failure.

The damage was later repaired to some extent at the London Naval Conference of 1930, but for the time being only misunderstanding and ill will emerged from the Geneva Conference, and it colored Anglo-American relations for several years. It was in striking contrast to the results of the Washington Conference five years earlier. In one case understanding and good will predominated; in the other misunderstanding and concern. In the first instance the Department of State prevailed; in the second it acquiesced readily. Perhaps the only moral that can be drawn with assuredness is that in great issues the Department cooperates with the Navy, sometimes wisely, at other times less wisely, but at all times with the White House and public opinion exercising a controlling influence.

CHAPTER XVI

RELATIONS WITH OTHER DEPARTMENTS

RELATIONS of the Department of State are not restricted to those with Congress and the Army and Navy. They extend into every other department and many of the independent agencies of the government. Without them it would be impossible to protect the interests of the country and conduct foreign affairs properly. Obviously, the Department of State in developing its policies must consult the others, for while it is in touch with foreign governments and keeps its ears attuned to public opinion at home, these other agencies are in direct contact with the internal affairs of the country. The problem is one of integrating policy so that it will accord as far as possible with the broad objectives of the government in external affairs and at the same time meet the needs of the country at home.

The process of coordination has been improved greatly in recent years under force of necessity, for as the country has grown and its interests expanded abroad, pressure has increased on the Department of State, its responsibilities have become wider, and the ramifications of its operations unavoidably more complex. Without constant contact within the government an adjustment of specific national questions to foreign relations would be impossible.

The Department of Agriculture may propose a particular program covering the export of commodities and in so doing reflect not only its own views but the attitude of farmers.

On the other hand, the program might set in motion a train of events running along the entire foreign front and causing resentments that would impair international understanding and paralyze foreign policy in many directions. In this situation the Department of State would not necessarily seek to impose its views, but it would consult for the purpose of ascertaining to what extent adjustment might be advisable to protect the position of the country abroad and at the same time permit interests at home to be served.

These questions are constantly arising. In many other cases, however, the Department of State does no more than act as the transmitting agency, the channel of communication for other departments to foreign governments. If the Post Office Department desires to make some detailed arrangements in mail service abroad through international agreement, the Department of State will forward its correspondence and leave the matter entirely to that Department. If the Department of the Treasury has a technical financial question to take up with another government involving foreign policy in no way, the same procedure will be followed. This is a service that is carried on frequently, in fact so often that the Department of State is known as the post office for other sections of the government in their dealings abroad.

Nevertheless, its services are far from perfunctory. Nor are thrilling episodes limited to the emergencies in which the Foreign Service and the military arms afford protection to Americans abroad. There are mystery and drama as well as thrills, for the Department of State in carrying on cooperative activities with other organizations in the executive branch of the government even has its own secret service. It assists in trailing international crooks, spies, and foreign conspirators, in enforcing treaties and domestic law.

Few realize that the Department of State houses a virtual though small Scotland Yard. Though of course not called by that name, there is a section in the Division of Far Eastern Affairs directed by career diplomats which operates for the suppression of the illicit drug traffic and follows the movements of agents of illegal rings around the world. Constantly on the trail of traffickers, it pursues them relentlessly from behind the doors of quiet rooms giving from the corridor no indication of the character of the work carried on within their walls.

If the records ever were revealed, they would make fascinating reading, better than fabulously plotted detective stories. But they almost never are. It is a work that does not thrive on publicity and so the tales seldom get beyond the covers of confidential official records. It is generally known only that they hold accounts of intrigue, of agents of international rings crossing the oceans in disguise, of detections and apprehensions, and from time to time of suicides as police officers and Federal agents close in. Occasionally facts emerge at court trials but not otherwise.

In this work the Department cooperates with the Bureau of Narcotics of the Department of the Treasury, the Department of Justice, and foreign governments in consequence of international treaties for suppressing the traffic in narcotic drugs. Responding to the promptings of religious and civil organizations supported by public opinion, the United States has taken the leadership in this movement and for years has been represented by the astute and close-mouthed Stuart J. Fuller, assistant chief of the Division of Far Eastern Affairs and a career diplomat of thirty years' service. He has been present at international conferences in Geneva striving for more effective concerted action in discouraging the illicit business.

The obligations the countries have assumed for joint action in the work spring principally from the treaty of 1931 for the suppression of the traffic in narcotic drugs, while under an agreement concluded two years earlier, in 1929, twenty-three nations, including the United States, exchange information on this subject. The two arrangements have brought excellent results. Information concerning operations of rings abroad when obtained by consuls is telegraphed to the Department of State and then transmitted to the Treasury, which also receives information from its own agents abroad. Both the consuls and the Treasury agents also make reports to local police in the countries where they are stationed, if they concern activities only in those countries. If the information points to operations in the United States, it is transmitted to Washington. When the Treasury receives it, orders are sent by telegraph for arrests to be made on charges of violating or planning to violate the law.

How successful this system has been may be judged from the fact that in 1937 there were no seizures of raw opium on the Atlantic coast of the United States, although prepared opium was seized. Prepared opium is used only by Chinese in this country. And, whereas, ten years earlier there were 100,000 addicts in the United States, by 1938 there were only 35,000.

The Department of State also conducts investigations along other lines. With equal secrecy it directs its attention to the activities of spies, although this work falls more directly under the Department of Justice and the military services. However, the Department of State finds opportunity to cooperate by checking records and developing information concerning their activities. Here again it remains much in the background, merely giving its information

quietly to the other agencies and thence into the possession of district attorneys for use in prosecutions in the courts.

It also keeps a vigilant eye through its Division of Controls on the munitions business and seeks to detect any violation of embargoes against the exportation of arms, ammunition, and implements of war to belligerents abroad. It maintains close liaison with American manufacturers and with customs officials at the various ports of the United States. Foreign Service officers abroad, whenever suspicions have been aroused, check shipments as they arrive in the countries where they are stationed to ascertain whether there has been evasion of American law. If evidence of violations is discovered, it is sent by the Department of State to the Department of Justice for further investigation and legal action.

In addition, the Department has a section with subsidiary offices in New York and several other cities for the protection of official records and of distinguished foreign officials when they come to the United States. It works closely with local police authorities in such matters, always in the background but persistently.

However, cooperation with other departments does not stop here. On the contrary, the relations cover a host of other subjects, particularly financial and economic. There is daily consultation that usually, although not always, is marked by a spirit of complete harmony. If there is lack of teamwork, if another department is moving in an opposite direction, or if another Cabinet officer lifts his voice with a tone of authority on foreign affairs, the Secretary of State is called upon to exercise his best political talents to safeguard the prestige of his office, make his views prevail or reach a compromise adjustment. Well may he exclaim on some of these occasions —and some have in private outbursts of exasperation—

"Every morning I open my newspaper with trepidation to see what some other official has been saying about my business."

The observation, it should be remarked parenthetically, might even be extended at rare intervals to include the White House, for every Secretary of State has to keep in step with the President, and some have had to bring all their political skill to bear in discouraging an impulsive President from unwise action. The country may have been the gainer, although it has known little of what went on. It is a part that illuminates the political character of the office of Secretary of State. His role is not confined to dealings with foreign governments.

Usually the Secretary of State has sufficient political skill to avoid open conflict with a Cabinet colleague over foreign policy. Secretary Hull, outwardly at least, took it calmly when Harold L. Ickes, the Secretary of the Interior, in 1938 broadcast a speech by radio to the British Isles in which he discussed foreign questions. However, Secretary Ickes carefully explained at the outset that he was speaking as a private citizen. When late in that same year he attacked Germany vigorously in the Cleveland speech that produced the sensational but unsuccessful effort at a diplomatic protest from Berlin, Secretary Hull was temporarily absent from his post attending the Pan-American Conference at Lima, Peru. The incident had blown over by the time he returned to his duties in the Department.

Ordinarily relations of the Department of State proceed smoothly with the other departments and agencies of the government. And this is the more exceptional because every department of the government and many of the independent agencies enter the field of foreign affairs at some place. It is a subject that is not confined to the Department of State.

[273]

Even the Post Office Department negotiates postal treaties and conventions.

Especially close relations are required with the Department of Justice, the legal arm of the government. From time to time the Department of State requests the Attorney General to render opinions for its guidance in construing domestic law, particularly in reference to visa, passport, and similar matters. These opinions are usually on routine questions. They almost never are requested where broad diplomatic policy is at stake. The Department of State relies upon its own legal division, staffed as it is by a score of lawyers, for guidance in that field. Furthermore, when the Attorney General renders an opinion it is only advisory, not mandatory on the Department. It may be accepted or not, as the Department prefers.

The Department of Justice prosecutes for the Department of State violators of arms embargoes, counterfeiters of consular invoices and passports, and unlawful users of the Seal of the United States, of which the Secretary of State is custodian. It also prosecutes extradition cases that include Federal offenses. The Attorney General, in addition, defends cases for the Department in the courts. He so acts in proceedings against the Secretary of State involving any question where the Secretary has a discretionary right of action. Examples of this are to be found in passport cases and less frequently in suits over the distribution by the Department to American claimants of funds that have been paid as a result of international arbitration proceedings. The Attorney General also defends other officials of the Department besides the Secretary when cases are brought against them in matters involving their execution of official duties.

In another category of cases, the Department of Justice cooperates with the Department of State in extradition pro-

ceedings for foreign governments, using its machinery to apprehend a fugitive sought in this country and bring him before a magistrate for hearing.

There are many matters in which the Department of State cooperates closely with the Treasury. The question of the war debts is of equal concern to them, for it involves in the present uncertain status problems of both finance and foreign relations. The two departments have also worked closely together in recent years in connection with the operation of the Tripartite Monetary Agreement among the United States, Great Britain, and France. This Agreement was brought about by a combination of events. In the first place, the Gold Reserve Act of 1934 gave the President discretionary power over the gold value of the dollar, so placing in his hands great power to influence world monetary values. Other countries were off the gold standard and employing managed currencies, while world events threw the three democracies into a relationship of close sympathy and understanding. Out of these factors, and as the great depression wore its way along, emerged the Tripartite Agreement for collaboration in maintaining monetary stability within certain reasonable limits.

To operate the agreement daily consultation is required. Cable messages are exchanged by Washington with London and Paris. The overseas telephone is utilized; in one week alone Henry L. Morgenthau, the Secretary of the Treasury, made twenty-seven telephone calls to London. In addition, with the approval of the Department of State, the British and French Embassies in Washington maintain constant contact with the Treasury, while the American Embassies in London and Paris keep the same vigil with the financial offices of those governments. Foreign Service officers in the London and Paris Embassies periodically return to Wash-

ington to report directly to the Secretary of the Treasury on the operations of the agreement, while the Adviser on International Economic Affairs in the Department of State or his assistant attend all important conferences on the subject at the Treasury, so that the Department may be informed of every step that is contemplated or that is taken.

The same practice is followed in reference to other subjects. As a matter of fact, conditions have reached the point where any Treasury policy is now of interest to the Department of State; and to a certain extent foreign policies are of concern to the Treasury. This is recognized in the close liaison maintained between them. Whenever any questions of a general character arise in the Treasury or whenever any of its decisions are of real importance with regard to foreign policy the Adviser or the Assistant Adviser on International Economic Affairs of the Department of State goes to the Treasury and participates in the discussions.

Meanwhile the Treasury has gradually built up a force of its own agents in the foreign field who report to it on key policies in monetary and financial matters. At the same time the Department of State has trained Foreign Service officers in embassies and legations who are specialists in these subjects, make their own observations and reports, and cooperate with the Treasury agents.

When foreign diplomats on special financial missions or finance ministers from abroad come to Washington on matters in their particular field they call first at the Department of State before going to the Treasury, in order not only that the official proprieties may be observed but also that the Secretary of State may be informed concerning their objectives and the questions that they plan to bring up.

As for cooperation between officials and experts of the two departments, the lines of relationship on the many special

topics that so constantly arise may run anywhere. The question of applying countervailing duties, for instance, used to be handled by the Treasury alone. Now, when it is to be taken up by the Treasury, the Department of State is informed in advance. This notification is usually given to the office of the Adviser on International Economic Affairs, but not always if no high economic interest is involved. When the Treasury late in 1938 took under consideration the question of amending its customs regulations to have the Sudeten area of Czechoslovakia, after its absorption by Germany, considered part of Germany, that was discussed with the European division of the Department of State, for it involved broad political rather than economic policy.

There is not always plain sailing. Sometimes the Department of State has found itself powerless in the face of policies of the Treasury and other departments that have been approved by the President for reasons that he considered overshadowed foreign considerations. Such a case arose when the United States attempted to pay the Republic of Panama in 1935 for the annual rental of the Panama Canal under the Treaty of 1904 in depreciated dollars instead of gold dollars of the standard of 1904. While it never was publicly admitted, there appears no question but that the Department of State would have wished the payment to be made in the customary form of standard currency. However, payment was tendered in depreciated dollars— and Panama returned the check.

The reason for the form of payment that was tendered was obvious. The Treasury and the Department of Justice, it appeared, had recommended to President Roosevelt that payment be made in this form after giving a highly technical construction to the terms of the Treaty, because of the effects a payment in gold coin of the standard of 1904 would

have had on the entire monetary policy at home. That the Department of State maintained silence was as obviously due to the fact that it realized that all policies are decided as far as possible from the standpoint of what are considered the best interests of the country. In deciding what those interests are all the departments are consulted, and the White House reaches the final decision.

Eventually the issue with Panama was adjusted by the Department of State in the course of the negotiation of a treaty to replace the one of 1904, into which was written a provision for a new basis of rental payments.

This experience represents the exception rather than the rule, for in most matters requiring cooperation there is harmonious action. That was the case when President Franklin D. Roosevelt directed steps to be taken for asserting the sovereignty of the United States over some of the small islands that dot the central Pacific. They had been permitted to slumber undisturbed by the United States since their accidental discovery by American whalers more than a century earlier. When the arrival of trans-Pacific aviation put a new face on their potentialities, because they could be developed as airplane bases, it was decided that claims should be advanced for their possession by right of discovery.

This required diplomatic negotiations with Great Britain, which as a great sea power had asserted claim to them in the intervening century as a matter of course. The Department of State conducted the negotiations, but two other departments were employed to reinforce American claims. The Department of the Interior, because it has jurisdiction over insular possessions, took practical steps by sending small colonizing parties to Enderbury and Canton islands, while the Department of the Treasury placed Coast Guard cutters at the disposal of the colonists to transport them to their

destinations and keep them supplied with necessities of life. Thus reinforced, the Department of State pressed the negotiations and reached agreements for the exercise of a form of joint sovereignty over the two islands with Great Britain.

It was this same Coast Guard service that combated the international fleets of liquor smugglers that hovered off American coasts during the prohibition era. Their activities called for close cooperation between the Treasury and the Department of State in respect to tactics that should be followed in preventing the landing of cargoes and tracing responsibility when the cordon was penetrated. It was a ceaseless source of international irritation during the ill-fated era, one that caused a long list of diplomatic protests requiring skill and tact of the Department of State in its relations with foreign offices abroad and in dealing with claims that constantly arose out of brushes between the Coast Guard and smugglers.

Other departments are equally as important to the Department of State. The Department of Commerce has representatives abroad (now blanketed into the Foreign Service for administrative purposes) reporting upon business and financial trends, and is the principal source of information of the Department of State in this field. It also is in charge of fisheries, a subject that often has raised its head in North Atlantic, Alaskan, and other waters, to complicate the foreign relations of the United States with Great Britain, Japan, and Russia. The Department of Labor is in charge of immigration questions, while the Department of State supervises passport administration and the issuing of visas, subjects that are very much interrelated and call for constant exchange of information and consultation on policy.

Although it may seem a long step from the farm to foreign affairs, the Department of Agriculture is an important cog

in the machine. In matters falling under its purview its voice carries great weight with the Department of State in international negotiations. Its officials and experts are in constant contact with the Department of State.

The views of the Department of Agriculture prevail on the question of whether a sanitary embargo should be laid down against a foreign country on account of plant or animal disease, even though stopping the importation of certain products may cause resentment abroad and react to complicate the conduct of relations for the Department of State along other lines. The Department of Agriculture is one of the most important of the many departments and agencies that cooperate with the Department of State in the negotiation of reciprocal trade agreements, because so many farm products are covered by tariff rates, and its officials and experts necessarily have in mind the needs and sentiment of the great farming regions of the country.

There are questions as to whether the Department of Agriculture should engage in a program of subsidizing farm exports, for that may affect a long line of American relations with other countries and reactions in many directions. There are policies to be considered with reference to the flow of commerce in farm products of Latin America that are non-competitive in the United States. Then there are international commodity agreements on sugar and wheat, the details of which are problems for the Department of Agriculture, but the broad policy involved is something of direct and immediate concern to the Department of State.

Consultations on all these matters require not only joint meetings of experts of the two departments but of the Secretary of State and the Secretary of Agriculture. And they do not stand on ceremony or order of precedence, for as convenience dictates, the Secretary of State one day will go

to the Department of Agriculture, and the next time the Secretary of Agriculture will go to the Department of State to confer with the Secretary of State. It matters little as long as there is cooperation and understanding.

Similarly, the Department of State consults on commodity agreements with the Department of the Interior for tin, a commodity of great importance in the import trade of the United States, and with the Department of Commerce on international rubber restrictions. In these activities it seeks to protect the consumer interests of the United States.

Apart from the executive departments stand the independent agencies of the government: the United States Tariff Commission, the Export-Import Bank, the Maritime Commission, the Civil Aeronautics Authority, and the Federal Communications Commission, to name a few, with which the Department of State must coordinate policies. While regularly in touch with the Tariff Commission, their relations concern technical details of tariff rates and duties more often than broad policies. Questions involving shipping are constantly arising with the Maritime Commission.

International radio problems involving the use of broadcasting channels and other facilities are dealt with through intergovernmental committees on which the Department of State is represented. And when arrangements are to be made for trans-Atlantic or other international aviation service with foreign governments, it is the Department of State which consults with the Civil Aeronautics Authority and then conducts the diplomatic negotiations to arrange the details of schedules and services by formal agreements.

Financial relationships are maintained not only with the Department of the Treasury when foreign policy is involved, as in the case of silver purchase agreements with Mexico, but also through the Export-Import Bank, which as a

[281]

subsidiary of the powerful Reconstruction Finance Corporation is the chief agency of the government in stimulating the flow of trade through extension of credits in Latin America, the Orient, and other regions. Yet none of these arrangements is made without the assent of the Department of State, for most or all of them have political aspects.

Will the extension of credits to China help prolong the war in the Far East and antagonize Japan? Will the extension of credits to a West Indian country for commercial purposes or for carrying out a public works program assure continued stability for the government in power and lessen the prospect of a revolution? All these and many other questions must be considered in the Department of State and its approval obtained before the Export-Import Bank will make an important decision.

And to assure the right degree of collaboration, officials of the Department serve on the Board of Trustees of the Bank, while officials of the Bank report regularly to the Department their observations and impressions of conditions and the attitude of governments in foreign lands. The Bank is not only a subsidiary of the Reconstruction Finance Corporation but in all practical ways it is also an arm of the Department of State. Its decisions can be even more important in terms of politics and diplomacy than in finance.

So it goes all along the line. There is collaboration in fields through which it is difficult or even impossible to draw lines of demarcation to define exactly where the Department of State leaves off and others begin. This is partly due to the variety of interests involved. They are growing all the time as the number of government interests increases, so that a rule laid down today may not be accurate in a year or even a few months. But the fact remains that practical ways are

found for affording the broad treatment that is demanded by circumstances.

In the Department of State itself there is the utmost flexibility. Not all subjects go by rigid rule to any one division or office. It may be the adviser on international economic affairs at one time, a geographical division at another, and a political adviser to the Secretary of State at still another.

Everybody at times takes in everybody else's washing. They have to. Within the Department this is true, just as it is between the Department and other agencies of the government.

CHAPTER XVII

INTERNATIONAL CONFERENCES AND ORGANIZATIONS

THE political talents of the Secretary of State are never brought more into play than at an international conference. There when he is chief of his government's delegation he is confronted with a swirling vortex of varied national interests as diverse as the number of countries represented and the diversified aspects of their national economies, political and social problems, and their ambitions. In addition to attempting to attain his objectives by obtaining the acceptance of his own program, he must tread warily to avoid wounding national pride and susceptibilities lest he arouse resentments that will plague him and his successors for years in their dealings with those same countries.

As if this were not enough, he must at the same time keep an eye over his shoulder toward home, attentive to the reaction of his own countrymen and particularly to the attitude of the Senate, for the treaties he signs will be only scrap paper unless the Senate gives its approval by a two-thirds vote. It is a vote not always easy to obtain, for suspicions must be allayed and doubts resolved in a body whose rules give exceptional power of obstruction to a single member.

The position of the chairman of the delegation, placed as he is in the midst of delegations each with its own program and objectives, is much like that of the chairman of a political party at its national convention. His hand must

be on all controls, his eyes and ears alert to the slightest movement; ambitions must be reconciled, discordant elements placated, team play encouraged, and at the same time his own objectives attained as far as possible. Only the closest attention to details and fine political skill will bring success.

It is why at so many international conferences of real political significance the Secretary of State is selected to head the delegation. It is why on a number of occasions Presidents themselves have graced the opening sessions and delivered addresses of good will. President Harding, as host, opened the Washington Conference on Armament Limitation and Pacific Questions in 1921, President Coolidge went to Havana on a warship for the opening of the Pan-American Conference in 1928, and President Roosevelt raced down the East coast of South America in 1936 to attend the Inter-American Peace Conference at its opening in Buenos Aires.

The technique is quite different from that required in the ordinary negotiation of treaties, for with the exception of occasional multilateral pacts such as the Kellogg-Briand Peace Treaty, these consist of bilateral arrangements. A proposal is made to another government for a treaty on a commercial, arbitration, or some other subject. Preliminary soundings are taken through diplomatic conversations and exchanges of notes until an agreed basis of discussion is reached.

Then the negotiations are undertaken formally, either in Washington or the capital of the foreign country concerned, depending upon convenience. The Secretary of State and the foreign ambassador in Washington, or the foreign minister and the American ambassador abroad, as the case happens to be, take up the proposals point by point, questions are referred to the capital of the other country as circumstances

[285]

require, until all issues are resolved. The treaty is drafted and its text scanned word by word, and it stands a completed document satisfactory to both parties. It is then initialed and the time set for signing, a formality that is carried out with due ceremony.

At an international conference, however, several treaties may be negotiated, not merely between two governments but among a half dozen, or in the case of pan-American conferences the full number of twenty-one American republics. Not only is the negotiation of a single one of these instruments infinitely more difficult than a routine treaty-making procedure, but the several that are concluded may make a composite pattern in which each is dependent on the other. They are intended to stand as the integrated whole of a broad program. That was the case at the Washington Conference when the Naval Treaty had a definite place in relation to the Four Power, the Nine Power, and the Chinese Tariff Treaty. That was the basis on which they were concluded. Concessions by a power in one of them were compensated by concessions in the opposite direction in another one.

Obviously the process is involved, one that requires careful preparation and then negotiations extending over a period of many weeks. That is why the delegation must be selected with exceptional care and why so often the Secretary of State is designated by the President to lead it. There is also another reason. International conferences present an excellent opportunity for increasing good will and common understanding that come from a better appreciation of the problems of others. Sympathy and a readier comprehension of the viewpoints of others tend to flow from conversations that proceed almost without cessation in conference rooms and hotels, at luncheons and dinners, with foreign ministers,

delegates, and experts mingling freely and discussing national and international questions.

This is one of the most valuable features of international conferences. Secretaries of State have often remarked on it, saying that the informal discussions, rubbing elbows, meeting on a common plane, are worth almost as much as the formal resolutions, treaties, and conventions that emanate from the plenary sessions of the conferences themselves. And so at the principal conferences they are usually found at the head of their delegation.

Because of the predominant importance of the Versailles Peace Conference at the close of the World War and his own intense, personal interest, President Wilson unprecedentedly headed the delegation in 1919, but his Secretary of State, Robert Lansing, was a member. In 1921 Secretary Hughes was chairman of the delegation at the Washington Conference, and also, by reason of the United States being host, chairman of the Conference itself. In 1930 Secretary Stimson headed the delegation to the London Naval Conference and two years later, in 1932, was chairman of the delegation at the General Disarmament Conference at Geneva. Secretary Hull in 1933 was chairman of the delegation at the London Economic Conference. Similarly, Secretary Hull was chairman of the delegations at the Buenos Aires Conference in 1936 and at the Pan-American Conferences in Montevideo in 1933 and in Lima in 1938. In 1928 Charles Evans Hughes, who had relinquished the office of Secretary of State only three years previously, was chairman of the delegation at the Pan-American Conference at Havana.

There have been only three other important exceptions to this virtual rule at conferences since the World War, and there were special reasons to account for them. In 1923 Henry P. Fletcher was chairman of the delegation to the

Pan-American Conference at Santiago. But he had previously been Under Secretary of State and Ambassador to Chile. In 1927 Hugh S. Gibson, the leading diplomatic expert of the Department of State on armament limitation, was chairman of the delegation to the Tripartite Naval Conference at Geneva, and because the United States had convoked it, chairman of the Conference itself. And Norman H. Davis, who had a quite similar record as a disarmament expert and was close in the confidence of Secretary Hull and President Franklin D. Roosevelt, was chief of the delegation at the London Naval Conference in 1935.

The post carries great responsibilities, for the chairman of the delegation, although he invariably refers major decisions to the Department of State for approval and although he has the facilities offered by modern communications to do so, nevertheless is often far from Washington where he does not have the Department at his instant service, and must make some decisions himself, even though he has the guidance of general instructions.

Senators are appointed members of the most important delegations in recognition of the fact that the Senate will pass upon the treaties that emerge and because the knowledge and sympathy that can be gained only through participation in the negotiations will be a powerful factor in the debate preceding the final vote in the Senate. It is only natural that the chief of the delegation, when he has never served in the Senate, will not have as complete an understanding of that body's point of view, its attitude, prejudices, and convictions.

If, in addition to being chairman of the delegation, the Secretary of State is also chairman of the conference itself, as Secretary Hughes was at the Washington Conference, he

will be bound by proprieties that surround a presiding officer and not speak as freely as other chiefs of delegation. Secretary Hughes knew that he disappointed more than once the two hundred correspondents who crowded his press conferences at the Washington conference and that other chiefs of delegation were speaking with greater freedom, but that knowledge did not influence him. He accepted the situation as an inevitable handicap of his conference position.

On the other hand, Senators who are members of the American delegation but do not have a dual status, not only can speak but by influencing the course of negotiations can guard against the adoption of provisions that could cause serious trouble later in the Senate. Obviously, Senate members of a delegation all during the negotiations have their thoughts attuned to Senate probabilities. They know their task is twofold—to assist in the negotiations and to effect Senate approval of the completed projects afterward. And, although the chief of delegation may seek to surround the negotiations at delicate moments with a cloak of secrecy in order to prevent leaks that might raise questions prematurely in several countries and so complicate the negotiations in the yeasting stage, the Senators may think beyond to the consequences of floating rumors, many unjustified, that could rise later to plague a treaty.

Confident that if the facts are made known a threatened cause of opposition will subside, they can quietly let the true situation become known, perhaps to the dismay of the Secretary of State but nevertheless for the good of the cause. Anyone who sat in the Senate gallery and witnessed the clocklike precision with which the Senate rejected emasculating reservations and then approved by comfortable margins the treaties of the Washington Conference must have

realized the effective preparatory work done during the conference by its two members of the delegation, Henry Cabot Lodge and Oscar W. Underwood.

True, other Senators have resented this part. When Senator David A. Reed of Pennsylvania who had been a delegate at London was laboring in the Senate for approval of the Naval Treaty of 1930, Senator Hiram Johnson of California charged that he was appearing as an advocate of the Treaty rather than as a Senator dispassionately passing upon it. Probably the California Senator was right, yet that has not discouraged the practice.

In one important field, however, Senators have not appeared in the role of delegation members. That is at pan-American conferences. There are several reasons for this. The treaties that are concluded do not present as controversial features as those negotiated at conferences with European and Asiatic nations. Pan-American treaties do not involve questions of political entanglement abroad or high naval policy. The nations concerned, notwithstanding their different racial strains, have a common continental background, and pan-American conferences are held more for adjustment of questions within the family. Also many of the treaties are on cultural and educational subjects, or designed to solve local disputes by pacific means. Consequently, it has never been found essential to have Senators on the delegations, for there is little prospect of serious Senate opposition.

Instead, with continental solidarity and peace the watchwords, the practice has been to select a large delegation of a broadly representative character. The Secretary of State usually heads it to signify the importance attached by the United States to pan-American relations, but other delegates are more representative of the citizenry than the govern-

ment. To be sure, the Under Secretary and an assistant secretary of state may serve on the delegation as chief aides of the Secretary of State in the work of negotiation, for problems arise that call for careful treatment and technical diplomatic skill but there is room for others. So it happens that professors of international law at universities, leaders of civic and women's organizations, and always, as in the case of most international conferences, one or two representatives of the opposition political party are selected. J. Reuben Clark, Jr., former Under Secretary of State and a prominent Republican, was a member of the delegation to the Pan-American Conference at Montevideo in 1933, and Alfred M. Landon, Republican candidate for President in 1936, was a delegate to the Pan-American Conference at Lima in 1938. Their presence emphasized the national and nonpartisan character of the delegation.

With European or other world-wide conferences circumstances are different. The Senate is then wooed because of the more highly controversial character of the policies that will be written into treaties. The lesson was learned years ago. President McKinley pointed the way in 1898 when he appointed three Senators to the delegation that negotiated peace with Spain in Paris. His foresight was amply demonstrated when the Senate gave its approval to the peace treaty, in the face of stormy opposition that raged for years over retention of the Philippines.

On the other hand, as we have already seen, President Wilson chose to ignore these safeguarding tactics when he went to Paris for the conference at the close of the World War. He passed the Senate by, and what the Senate did to the Versailles Treaty will be remembered as long as there is a history of American diplomacy. Not that the treaty would necessarily have been accepted, but at least its rejec-

tion would have been more difficult, if there had been members of the delegation in the Senate to defend it.

President Harding and Secretary Hughes had these contrasting experiences of 1898 and 1919 much in mind when they came to select the delegation for the Washington Conference in 1921, and they chose shrewdly. The delegation consisted of four members. Secretary Hughes was chairman. The other three were Senator Lodge, chairman of the Committee on Foreign Relations and Republican leader in the Senate; Senator Underwood, Democratic leader in the Senate, and Elihu Root, who had served both as Secretary of State and as a member of the Senate.

Nine years later when the delegation was selected for the London Naval Conference of 1930, Secretary Stimson was its chief, and Charles G. Dawes, Ambassador in London, Hugh S. Gibson, Ambassador to Belgium, and Charles F. Adams, Secretary of the Navy, were included. The others were Senator Reed, a Republican, Senator Joseph T. Robinson of Arkansas, Democratic leader in the Senate, and Dwight W. Morrow, Ambassador to Mexico, who, as events turned out, was soon to take his place in the Senate. Nor should the observation be omitted that no one worked harder first at the conference or later in the Senate for approval of the treaty than Senator Robinson, the opposition leader. He performed titanic service. And the treaty was approved.

Senator Claude A. Swanson of Virginia, who later became Secretary of the Navy, was a member of the delegation at the abortive General Disarmament Conference of 1932. When the London Naval Conference of 1935 rolled around it was obvious that under pressure of power politics of the totalitarian states the principle of naval limitation was only a shell, that little could be salvaged of a system that had worked well for a dozen years. All governments were recon-

ciled to that fact. It was known that what little could be written into treaty under no circumstances could cause serious opposition in the Senate, and so no special safeguards directed to that quarter were necessary. The delegation that year consisted of Norman H. Davis as chairman, who like Ambassador Gibson had long specialized in armament limitation and had conducted the preliminary discussions looking to the 1935 conference, and Admiral William H. Standley, Chief of Naval Operations. No Senators were included.

However, two years earlier, in 1933, at the London Economic Conference where Secretary Hull was chief of the American delegation, both the Senate and House of Representatives were represented. The members included Senator Key Pittman of Nevada, chairman of the Committee on Foreign Relations; Sam D. McReynolds of Tennessee, chairman of the Committee on Foreign Affairs of the House o Representatives, and Senator James Couzens of Michigan, a close friend of President Roosevelt. However, they had no subsequent service to perform, for the conference collapsed in failure.

The Economic Conference did not collapse for lack of preparation. The utmost efforts were made in advance to assure success. The collapse came about because of the difficulty in dealing with the problems in the sorry economic state of the world at that time and because President Roosevelt decided that his monetary policies would be handicapped by stabilization of currencies. Before reaching that decision he had pressed the preparations vigorously. They had been started by President Hoover and Secretary Stimson, and the Roosevelt administration took up where they left off. President Roosevelt circularized the heads of foreign states urging that every effort be made for success and invited

[293]

delegations from many countries to come to Washington for discussions with him. Prime Minister Ramsay MacDonald represented Great Britain on what proved to be his last official visit to the United States, and Edouard Herriot represented France in these deliberations. It was not lack of preparation that doomed the conference to failure.

It is sometimes maintained that lack of preparation did wreck the Tripartite Naval Conference at Geneva in 1927. That is open to question. The collapse would appear to have come about more because of the irreconcilable policies of the American and British navies over cruisers and a belief of the Americans that Britain was retreating from her concession of naval equality made to the United States at the Washington Conference five years earlier.

The fact that no preparation was made was deliberate. The United States in summoning the conference decided at the instance of the Department of State to issue the invitations without preliminary soundings, and for a very definite reason. For two years the Department had been wrestling with the Preparatory Commission which was meeting in Geneva to pave the way for the General Disarmament Conference, which years later, in 1932, sought unsuccessfully to reach agreements for the reduction and limitation of land armies. By 1926 the Department had found in the Preparatory Commission that some European nations were little disposed to make progress toward armament reduction. In fact, they used the Commission as a device for delay and for whittling down proposals.

In the face of that experience, the Department of State decided that there would be less chance of whittling if the 1927 conference were called without advance warning. Perhaps it was a mistake. If preparations had been undertaken, it might have been discovered that it would be futile to call

the conference. There will never be any satisfactory answer to the question, but at least when the world recoiled from the failure at Geneva the way was opened for constructive action at London three years later, and the Naval Conference of 1930 finally did deal successfully with the issue of cruisers.

That was the one exception to the rule of careful preparation for a conference. The preliminaries to the Washington Conference occupied months. Exchanges proceeded between all the interested world capitals through diplomatic notes and conversations, and in time an agenda was agreed upon for the conference. No more valuable service was performed at this stage than by Charles B. Warren, American Ambassador in Tokyo. In the weeks before Japan accepted the invitation he greatly facilitated matters by informing her of America's real intentions, save possibly for the details of Secretary Hughes' formula for scrapping ships which was tossed into the Conference with the force of a bombshell at the opening session.

Prior to the 1930 Naval Conference, Prime Minister MacDonald came to Washington to discuss naval problems and the Kellogg-Briand Pact. It was the occasion made picturesquely friendly by his sitting on a log with President Hoover at the Rapidan camp. And, likewise, prior to the 1935 Naval Conference, Norman H. Davis conducted thorough explorations through conversations in Europe with leading statesmen.

Contemporaneously with these international preparations, measures are undertaken within the government through discussions with the Secretary of State to prepare the American delegation for its part in a conference. If a naval conference is approaching, the Secretary of the Navy, the Chief of Naval Operations, and their technical assistants confer with the Secretary of State and his aides day in and day out

for weeks, canvassing possibilities and defining the American position. If economic questions are to be taken up, officials of the Treasury, Commerce, Agriculture, and other interested departments and agencies participate in the discussions. If army questions are at stake, officers of the War Department contribute to the studies. From time to time they all confer with the President at the White House, until finally agreement is reached on the American position and instructions are framed and approved by the President for the guidance of the delegation.

The broad position of the government is usually announced in the opening speech to the conference delivered by the chief of the delegation. This is prepared with the utmost care. Usually it is practically completed before the delegation leaves the country, but after the group sails revisions are frequently necessary. They are made with the aid of constant interchanges by radio with the Department of State. At the same time the delegation on shipboard begins its task of organizing for the work of the conference. Daily consultations are held, committees are formed, and subjects assigned to different members of the delegation for specialization at the conference. When the delegation arrives it is ready to go forward with the main task.

As the conference proceeds the operations cover all the interested countries. They are not confined to the conference sessions. Discussions are held in the quiet of hotel rooms, and at small dinner parties of delegates and technical advisers. The delegates are supplemented by technical staffs made up of expert officials from the various departments of the government concerned with the subject matter, of officials of the Navy Department, the Department of State, and of Foreign Service officers in the field who have been ordered to the conference as expert assistants.

[296]

The delegation is organized on the basis of subject matter. One member will specialize on this detail, another on that, for the conference itself is divided into committees and sub-committees, and specialized treatment is necessary. Occasionally various delegates will also be assigned to maintain personal contact with other national delegations. One may be instructed to give his particular attention to the British, another to the French, and another to the Japanese. However, this is not often done, for it usually is unnecessary. It was done at the London Naval Conference of 1930; on the other hand, it is never done at pan-American conferences. The problem, it has been found, can be successfully met by calling to the conference Foreign Service officers in the field, officers who know thoroughly the countries to which they are assigned. They can interpret accurately the viewpoints of other nations to their delegation.

At the same time that all this is going on there are occasional discussions of interested officials in the various capitals. An ambassador of a participating country may call at the Department of State in Washington to discuss certain phases of the conference on instructions of his government. Often this clarifies national viewpoints, and it can be of the utmost service in allaying apprehensions. For example, William R. Castle, Jr., while an assistant secretary of state was sent to Tokyo as United States Ambassador during 1930, especially to interpret to the Japanese authorities the American naval position during the London conference that year. He performed admirable work without which the efforts at London might have been far more difficult than they were.

The Department of State and the White House also keep in close contact with the delegation, a task that is now facilitated not only by the cable and wireless telegraph but by the wireless telephone, for the Secretary of State does not

hesitate to talk with the Acting Secretary of State in Washington or the President by telephone from the conference when occasion arises. Simultaneously, the Department of State keeps the delegation informed of the state of public opinion in America, a most important consideration to any diplomat. Every day the Department also compiles a summary of press reports of the conference that have been cabled by the American correspondents on the scene and telegraphs it to the chairman of the conference delegation in order that he may know what the American public is being told about the conference. In addition, the Department watches editorial comment and other pertinent reactions, and telegraphs this information to the delegation.

But beyond this it does not go. Lest wires be crossed by announcements at different places, it consistently refrains from discussing the progress of the conference, letting announcements be made solely by the delegation itself. It is informed promptly of what is to be said by the chief of the delegation at the conference, and is in touch at all times with the progress of affairs through confidential reports from the delegation. When a major speech is to be delivered by the chief of the delegation its text is sent to the Department for suggestions and approval of both the Department and the President. Then it is given out for publication at a prearranged time in order that the American press may have it in full and not have to hesitate about the expense of cable tolls. It assures a wider public treatment of the conference than otherwise might be accorded it.

It is a complex process, one that requires infinite attention to detail, comprehension of national viewpoints, understanding of public opinion, close liaison with the government at home; in short, use of all the facilities that the modern age has made available to the Department of State for conducting foreign affairs.

International conferences of a political character, however, are not the only ones that occupy the attention of the Department of State. There are many others devoted to scientific, educational, and cultural questions. Their value is recognized by the Department. In the words of Secretary Hull they are "powerful influences in assisting the stream of new ideas, of new discoveries, of learning and culture, to flow throughout the world."

These conferences are held in Washington and other capitals and cities of the world, as the organizations concerned prefer. They have to do with health, education, agriculture, commerce, industry, communications, and many other topics. The list is somewhat bewildering. There are conferences on high-tension electric systems, seed testing, vacation colonies, public health, applied meteorology, sugar, hospital associations, grasslands, sanitation, modern languages, architecture, public instruction, hygiene, geology, infant psychiatry, art education, problems of the deaf, utilization of unfermented fruit juices, universal documentation, and folklore. It is an extensive and varied list.

They average two a week, for in the course of a year about one hundred are held. They are attended by an average of nearly 400 Americans who come to Washington or go abroad for that purpose. All are held by invitation of different governments, and the United States government designates the American delegations in consultation with the interested groups in the country. The arrangements are made by the Division of International Conferences in the Department of State in collaboration with organizations like the American Medical Association, Rockefeller Foundation, and the Carnegie Institution.

While the government contributes to the expenses and spends annually nearly a quarter of a million dollars for this purpose, 75 percent of the expenses are paid by the delegates

themselves or their organizations. When the conferences are concluded the delegates write reports that are submitted to the Department of State, which publishes an annual digest of them and the sources, in order that the information may be available for further research.

In addition to these conferences, there are many international organizations of which the government is a member. The Department of State annually contributes more than half a million dollars toward their maintenance. There are more than twenty-five of these organizations. Among the more important is, of course, the Pan American Union in Washington, which is a focal point of good relations in the Western Hemisphere and in which all the Latin-American governments also hold membership. The Secretary of State is always chairman of its Governing Board. Then there are the International Labor Office at Geneva, the Opium Section, and other organizations important in their own spheres that are fostered by the League of Nations and, therefore, agencies through which the United States maintains its principal cooperative contacts with the League.

Also, there are a number of organizations with headquarters in various capitals and other cities of the world—Washington, Rome, The Hague, Mexico City, Southampton, and others, in which membership is maintained. Among them are the International Institute of Agriculture, the International Hydrographic Bureau, the Interparliamentary Union, the American Institute of Geography, the Pan American Sanitary Bureau, the International Office of Public Health, the Permanent International Association of Road Congresses, the Radio Section of the Telecommunication Union, the Inter-American Trade Mark Bureau, the International Bureau of Weights and Measures, the International Statistical Bureau, the Institute for the Protection

of Childhood, and even the Bureau of the International Map of the World on the Millionth Scale.

Membership in all of them is under treaties or conventions, or laws authorizing participation. They represent, along with the Foreign Service stationed abroad in embassies, legations, and consulates, the far-flung organization of the Department of State.

The Department has its home service, and its relations with the public, Congress, and departments and agencies of the government. It stands on a background of steady growth over a period of a century and a half. To the casual passer the monumental building that houses it, across West Executive Avenue from the White House, is merely another government building, but to the initiated that is only the beginning, for from there its tentacles reach out in all directions embracing Washington, the country, and the world at large. No one can comprehend it without an understanding of the wide scope of its activities, the bases from which it acts under administrative practice and national tradition, its sensitiveness to public opinion, and its responsibility to the law both domestic and international.

Housed in the structure so much the bane of present-day architects, it stands as Presidents and Secretaries of State and their administrations come and go, devoted to purposes of peace, a living organization that will continue as long as the nation endures.

ORGANIZATION OF
THE DEPARTMENT OF STATE—1939

The Secretary of State
CORDELL HULL

Special assistants to the Secretary of State
LEO PASVOLSKY
LYNN R. EDMINSTER

The Under Secretary of State
SUMNER WELLES

The Counselor for the Department
R. WALTON MOORE

Assistant Secretaries of State
FRANCIS B. SAYRE
GEORGE S. MESSERSMITH
ADOLF A. BERLE, JR.

Office of the Legal Adviser
GREEN H. HACKWORTH, LEGAL ADVISER

Advisers on Political Relations
JAMES CLEMENT DUNN
STANLEY K. HORNBECK

Adviser on International Economic Affairs
HERBERT FEIS

The Chief Clerk and Administrative Assistant
EDWARD YARDLEY

Board of Foreign Service Personnel
GEORGE S. MESSERSMITH, CHAIRMAN

Board of Examiners for the Foreign Service
GEORGE S. MESSERSMITH, CHAIRMAN

Division of Foreign Service Administration
NATHANIEL P. DAVIS, CHIEF

Foreign Service Buildings Office
FREDERICK LARKIN, CHIEF

Division of Foreign Service Personnel
G. HOWLAND SHAW, CHIEF

Foreign Service Officers' Training School
GEORGE S. MESSERSMITH, CHAIRMAN
J. KLAHR HUDDLE, DIRECTOR

Division of Far Eastern Affairs
MAXWELL M. HAMILTON, CHIEF

Division of the American Republics
LAURENCE DUGGAN, CHIEF

Division of European Affairs
JAY PIERREPONT MOFFAT, CHIEF

Division of Near Eastern Affairs
WALLACE MURRAY, CHIEF

Division of Current Information
MICHAEL J. MCDERMOTT, CHIEF

Office of Coordination and Review
BLANCHE RULE HALLA, CHIEF

Passport Division
RUTH B. SHIPLEY, CHIEF

Treaty Division
CHARLES M. BARNES, CHIEF

APPENDIX I

Translating Bureau
    EMERSON CHRISTIE, CHIEF

Division of Communications and Records
    DAVID A. SALMON, CHIEF

Visa Division
    AVRA M. WARREN, CHIEF

Division of Research and Publication
    CYRIL WYNNE, CHIEF

Division of Trade Agreements
    HARRY C. HAWKINS, CHIEF

Division of Controls
    JOSEPH C. GREEN, CHIEF

Office of Philippine Affairs
    JOSEPH E. JACOBS, CHIEF

Division of International Conferences
    WARREN H. KELCHNER, ACTING CHIEF

Division of Protocol
    GEORGE T. SUMMERLIN, CHIEF

Division of Cultural Relations
    BEN M. CHERRINGTON, CHIEF

Office of the Editor of the Treaties
    HUNTER MILLER, EDITOR

Division of International Communications
    THOMAS BURKE, CHIEF

Division of Accounts
    LAURENCE C. FRANK, CHIEF

Board of Appeals and Review
    GEORGE S. MESSERSMITH, CHAIRMAN

Conciliation Committee
    JOSEPH R. BAKER, CHAIRMAN

SECRETARIES OF STATE, 1789—1939

(*Ad interim* Secretaries omitted)

Secretary of State	*Administration*
*THOMAS JEFFERSON, Virginia	GEORGE WASHINGTON
March 22, 1790–December 31, 1793	
EDMUND RANDOLPH, Virginia	
January 2, 1794—August 20, 1795	
TIMOTHY PICKERING, Pennsylvania	
December 10, 1795——	
TIMOTHY PICKERING	JOHN ADAMS
Continued from previous administration to May 12, 1800	
JOHN MARSHALL, Virginia	
June 6, 1800–February 4, 1801	
JAMES MADISON, Virginia	THOMAS JEFFERSON
May 2, 1801–March 3, 1809	
ROBERT SMITH, Maryland	JAMES MADISON
March 6, 1809–April 1, 1811	
JAMES MONROE, Virginia	
April 6, 1811–September 30, 1814; March 1, 1815–March 3, 1817	
JOHN QUINCY ADAMS, Massachusetts	JAMES MONROE
September 22, 1817–March 3, 1825	

* Jefferson was commissioned September 26, 1789, but did not enter upon his duties until March 22, 1790. Until he did, John Jay, of New York, Secretary for Foreign Affairs under the former government of the Confederation, unofficially superintended the Department.

HENRY CLAY, Kentucky   JOHN QUINCY ADAMS
    March 7, 1825–March 3, 1829

MARTIN VAN BUREN, New York   ANDREW JACKSON
    March 28, 1829–May 23, 1831
EDWARD LIVINGSTON, Louisiana
    May 24, 1831–May 29, 1833
LOUIS McLANE, Delaware
    May 29, 1833–June 30, 1834
JOHN FORSYTH, Georgia
    July 1, 1834——

JOHN FORSYTH   MARTIN VAN BUREN
    Continued from previous administration to March 3, 1841

DANIEL WEBSTER,   WILLIAM HENRY HARRISON
      Massachusetts
    March 6, 1841——

DANIEL WEBSTER   JOHN TYLER
    Continued from previous administration to May 8, 1843
ABEL P. UPSHUR, Virginia
    July 24, 1843–February 28, 1844
JOHN C. CALHOUN, South Carolina
    April 1, 1844——

JOHN C. CALHOUN   JAMES K. POLK
    Continued from previous administration to March 10, 1845
JAMES BUCHANAN, Pennsylvania
    March 10, 1845——

JAMES BUCHANAN   ZACHARY TAYLOR
    Continued from previous administration to March 7, 1849
JOHN M. CLAYTON, Delaware
    March 8, 1849——

JOHN M. CLAYTON   MILLARD FILLMORE
  Continued from previous administration to July 22, 1850
DANIEL WEBSTER, Massachusetts
  July 23, 1850–October 24, 1852
EDWARD EVERETT, Massachusetts
  November 6, 1852–March 3, 1853

WILLIAM L. MARCY, New York   FRANKLIN PIERCE
  March 8, 1853——

WILLIAM L. MARCY   JAMES BUCHANAN
  Continued from previous administration to March 6, 1857
LEWIS CASS, Michigan
  March 6, 1857–December 14, 1860
JEREMIAH S. BLACK, Pennsylvania
  December 17, 1860–March 5, 1861

WILLIAM H. SEWARD, New York   ABRAHAM LINCOLN
  March 6, 1861——

WILLIAM H. SEWARD   ANDREW JOHNSON
  Continued from previous administration to March 4, 1869

ELIHU B. WASHBURNE, Illinois   ULYSSES S. GRANT
  March 5, 1869–March 16, 1869
HAMILTON FISH, New York
  March 17, 1869–March 12, 1877

WILLIAM M. EVARTS, New York   RUTHERFORD B. HAYES
  March 12, 1877–March 7, 1881

JAMES G. BLAINE, Maine   JAMES A. GARFIELD
  March 7, 1881——

JAMES G. BLAINE   CHESTER A. ARTHUR
  Continued from previous administration to December 19, 1881

FREDERICK T. FRELINGHUYSEN, New Jersey
December 19, 1881–March 6, 1885

THOMAS F. BAYARD, Delaware   GROVER CLEVELAND
March 7, 1885–March 6, 1889

JAMES G. BLAINE, Maine   BENJAMIN HARRISON
March 7, 1889–June 4, 1892
JOHN W. FOSTER, Indiana
June 29, 1892–February 23, 1893

WALTER Q. GRESHAM, Illinois   GROVER CLEVELAND
March 7, 1893–May 28, 1895
RICHARD OLNEY, Massachusetts
June 10, 1895–March 5, 1897

JOHN SHERMAN, Ohio   WILLIAM McKINLEY
March 6, 1897–April 27, 1898
WILLIAM R. DAY, Ohio
April 28, 1898–September 16, 1898
JOHN HAY, District of Columbia
September 30, 1898——

JOHN HAY   THEODORE ROOSEVELT
Continued from previous administration to July 1, 1905
ELIHU ROOT, New York
July 19, 1905–January 27, 1909
ROBERT BACON, New York
January 27, 1909–March 5, 1909

PHILANDER C. KNOX, Pennsylvania   WILLIAM H. TAFT
March 6, 1909–March 5, 1913

WILLIAM JENNINGS BRYAN, Nebraska   WOODROW WILSON
March 5, 1913–June 9, 1915

INSIDE THE DEPARTMENT OF STATE

ROBERT LANSING, New York
  June 24, 1915–February 13, 1920
BAINBRIDGE COLBY, New York
  March 23, 1920–March 4, 1921

CHARLES EVANS HUGHES, New York   WARREN G. HARDING
  March 5, 1921——

CHARLES EVANS HUGHES   CALVIN COOLIDGE
  Continued from previous administration to March 4, 1925
FRANK B. KELLOGG, Minnesota
  March 5, 1925–March 28, 1929

HENRY L. STIMSON, New York   HERBERT HOOVER
  March 28, 1929–March 4, 1933

CORDELL HULL, Tennessee   FRANKLIN D. ROOSEVELT
  March 4, 1933——

APPENDIX II

COUNSELORS FOR THE DEPARTMENT
OF STATE, 1909—1919

HENRY M. HOYT, Pennsylvania
August 27, 1909–November 20, 1910
CHANDLER P. ANDERSON, New York
December 16, 1910–April 22, 1913
JOHN BASSETT MOORE, New York
April 23, 1913–March 4, 1914
ROBERT LANSING, New York
April 1, 1914–June 23, 1915
FRANK L. POLK, New York
September 16, 1915–June 30, 1919

UNDER SECRETARIES OF STATE,
1919—1939

FRANK L. POLK, New York
July 1, 1919–June 15, 1920
NORMAN H. DAVIS, New York
June 15, 1920–March 7, 1921
HENRY P. FLETCHER, Pennsylvania
March 8, 1921–March 6, 1922
WILLIAM PHILLIPS, Massachusetts
April 26, 1922–April 11, 1924
JOSEPH C. GREW, New Hampshire
April 16, 1924–June 30, 1927
ROBERT E. OLDS, Minnesota
July 1, 1927–June 30, 1928
J. REUBEN CLARK, JR., Utah
August 31, 1928–June 19, 1929

JOSEPH P. COTTON, New York
  June 20, 1929–March 10, 1931
WILLIAM R. CASTLE, JR., District of Columbia
  April 2, 1931–March 5, 1933
WILLIAM PHILLIPS, Massachusetts
  March 6, 1933–August 23, 1936
SUMNER WELLES, Maryland
  May 21, 1937——

APPENDIX II

CHAIRMEN OF THE SENATE COMMITTEE ON FOREIGN RELATIONS, 1816—1939

JAMES BARBOUR, Virginia, 1816
NATHANIEL MACON, North Carolina, 1818
JAMES BROWN, Louisiana, 1819
JAMES BARBOUR, Virginia, 1820
RUFUS KING, New York, 1821
JAMES BARBOUR, Virginia, 1822
NATHANIEL MACON, North Carolina, 1825
NATHAN SANFORD, New York, 1826
NATHANIEL MACON, North Carolina, 1827
LITTLETON W. TAZEWELL, Virginia, 1828
JOHN FORSYTH, Georgia, 1832
WILLIAM WILKINS, Pennsylvania, 1833
HENRY CLAY, Kentucky, 1834
JAMES BUCHANAN, Pennsylvania, 1836
WILLIAM C. RIVES, Virginia, 1841
WILLIAM S. ARCHER, Virginia, 1842
WILLIAM ALLEN, Ohio, 1845
GEORGE McDUFFIE, South Carolina, 1846
AMBROSE H. SEVIER, Arkansas, 1846
EDWARD A. HANNEGAN, Indiana, 1848
THOMAS H. BENTON, Missouri, 1849
WILLIAM R. KING, Alabama, 1849
HENRY S. FOOTE, Mississippi, 1850
JOHN H. CLARKE, Rhode Island, 1851
JAMES M. MASON, Virginia, 1851

[313]

CHARLES SUMNER, Massachusetts, 1861
SIMON CAMERON, Pennsylvania, 1871
HANNIBAL HAMLIN, Maine, 1877
WILLIAM W. EATON, Connecticut, 1879
AMBROSE E. BURNSIDE, Rhode Island, 1881
GEORGE F. EDMUNDS, Vermont, 1881
WILLIAM WINDOM, Minnesota, 1882
JOHN F. MILLER, California, 1883
JOHN SHERMAN, Ohio, 1886
JOHN T. MORGAN, Alabama, 1893
JOHN SHERMAN, Ohio, 1895
CUSHMAN K. DAVIS, Minnesota, 1897
SHELBY M. CULLOM, Illinois, 1901
AUGUSTUS O. BACON, Georgia, 1913
WILLIAM J. STONE, Missouri, 1915
GILBERT M. HITCHCOCK, Nebraska, 1918
HENRY CABOT LODGE, Massachusetts, 1919
WILLIAM E. BORAH, Idaho, 1924
KEY PITTMAN, Nevada, 1933

INDEX

INDEX

INDEX

Tinkham, George H., 239

Trade agreements, reciprocal, 68, 230–231, 245

Trade Agreements Division, 30, 68

Trans-Siberian railroad, 255

Treasury Department of the, relations with Department of State, 54, 269, 270–271, 275–279, 281

Treaties, consent to, by Senate, 242, 289
  how negotiated, 285–286
  ratification of, 12

Treaty of 1904, 277–278

Tripartite Monetary Agreement, 275

Tripartite Naval Conference, 266–267, 294

Trist, Nicholas P., 174–175

Tweed, Boss, 25

Tweedsmuir, Lord, 183

Typewriter, history and present use of, 157

U

Under Secretary of State, 16, 17–18, 58, 59–62, 65, 67, 70
  comparison with Permanent Under Secretary of British Foreign Office, 64
  office of, when established, 17, 29
  as political appointee, 64
  regular reception of foreign envoys by, 11, 61, 190

Underwood, Oscar W., 290, 292

Upshur, Abel P., 41

V

Van Buren, Martin, 42, 107

Venezuelan controversy with Great Britain, 48, 49

Vera Cruz, occupation of, 259

Versailles, Peace Conference at, 28, 53, 83, 232
  (See also Versailles, Treaty of)

Versailles, Treaty of, 74, 235, 291–292
  Senate opposition to, 291–292
  (See also League of Nations)

W

Wallace, Lewis, 108

War debts, 54–56, 220, 234
  Hoover moratorium on, 220

War Department, 14
  (See also Army)

Warren, Charles B., 102, 295

Washburne, Elihu B., 108

Washington Conference on Armament Limitation and Pacific Questions, 50, 226, 265, 286, 289–290

Watson, James E., 198

Webster, Daniel, 12, 19–20, 41, 44, 47

Welles, Sumner, 65–66, 184, 194, 207, 217–219

Wendelin, Eric C., 32, 33, 80

Wharton, William F., 21

Wheaton, Henry, 109

White, Andrew D., 108

White, Edward D., 35

White, Henry, 86–87

White House, 14, 16, 59, 61, 73, 101, 267
  annual diplomatic dinner at, 200–201
  annual reception at, 201
  seating arrangements for dinners at, 23, 24

White House press conference, 53, 135, 144–146
  and President Wilson, 144

Whitlock, Brand, 108

Wilson, Hugh R., 69, 104–105, 173, 180, 204, 207

Wilson, Huntington, 22

Wilson, Woodrow, 26, 42, 45, 50, 51, 53, 63, 74, 113, 114, 143, 144, 185, 232, 248, 259, 291
  and the League of Nations, 74–75, 113
  and the White House press conference, 144

[327]